Critical Stages
Canadian Theatre in Crisis

Gordon Vogt

Unless otherwise indicated, these reviews were written for broadcast on CBC Stereo Morning.

This book was published with the assistance of the Canada Council, the Ontario Arts Council and others. We acknowledge the support of the Canada Council for the Arts and the Government of Canada through the Book Publishing Industry Development Program for our publishing activities.

ISBN 0 7780 1085 6 (hardcover)
ISBN 0 7780 1086 4 (softcover)

Photograph facing page 17 by Tess Steinkolk
Cover art by Ghitta Caiserman-Roth
Book design by Michael Macklem

Printed in Canada

PUBLISHED IN CANADA BY OBERON PRESS

This book is respectfully and lovingly dedicated to our parents.

Introduction

Rick Salutin

"But about the play—" wrote Gordon Vogt of a now-forgotten work he was reviewing for CBC radio, "and I would be happy to be challenged on this—I found it schematic." How I long to hear this tone in a reviewer: the courage to be unsure. Can these folks really attend dozens, maybe hundreds of performances, films, concerts in a year, and never have a doubt about their judgments? Are they ever uncertain? And if they are, why don't they let us in on it, as Vogt does here? Don't they occasionally find themselves without an opinion—like normal mortals? And if they are human, why don't they say so? Personally, I find that the instant an ostensible authority acknowledges uncertainty or doubt ("It's very hard to be sure about this...."), it's then that I start to trust. Expertise is a qualified attribution, even in realms like medicine or auto mechanics; it's so easy for an expert to get it wrong, and they disagree among themselves all the time. All the more so in aesthetic judgments. By admitting uncertainty, you're just being honest and treating your own audience with enough respect to let them in on the real situation. Once you've extended that respect, it's possible to extend it further. "I suggest that you make up your own mind about it if you get the chance," Vogt concluded his review. "One of the things that made me most uncomfortable about the piece was my own response to it."

By extending this kind of invitation to his listeners, Vogt proposed a dialogue which included not just him and them, but also the artists and the work of art under discussion. In other words, he saw his reviews as part of a living cultural community, rather than as tips to individual consumers on how to spend their entertainment dollars; the kind of review which culminates in a thumbs-up or thumbs down or an array of stars—which render the preceding review more or less superfluous. That form of review is now so common that it's grown hard to even imagine the kind of alternative which Gordon Vogt's own pieces exemplify.

The reduction of the review to a consumer advice column has social implications, particularly for the democratic process. I know this sounds as if I may be taking the reviewing process too seriously. But what can I say? It seems to me that the yea-nay style of review trains members of our society to distrust their own ability to make judgments; and to count on experts for opinions in areas where they are perfectly capable of judging for themselves. (Oddly, this kind of reliance on expertise does not attach to spectator sports. Hockey fans don't wait till the morning after a game to be told whether they enjoyed it or not—or should have.) It's clear from this collection of his writings that Gordon Vogt took the social responsibility of reviewing seriously.

In this respect he was a successor to Nathan Cohen, who also reviewed theatre on CBC radio, in the late nineteen-forties; then for twenty years was drama critic of the Toronto *Star*, until his death in 1971. Cohen saw the role of critic as that of a teacher; he believed he could educate the Canadian public to appreciate the arts until it became capable of forming its own judgments; at that point critics like himself, much like the state in the marxist view of the world (which Cohen knew well) would be able to wither away, having served a historical function no longer necessary. To his dismay, Cohen found as the years passed that he was not fading away to make room for a discerning Canadian audience, but that on the contrary his role as critic was growing ever more prominent; he had become an element of the culture he had originally yearned only to herald. He died in despair about the value of his life's work.

So you could say Cohen felt his task as a critic was to teach his audience to think for themselves. That's think, not react. "Anyone can have opinions," wrote Cohen. "But the critic knows the reasons for his opinions." This is a deceptively simple requirement. I could draw on some examples, but instead let me suggest that you read through the reviews in any newspaper—on movies, books, theatre, whatever. See how often opinions are simply stated, rather than argued or explained: So-and-so gives a flawless performance; the script was lumpy; the direction was dazzling—as if reviewing is really reacting with a tone of authority. Twenty-seven years after Cohen's death, the Toronto *Star* was promoting its movie reviewers with an ad that read, "Lights. Action. Reaction." The substitution of opinion for thought in the reviewing process has become normal. An actual reason behind an opinion may slip through occasionally, though restating the opinion in different words doesn't count. (So-and-so was flawless because of her talent.) But it's rare. This is another good place to fear the effects on democracy. If a reviewer gives no reasons for judgments, then we are being asked to accept them on authority. Debate and discussion are ruled out, since there's no basis on which to talk. A reader may take a contrary view, as may another reviewer; what cannot happen is discussion, debate, change of views—all the things that ought to mark a democratic society. There is a similarity here to processes which have occurred regarding other subjects of concern to our society—like our economic and political options—formerly open to discussion and debate.

I'll admit it's not always easy to distinguish between an opinion and a reason, when talking about the arts. But the least a reviewer can do is give some idea of the thinking or reasoning involved. In his discussion of the NDWT company's production of James Reaney's *The Donnellys*, Vogt explains why he found the naturalistic staging of a brawl ineffective. The level of realism "served only to make me notice how unsuited were the actors' bodies...how unconvincing was violence when literally acted out onstage...." He contrasted that scene with a violent scene staged by George Luscombe in his play on the Depression, *Ten Lost Years*, which was performed as "one simple stylized action." Vogt calls the latter "a case of embracing the artificiality of the stage and using it as a lever on reality to achieve your theatrical ends." I grant this argument for his preference of one style over the other isn't definitive the way a mathematical proof is; but you're at least invited into the process taking place in the reviewer's mind; you can question, admire or dispute it; you're not expected to simply take it or leave it. Even if you disagree with the conclusion, it's possible to learn something about ways of seeing and evaluating theatre from this kind of reviewing.

It's typical that Vogt turns to George Luscombe for an understanding of what works and what doesn't in the theatre. Luscombe was the artist to whom he referred most often and about whom he wrote his longest, most carefully considered work. Luscombe became his baseline, you could say, for the judgment of Canadian theatre. Cohen too had paid close, respectful attention to Luscombe's work, and I'd have to say that in my own view, Luscombe is a case of true theatrical genius in Canadian theatre. At any rate, there is special value in the choice to concentrate on a particular artist, to think about his work over time, to ponder and re-evaluate your earlier assessments, as Vogt did of Luscombe. "This is the most solemn Luscombe I've seen," he wrote about *The Mac-Paps*, Luscombe's play on the Canadians who fought in the Spanish Civil War. What a respect for history and achievement is in that line.

9

How rarely have we had critics who accept responsibility for knowing the body of an artist's work, and show it the respect of viewing it in historical and biographical context; assuming that an artist's career, like a human life, has some continuity. Far more often we've had, as Vogt himself noted, a kind of premise that Canadian artists are meant to disappear after a youthful burst of activity, relieving critics of the need to maintain an interest or develop a perspective about them.

Vogt knew the role Cohen had played during his career as a critic, and what he termed "the subsequent deterioration of theatrical comment and debate in the Toronto papers" following Cohen's death. Of course so did anyone who lived through the so-called "golden age of Toronto theatre," which Vogt located in a narrow period between 1971 and 1974 , followed by years of difficulty for many theatre artists, including George Luscombe. He wrote about the impact of journalists and critics "whose secret function is to reflect fashion" and who "tend to be bold champions of orthodoxy." Unlike current Toronto *Star* book reviewer Philip Marchand, who recently claimed no good book has ever been killed by hostile reviews, Vogt was aware of damage, both to individual works and to a culture, which can be done by a "blind and tone-deaf press reaction." I hope this doesn't sound like a special plea or whine on behalf of a generation of people in theatre with whom I worked. There are others in our society who suffer far more from the stifling effects of imposed fashion (in the economy, in government, in social policy) than its artists. We can be grateful to have works which survived to inspire us; still, there's no way to number those which may have been lost by the foolish and narrow judgments of those with the power to dismiss without much thought.

That wasn't Vogt's kind of reviewing, what he described as a "tedious charade of saying that this actor was good but that actor was bad...a charade because observations of that sort when unconnected to a larger sense of the play really come down to personal reaction or lack of it." He thought hard about the larger sense of the play and many other matters. He felt a commitment to get it right. He had deadlines which distressed him when he wrote for radio, but he didn't rush back to the office and zip off a review in 20 minutes in order to get back to the post-opening party. He mulled his judgments over and returned to them, when he got a chance, as a reader of this collection can see by comparing his original reviews of

The Mac-Paps and *Ain't Lookin'* to his more considered reflections in the long piece on George Luscombe. In it, Vogt comes closest to what you might call criticism as opposed to reviewing, a distinction I've skirted so far and would rather not spend a lot of time on. But it's not just a matter of having time and the inclination to use it to rethink and hone your earlier conclusions; it's also a matter of being freed from the pressure of providing consumer tips on what to do with those entertainment dollars this weekend, and from the temptation to wield what power a critic has in the service of their particular vision of culture—a temptation from which Vogt was largely spared by the limited reach of the outlets he wrote for, and the shortness of his life.

But what I think really distinguishes Vogt's writing about art, however you categorize it, is not just that rare ability to give reasons for opinions; there's something else. He uses his analytical skills, his literacy and his sense of observation to get inside the plays, even when he doesn't particularly like them. As a result, reading him, you don't have the feeling of a critic looking on and judging, but of one whose mission is to penetrate the work and comprehend it. As a result, even when his assessment is negative, his mood feels more like disappointment than dismissal. So in his review of *The Mac-Paps*, Vogt writes that Luscombe's respect and reverence for the direct experience of the young men who fought in Spain "sometimes muddies the theatrical clarity and may give some viewers the feeling of a show which has not quite taken the step from life into art. But that respect gives the show its own solid warmth and dignity." What a fine way of saying the show indeed has not quite taken that leap, while at the same time understanding why it failed to do so; and simultaneously exploring the value the show has for an audience in spite—or because—of the fact it did not make that transition from life to art. It's hard to express how deft and rare this stance is for a critic-reviewer. Vogt gets to make a negative critical judgment and be generous at the same time, on the same point; and when you see him do it, you realize it's not nearly as tricky as it might sound. In fact it's not mysterious at all, if you think that, out in real life, positive and negative judgments aren't mutually exclusive. They normally cohabit, when we think of our friends or family; it's only in a fabricated context like mainstream reviewing (or editorial page punditry) that one is usually required to separate things neatly and take a definitive stand—or pretend to. At any rate this kind of ability to get inside a work, where he can be both critical and sympathetic at the same time, typifies Vogt; it is his characteristic stance as a writer on the arts. He called Linda Griffiths' play *Maggie and Pierre*, which was already a "hit" at the time he reviewed it, "a serious attempt at analysis of a public myth." Then he immediately added, "The fact that it's a pretty clear failure as theatre makes it only slightly less interesting." What's implied here is that the value of an evening in the theatre can be determined by a variety of things and doesn't solely depend on whether the play "works" or satisfies the reviewer's and audience's preconceptions about what a play should do. In fact, a badly done play might in some cases make for a better-spent evening in the theatre than a flawless production. In this respect, it seems to me, Vogt as critic-reviewer maintained the attitude of a typical audience member rather than a privileged expert, i.e., having devoted the time and money to go out, you'll look for something of value in the experience. "I'd like to be able to report on the nasty little scene that has caused [Jim Garrard's play] *Getting Even* to protect itself with a restricted rating," he wrote. "Unfortunately my view of that scene was obstructed by one of those ridiculous pillars that make the Theatre Second Floor such a perverse and lovable place." See what I mean about even his negative reactions having a sympathetic quality? You could call it reviewing with soul and in a culture like ours, drenched in condescending reviews and judgments, it's refreshing—even if many of the works Gordon Vogt exercised it on have faded from memory.

Vogt's reviews of plays at the Stratford or Shaw festivals many years ago remain astute; his insights into Shakespeare, Shaw, Chekhov and the rest are as good as you'd get anywhere. But that's also what characterizes them: you do get them almost anywhere. What you don't get elsewhere is insights into our own culture. Vogt's passion was with the Canadian reality and what he called "my attempts to understand what it is to exist in the civilization that has spread itself so thinly across the northern half of the North American continent."

But in fact, for this very reason, what comes through in his writing on Stratford and Shaw is exactly his sense of the role these institutions played in a still-colonized culture. "I sat meekly and obediently among the note-takers and the hungry-eyed actors and the stuffed tuxedos," he wrote about a Stratford opening, "breathing in the stale intimidating air of officially sanctioned culture and fleshing out the prosaic doodlings of the production with a willing imagination." It's true this could be a critique and condemnation of sanitized, authorized culture anywhere, but it has a special sav-agery, it seems to me, owing to the imperial provenance of that culture, and the humiliating, supine way the locals lap it up. His patience grew shorter as the theatre seasons passed. He described a Stratford repertoire of "sequined mediocrity" in which, under the direction of Robin Phillips, "dullness conquers all." It was as if, over time, he refined his feelings about those institutions and what they represented, till it became the pure, satisfying hatred Fanon rec-ommended to the colonized. That doesn't mean Vogt felt either contempt or disinterest for the art of other cultures. On the con-trary, he was a fan and critic, as the current selection shows, of both the classics and commercial culture. He knew enough of French cinema to correct Canadian critic Martin Knelman's screaming misuse of a line of Jean Renoir's; he called Francis Ford Coppola's *The Cotton Club* a "multimillion dollar art film;" and he considered Fred Astaire (an opinion which sounds carefully considered) "one of the three or four greatest popular artists of the century." He even praised some of the productions at Stratford.

Now, more than ten years later, we have not just the festivals outside Toronto, but in the city, theatres and megamusicals— Broadway-derived or Broadway-bound—which also squander and divert our theatre resources. Their audience could also be described, as Vogt put it, as "people who don't necessarily like theatre, almost certainly know little of what kind of work is being done in other companies, and who yet make a pilgrimage to"—here substitute the Ford Centre or the Princess of Wales Theatre for Stratford— "every season to see a new batch of frozen culture slightly thawed." At least these days they don't have to wearily drive all the way to Stratford and back to take advantage of the fact, as Vogt wrote at the time, "Stratford is as close to Broadway as Canada gets." Today it's even closer.

I want to acknowledge how deeply I feel when I read Vogt's brief review of a 1981 play of mine about Nathan Cohen. I wrote that play largely as an attempt to deal with the experience of being reviewed. I believe this is something that affects almost everyone working in the arts. We would rather not think that the reviewing process touches us in important ways, but I think in most cases it does. It affects us externally, through consequences for our work: whether it will be seen, whether we will have the opportunity to do more. This is especially the case in theatre, which is so ephemeral: a play can't sit on the shelf like a novel or film, to be rediscovered and enjoyed a season or a generation later. Once its components: set, actors etc., disperse, it's simply gone. And reviews affect us internally; it's no simple thing to be damned (or praised) before thousands, maybe millions, of your fellow citizens. Some artists say they don't read reviews for these reasons, or ignore them. The difficult nature of being reviewed applies not just to negative but also to positive ones: for example, an audience which has been told it's going to see a hilarious comedy tends to laugh a touch too quickly and too loudly. In either case, the integrity of the work and the relation to the audience is compromised. At any rate, my play on Nathan Cohen was harshly reviewed, and closed. Vogt's short review, which I heard about but didn't hear, since it was on the radio, made an attempt to understand the problem of the play which I appreciated, as I told him the only time we spoke, briefly. I hadn't read it until I received the manuscript of this book from Gordon's brother, Bruce.

Canadian actress Diane D'Aquila used to fantasize about creating a play about, but especially for, reviewers; its title would be *What You Deserve*. Gordon Vogt, it seems to me, is what we really did deserve. What a difference such a voice could have made, had it reached even further than it did, and not been cut off at the age of 37. As I've already said, this shouldn't be interpreted as a special plea for artists. Reviewers have done and continue to do damage in the realm of culture. But they don't hire themselves. They serve media interests and owners who distort and ill serve other areas they "cover" just as fully. And after all we did have Gordon Vogt's reviews in our media: too briefly, but we had him and now have him again, in this collection, a record of a part of our cultural history. It takes that history seriously as a reflection of our experience and ambitions, not just as a series of successes or failures in marketplace terms. And it assumes those experiences and ambitions are as worth taking seriously as anyone else's.

Even though the productions Vogt writes about are long gone and you may well not be able to picture them, something of value comes through in his attentive, thoughtful responses to them. As he said of George Luscombe's play about blacks in baseball, *Ain't Lookin'*, a show Vogt doubted would ever be produced by anyone but Luscombe himself, the characters "are suspended in the fragile memory of the narrator. They are otherwise long gone. This production is a dream and a memorial." So is this book. But imagine a life which did not contain dreams and memorials. In the end what you may find in Vogt if you read him as I do, is joy, despite all his anger at targets like Stratford, cheapness, the reviewing scam: his real love of art, wherever he found it. It's in his thoughts on Fred Astaire: "The boring plots and creaky comedy that surround even the best of Astaire's movies are not his province or responsibility. But when the films flower into dance, the ineffable Astaire comes into his own. For the 25 years or so that Astaire danced on film (until he was almost 60), there was no poor, fair or even pretty good Astaire dance, there was only great Astaire and greater Astaire. And who would say which of his many dances was the greatest? Even when he was saddled with an inadequate partner, if you kept your eye on the man he had his own integrity.... His nearest rival, Gene Kelly, like the car rental people, was number two, tried harder, and it showed." If his joy was laced with anger about a culture and a world which, like his own life, could easily have been better and fuller, you could also say of him what he said about Luscombe: "his joy in humanity vies with the anger that is so much a part of his work, and often wins."

As to the question: why read a collection of old reviews of largely forgotten plays, you could respond to that too, as he did about Luscombe, and about all the ephemeral works of theatre: "Yet to say that his particular ongoing achievement is not fully as important as the work of those who carve on stone is to value the artifact over the art."

Gordon Vogt in February of 1984

Theatre Reviews
1978-80

The Leacock Festival of Humour

Orillia, Ontario

At the Leacock Festival of Humour (The Merry-Posa Revue, it says here), the smell of mothballs is heavy on the Orillia air. The number of more-or-less resuscitated old jokes proliferates overwhelmingly during the course of a long long long long long two-and-a-half hour evening. Vying for dominance over the mothballs is the most aggressive folksiness this side of the Mason-Dixon Line. The audience is enjoined, harassed and beleaguered to sing along to sad artifacts of hominess about sittin' lookin' at the sky and eatin' blueberry pie. It responds meekly, dutifully. Not responding at this show is akin to spitting on your mother's grave.

The whole program has a fierce undercurrent of family coziness. There's Grandpa Fred C. Dobbs (Canada's own Will Rogers, lingering well on past the machine age) sternly laying on admonishments and bitter reproval, sometimes forgetting to leaven his little lessons with humour. (The audience shifts in its seats; old Grandpa's gone too far again.) There's married couple Smith and Smith, taking the role of precocious young brother and sister, singing their pleasant young songs and making their pleasant young jokes, while the audience claps indulgently, charmed by the promise of youth that knows its place. There's John Allan Cameron, embarrassing extroverted cousin, anything for a laugh, full of camp songs and good times and bullyrag humour ("a natural phenomenon!" it says here). There's Sears and Switzer, those smart-aleck second cousins from the city (Kingston, and therefore aggressively urban) who have lots of talent but the family finds them a bit uppity. There's host Bill Langstroth in the role of unsuccessful uncle whom everybody loves probably because he's unsuccessful. And then there's successful Uncle Gordie Tapp who graces the little gathering with his big-time presence ("the most loved performer in Canadian Show Business" it says here) expansively imparting the unction and humility which can only come from rubbing elbows with the Great (Buck Owens, Johnny Cash).

To be sure, this rag-tag gathering of minor show business phenomena has little to do with Stephen Leacock, a tough-minded and compact writer who used a small town persona to very shrewd ends. Easy to point out that the folksiness in which the more offensive of

18

these performers clothe themselves is a particularly crass manifes-tation of Show Biz dishonesty. (I here except Magee's Dobbs, who—no matter how often his creator misuses him—strikes me as a geuine creation, based on tight observation and a certain honesty.)

Oddly enough though, Gordie Tapp's Cousin Clem with his poo poo and wee wee jokes is less offensive than the persona of Gordie Tapp, Big-time Nightclub Entertainer, with his limp old cache of adolescent genitalia (Cousin Clem all growed up). Canada's Best Loved Performer resplendent in white safari jacket, white teeth and sincere open nostrils (a terrifying sight) is not above pandering to a good solid Canadian audience's closet racism. This emerged in a series of affectionate jokes about the many different nationalities who joined to make up this wonderful country of ours. This myriad of different nationalities turned out to be the English, the Scotch and the Irish. All were rendered in accents amazingly hard to dis-tinguish from Mr. Tapp's own. ("He can tell stories in fourteen di-alects with an authenticity to be envied," it says here.) As a post-script he added in a sudden change of manner:

"There are over 15,000 Italian people in Toronto, did you know that?"

Pause.

"But I know how to get rid of them."

The punch line is not important, having to do with the usual cosy assumption that all Italians like to do nothing but drink wine and fornicate. (Come to think of it, what's wrong with that?) What was important was the complacent assurance that the audience would feel along with the comedian that the Italian community was some-thing to get rid of. After that one Mr. Tapp found it necessary to add "only kidding." When a comedian has to assure his audience that he's being funny, he's in trouble.

Mr. Tapp went on after that. A member of the audience re-quested a Chinese story. Mr. Tapp responded with a Japanese story (all those orientals are the same anyway), and a story about a "Pakistani gentleman" (the one that ends "it's a knick knack Paddy Wack, give the Pak a loan"—if you don't know it, ask your Uncle Charlie). The fact that the audience tittered at the mere whiff of a Pakistani joke was enough to make this observer queasy.

It's embarrassing to acknowledge that perhaps Gordie Tapp's segment was the only portion of the show that touched on any part of the Leacock tradition. After all, Leacock is well known to have cherished the racist mentality of our forefathers. Maybe the Gordie Tapps of the world perform the useful function of reminding us of the worst aspects of our heritage.

Interestingly enough the French Canadian was conspicuous by his absence in Tapp's list of peoples who have helped to form Canada. In fact, I can't recall any allusion being made to the French at all. This despite the show's tendency to wax pompous about finding humour in everything we see around us. Perhaps that issue is too touchy for a show that by and large contents itself with licking the collective posterior of its audience.

To those who caught the show, may I recommend, as an antidote, catching *Codco*, one of Canada's great natural resources, which may, if you're lucky, play some church basement or public library near you before it collapses under the weight of its own brilliance. Also you might watch for Sears and Switzer away from Orillia. They show great promise and may just develop nicely despite the bad company they suffered in what might hopefully be described as Tapp's Last Crepe.

August 1978

Filthy Rich

Written by George F. Walker, directed by William Lane.
Toronto Free Theatre

Toronto Free Theatre came up with a strong opening for their season last Saturday. *Filthy Rich* is the second of George F. Walker's series of comic plays about Tyrone M. Power, reluctant private eye. The world which Power inhabits is suggested by a few hand-picked characters comically distorted from the pages of Raymond Chandler, and delineated by the cast with comic precision. Of course Chandler's mean streets are only implied here. The entire play takes place in a cluttered apartment. And it's wonderful how the designers, Arnott and Elchen, and the director, William Lane, have managed to coax from this tiny set the shadowy ambience of the film noir. Particularly clever is the contrasting use made of the two onstage entrances, one a glazed office wall and door, through which we can watch the distorted forms of the characters slowly approaching, and the other a window onto a fire escape through which figures materialize without warning.

Walker is clearly submitting a genre piece with *Filthy Rich*. That the laughs are never cheap, that the play never becomes a pastiche or a camp item, even in its comic mode, testifies to Walker's success in making a dead genre vital. The character of Power, although he clearly represents many other things to the author, revivifies the Chandler landscape largely because he's a legitimate reworking of the hard-boiled prototype. Walker chooses to exaggerate the self-pity that is such a disquieting undercurrent in Philip Marlowe. Power's self-pity all but incapacitates him, making him liable to drunken fits of blubbering. In fact, Power, despite Walker's assertion that he is the last of the great cynics, is a softie. Paralyzed from acting on his secret sentimental moralism, he has retreated into a squalid little hideaway with a bottle and a hopelessly unfinished novel which he stores in garbage bags rather than a filing cabinet. Even with his quick tongue, Power carries no personal authority whatsoever. He keeps the world at bay with a mechanical bluster-ing wit which he cannot check even when held at gunpoint or expressing grief.

David Bolt, giving a fascinating performance as Power, is remi-niscent of Elwy Yost with his grin surgically removed. A gifted comic actor, he uses his body like some dissolute Chaplin, rolling haphazardly on the balls of his feet but capable of quick deft moves that never fail to startle.

This poor middle-aged husk is bullied into action by a young street kid eager for a crack at the high life and together, forming an odd and touching partnership, they solve the case. More or less. Don't ask me the plot; Walker follows the glorious film noir tradi-tion of obscuring already convoluted plot lines which is just as well for they're hardly the point of the exercise.

The character of Tyrone M. Power functions as a kind of writer's self-parody. He evinces precisely that cutting self-contempt nur-tured by spending most of one's waking hours closeted away from humanity while trying to discern or impose patterns of meaning on life. This is a peculiarly Canadian writer's disease as this society does not value its serious writers beyond the handful who have achieved celebrity, an accepted goal. Because Power is a writer's surrogate we can accept the twisted ending in which the mur-dered young assistant suddenly springs back to life. After all, why shouldn't Walker change his mind about killing the guy? He's obviously intended as the life force of the play. Besides, as played by Angelo Rizacos, he's one of the most subtly ingratiating characters on stage.

You might be surprised to know that George Walker is Canada's most successful playwright outside of this country. Surprised, because although he has met acclaim in Britain and the States, none of his plays have been picked up by a Canadian company after their initial Toronto runs. Small wonder he is given to quoting Joyce's statement about the treatment accorded its artists by another colonized country. Perhaps Canada, like Ireland, is a mother pig that eats its young.

January 1979

Winter 1671

Written by Erika Ritter, directed by Leon Major. St. Lawrence Centre

Winter 1671 is a clumsily written melodrama disguised as a historical play. There's nothing wrong with melodrama, but by the time the play is forced to acknowledge its lineage—by virtue of some of the baldest plot contrivance this side of East Lynne—all of the stylistic decisions that could have floated it have been ducked. Erika Ritter apparently took her plot from a historical anecdote about the mysterious fate of one of the mail order brides sent from France to Quebec in the late seventeenth century as part of an effort to populate the new land. She's constructed a story around the character of the young woman, a country girl, escaping from a bad marriage of convenience. The woman, as imagined by Ritter, is a walking compendium of attitudes fashionable through this past decade. It's hardly surprising that such a woman should meet tragedy in the striated and transplanted society of seventeenth century New France. What is surprising is that this young woman should form such close alliances with the members of that society whom she meets. Her anachronistic ideas of personal freedom meet sympathetic ears in everyone from the embittered whore who causes all the trouble, to the well-born lady tragically married to a rogue, to the kindly old governor hoisted, Cleon-like, on his petard of duty, to

22

the proud widowed seigneur who falls in love with her and casts his dark masculine shadow over the proceedings. This is, of course, fantasy. And in Leon Major's production, that quality is unwittingly stressed by the odd mix-and-match costumes, white and shaded with shimmering pastels, hardly the sort of thing to suggest a pioneer settlement, even an established one with pretensions to civilization. But into this stolid fairyland of a seventeenth-century Quebec is injected actress Anne Anglin, playing the whore with the heart of flint. Anglin niggles around the edges of the production like a fidgety stagehand eager to get on with the real business. She nibbles away at her rather silly part, burrows into the ensembles, sending out gritty little sparks of reality that subvert all that noble female suffering and hollow male swaggering which postures so awkwardly about her. Just by being onstage, she is a reassurance. She tells us that a good actor never has an excuse to be anything less than good. Which brings us to *The Belle of Amherst*.

The Belle of Amherst

Written by William Luce, directed by Ray Whelan. Open Circle Theatre

Claire Coulter is one of the treasures of the Canadian stage. It wouldn't hurt most of our actors to sit at her feet for a while, if only to clear away the vestiges of Theatre School. For Coulter is an actress who works with an almost breathtaking lack of artifice and theatricality. Her technique has long since been so absorbed that it's invisible. One might think that she would be the perfect actress to play Emily Dickinson, the American poet, whose uneventful existence was balanced by one of the most eventful inner lives ever recorded. Yet *The Belle of Amherst* is a failure. This is partly due to the play itself, which wrestles mightily with the problem of how to dramatize life without event and fails. But finally the problem is in the nature of the one-character play and the nature of Coulter as an actress. The one-character play is a form that embraces artificiality, and the actor at its centre must do the same, carrying on conversations with invisible characters and changing ages in the blink of an eye. Coulter so absorbs herself in the textures of the woman she is playing that she fails to stand back and give the play the kind of shaping it needs. I suppose that's largely a director's responsibility.

But after all when one actor is alone onstage for an evening, that actor must provide the dramatic shape. As it stands, Coulter's is an exquisite characterization without a play to support it. And the final effect is numbing.

February 1979

The Pits

Written and directed by John Palmer. Adelaide Court Theatre

The main theatrical space of the Adelaide Court Theatre has been gutted. Where the audience would normally be is a great shambles of a boarding house designed by the talented team of Brian Arnott and Syvalya Elchen. The seats now surround the set on three levels of scaffolding, from which the audience observes the proceedings as if peering down into one of the pits of the title. In one corner room, a silent hulk switches television channels, bites the caps off beer bottles and punctuates the surrounding action with belches. Next door to him, a middle-aged telephone repairman, with pretensions to post-European refinement, sexually mounts the replica of a telephone pole which he keeps under his bed.

The beautiful young woman in the adjoining room observes the mating rituals of flat worms and initiates several rituals of her own. Across the hall an older woman lives in homely middle-class propriety, daydreaming about love affairs and mooning over her incarcerated son. Next door to her is a young couple: she a hopelessly incompetent child of 24 who rarely seems to get out of her nightdress and green socks; he an acrobatic dwarf obsessed with his private weather tower. As a couple they spend their time arguing about her pregnancy, and holding contests to see who can stage the most effective suicide attempts. On this last score the husband wins hands down, engineering a magnificent death by hanging in full clown make-up, while she flaps helplessly and empties the contents of a fire extinguisher on his face—and, incidentally, on the faces of half the east row of spectators who, I imagine, were not too happy about this rude violation of theatre's invisible wall.

This thin layer of grotesquerie is stretched over a lumpy core of drama. We know it's a comedy because the actors wear strange

24

clothes and do funny things. But if we were to take that away we would be left with the kind of thin little drama in which every character at some point in the play stops the action to speak a short monologue that reveals to the audience what is going on under the surface. This is by now a mechanical device. But it's also a very odd one in a play which fools around with grotesquerie. It's strange to hear the characters of a farce making cryptic allusions to previous events as if mysteries therein lie. Are the dwarf and the pregnant child/woman intended to be parodies of an Edward Albee couple, or is their allusion to a mysteriously dead child simply the result of a rather feeble workshop approach to character? It's hard to say.

But if it's hard to understand the little dramas of *The Pits*, it's also hard to understand the point of the comedy. Playwright/director John Palmer is certainly not simply making fun of his characters. He rather seems to like them, and that's nice. But why the weirdness? Whatever cross sections of society lurk in this boarding-house, it is not defined in any pointed way. The characters don't have the feeling of having been drawn from observation. The only point seems to be the most elementary of theatre school perceptions: that none of us are what we seem, that we are all of us slightly grotesque.

The ending is nice. A storm kills the lights and our cast of characters scurry about lighting candles, hopping in and out of beds, making up, making out, becoming some sort of small community in the process. It's a nice theatrical idea, the dark stage, the candles, the confusion. And for awhile, the play's rather soft and sweet nature emerges without apology. That softness is nice too, but it's also what's wrong with the play itself, which needs a hard eye somewhere.

It should be said that, under the circumstances, the actors are charming and surprisingly low key. Susan Rubes, in her first Toronto onstage appearance, is a friendly presence. And Claude Jutra, on sabbatical from film-making, is a skillful and appealing comedian within his oddly conceived role as a concupiscent technology freak.

February/March 1979

Sight Unseen

Written by Steve Petch, directed by Jack Blum. Tarragon Theatre

If *Sight Unseen* is Steve Petch's first play—and I believe it is—then he's a very promising playwright indeed. The play takes place in and around a Greek pension where three young Canadians pause during the course of a vacation. Around them two shadow figures hover, a decaying pederast in permanent exile and a young Swiss woman who operates on a plane of morality alien to our central characters. That's about all that the playwright starts with, but he explores the dramatic equations that the variables suggest with ruthlessness and compassion. The play is really about repression and about how it is bound up so closely with our sense of righteousness that it calls into question our whole structure of morality. But it works very nicely simply as a study of three people nearing the brink of their moral universe and trying to get their bearings. This is all good gripping theatre. Petch's first act is very strong. If he does tend to flop around a bit in the second, trying to get a handle on his themes, he is helped, in Tarragon's production, by director Jack Blum who himself has the benefit of one of the most balanced and uniformly strong casts I can remember seeing. It's a period play set, pointedly I think, in 1928. Richard Partington as the philan-dering husband catches just the right worldly breeziness that was that period's equivalent of cool. Richard Blackburn as his dogged repressed friend, and Maureen McRae as his wife, carry their rather dangerous roles with dignity, both resisting the temptation to tele-graph underlying tensions. Maureen McRae, on the evidence of this play alone, is a superb actress with an absorbing natural approach. We should see more of her, and of Steve Petch and his play. Tar-ragon Theatre still has the best eye for new material around.

Cop Shop

Written by Robert Lord, directed by Robert Robinson.
Toronto Arts Productions

The same can't be said for Toronto Arts Productions. New Zealand playwright Robert Lord's *Cop Shop* is probably the least appealing import Toronto has seen since last fall when a huge *Mackerel* slowly festered on the Adelaide Court main stage. This farce is about a pompous prima donna of a police detective who descends on a small New Zealand town to investigate a murder and in the process stirs up its muddy waters so that a nasty sludge of murder, abortion and general free-for-all fornication settles on all. The play is so tediously offensive on so many levels that it hardly seems worthwhile to catalogue them.

But beyond that, the production seems to miss in other ways. Like melodrama, farce must rely almost wholly on style to carry it. When a director approaches farce, he must have a very clear idea of what he wants to do with it. Unfortunately director Robert Robinson breaks the cardinal rule that farce must be deadly serious to its participants. He encourages Douglas Chamberlain as the detective to give a protracted vaudeville turn. The effect is exactly as if one of those character actors who people the edges of Hollywood screwball comedy had grabbed centre stage. In this case, the ghost of Eric Blore stalks the St. Lawrence Centre stage. The characters are walking exclamation points looking for a statement to punctuate. They carry even less substance when made to rush about Murray Laufer's characteristically solid set, all neat blocks of precisely detailed shape. Laufer is one of the best traditional set designers around. Lights up on a Laufer set and the mouth fairly waters with anticipation. But in this case the set also raises false expectation of substance. After a few moments of trivial post-Pinter dialogue one wants to crane, camera-like, through one of Laufer's beautifully lit rear windows and escape into the green New Zealand countryside which seems tantalizingly to be just beyond the sill.

March 1979

Getting Even

Written and directed by Jim Garrard. Theatre Second Floor

Getting Even is ostensibly a grim little story about two men, a woman and a card game that ends in jealousy and violence. Writer-director Jim Garrard coyly subtitles it a domestic comedy, but a mere plot outline would give the lie to that pretty quickly. Garrard

27

was closer to the point when he referred to it in an interview as a little exploration of the theatrical pause. But Garrard is too quiet about it all. I'm not sure that the play itself has any life outside of its immediate production, but that production seems to me a brilliant essay in theatrical style, and one that should be seen and digested by every theatre person who can get to it.

Garrard has pretty well subdued any hint of theatrical presentation. All of the production's considerable stagecraft is put in the service of mundane reality. Stage time is exactly parallel to real time. The actors make no apparent effort to play for the audience, and when their lines are drowned out by the inevitable Parliament Street sirens, they neither alter their delivery, nor wait out the aural intrusion. This approach may sound mannered but in fact it's rather easy to adjust to, and it's surprising just which things become theatrical in such a flattened context. For whole stretches of time there is nothing to watch but two men at a table playing cards while behind them in a kitchen a woman methodically prepares an early morning breakfast. To be sure a card game carries with it its necessary circular buildup of tension, and there is a slow winding up of frustration with each game, but over and above that it's remarkable how absorbing the natural pattern of two simple planes of action can become. There are moments—several of them in fact—in which one character stands motionless staring at a TV screen for a daringly long period of time. These dead moments are intriguing: the audience finds itself suddenly conscious of its role as audience, and the mind starts casting about for metaphors, grasping at significance that isn't there, and yet must be. Why else should such pieces of non-action be absorbing?

Finally, when the evening seems to be winding up in a conventional outburst of violence the audience knows where it is at last— the play is really just one of those slice-of-life melodramas. But no— the climax is not in the knife wielding, but in a logically climactic theatrical pause. For what seems an impossibly long period of time, one is left waiting for an offstage death scream, with nothing on stage to occupy one's attention but the terrible wait. The wait would be unforgivably sadistic were it not formally necessary. In fact Garrard ducks the conventional catharsis leaving a chastened audience holding its own frustrated expectations on its collective lap. It's Garrard's remarkable achievement that by the end of his production the very nature of theatrical reality is called into question.

We are left wondering whether theatre is at base merely the sum of an audience's projections. But Garrard makes it all an exhilarating experience.

I'd like to be able to report on the nasty little scene which has caused *Getting Even* to protect itself with a restricted rating. Unfortunately my view of that scene was obstructed by one of those ridiculous pillars that make the Theatre Second Floor such a perverse and lovable space.

April 1979

October Soldiers

Written by Alun Hibbert, directed by Clarke Rogers.
Theatre Passe Muraille

October 1970 is well on its way to becoming a touchstone date for Canadian playwrights, novelists and filmmakers. Last summer Quebec's Lennoxville Festival presented *Clouds of Glory*, a new play which dealt with the October crisis as it affected a power struggle in a small west-coast university. *Clouds of Glory* was one of those pieces which, although full of intelligence and witty lines, still managed to be a very bad play. It was fun, however, trying to work out the allegory behind the plot, which left the French-Canadian hero dead, caught in the crossfire between European fascist and American activist/power-monger.

There doesn't seem to be much allegory behind Alun Hibbert's *October Soldiers*. It seems to be what it seems to be: a story about five soldiers, in various stages of retarded development, spending a grim evening in a Montreal dive during the imposition of the War Measures Act. The cast is fleshed out with a couple of hookers, an impressive bartender, and a malignant little toadie of a hopeful pederast who tries to befriend the soldiers. And that's about it. The soldiers squabble, one of them loses his virginity to a hooker, another sets fire to a second hooker's macramé and a third undergoes a public crisis of conscience. As is usual with the kind of melodrama in which sexual tension strains under every masculine breast, the whole thing is wrapped up with violence, in this case a stabbing and a bludgeoning.

29

Playwright Hibbert, himself an ex-soldier, seems to have written the play as an act of expiation. But what he is trying to expiate is not clear. It might have something to do with having spent time in the service consorting with thoughtless bums such as those who spend an hour and a half in this Montreal bar. They are, without exception, stupid, violence-prone, racist louts, a fact to which the dialogue is constantly drawing our attention. The central character, Jeremy, the young conscience-prone soldier, spends the evening sneering at everybody around him, but finally proves himself at least as violent as his fellow soldiers.

I'm sure that Hibbert is aware of that irony in the behaviour of his central character. Yet I can't help feeling that Jeremy is little more than a device of the author's to disassociate himself from a past role with which he is uncomfortable. Therefore, even though Jeremy is finally guilty with the rest, we are asked to grant him forgiveness, simply for seeing beyond his role and not being like the other louts. In fact Jeremy demonstrates very little more understanding of his position than the others. His loud contempt merely masks confused thinking. And it's impossible to separate his confused thinking from that of his author. Finally, all of the characters are kept in a stranglehold by the playwright. They are being used to demonstrate a point of view and are given no room to breathe.

Over the soldiers' squabbling Raymond Belisle's bartender casts a cold eye. Belisle is one of my favourite actors, bringing dignity to every part he takes. I was very disappointed when his character proved to be a racist and a killer like the rest.

Mention should be made of David Clement's Gerry. He's the nasty little voyeur who attaches himself to the soldiers. If anyone successfully captures the tone of this play it's Clement. He skitters about the edges of the action during the first half, but in the second section he's centre stage with the perfect self-possession of one who has long since been bedfellow to humiliation and who, consequently, is impervious to insult. Our hero, Jeremy, the angry young soldier, is no match for this camp follower.

And I mustn't miss Michel Lefebvre's Frenchie, a prolonged drunk act that had many pleasurable moments. The rest of the actors too had their moments, but they were largely reduced to being Stupid or Bigoted or Drunk or Outraged—all in capital letters.

October Soldiers was developed at Factory Theatre Lab using funding from the Lee Awards. It will require more woodshedding if it is to become a successful play. It will also have to think through its attitudes to the event it depicts.

11 October 1979

Refugees

Written by Beverly and Raymond Pannell, directed by George Luscombe. Toronto Workshop Productions

Let's start with two privileged moments. The first belongs to the director and is the climax of the first act. Four people—a Jewish couple, a communist and a priest—have been huddled together in a tiny closet for months, hiding from the Nazis. On the night of their forced escape they turn their final evening into a celebration of friendship. The husband gets gloriously drunk for the first time in his life, and begins to dance, also for the first time in his life. Actor Jeff Braunstein, demonstrating once again his surprising physical talent, does a comic dance of graceful inebriation of which Chaplin would not be ashamed. Director George Luscombe takes that dance and orchestrates an entire movement around it from celebration to flight without losing momentum or mood. It's a curiously uplifting moment. We never lose sight of the fact that these people are in danger and their fragile gaiety is affecting.

The second moment belongs to the composers and comes at the end of the second act. The two principal refugees of the title are transformed into harmless symbols by the rest of the cast, who dance about them, singing an infectious and wonderfully bitter cabaret song which, even as it forces its buoyancy on us, cuts nastily against what we have experienced in the two previous hours, and leaves us with a very charged mixture of emotions.

This is all a roundabout way of saying that *Refugees* is a happy wedding of director and composers. In structure and concept it's not far removed from any number of previous Luscombe shows. Personal experiences of survivors of the depression shaped *Ten Lost Years*. *Refugees* is built around the reminiscences of refugee survivors of totalitarian regimes. The difference is that Beverly and Ray Pannell, who wrote the play, are composers. Their music is brilliantly theatrical, although only in a few instances is it anything approaching an operatic vein. Mostly it's closer to the kind of music that Weill wrote for Brecht, and like that music, it is intended to be serviceable as well as expressive. The Pannells soon inform us that they will plunder any idiom that best suits their needs. In one particularly strong number, a bright happy nursery melody and lyric tells a terrible story of children torn away from parents. The effect is terrifying, yet the song and lyrics never drop their cosy idiom. The lyrics throughout are very fine indeed; so fine that in the one or two instances when two of the singing cast failed to spit out their consonants and we lost the words, it felt like a severe loss.

And about our cast, well bless 'em. It's made up of actors who sing well and singers who act well. It's hardly surprising that Marilyn Lightstone and Jeff Braunstein bring off touchy scenes with ease. But it's very pleasantly surprising that the three principal singers should give them a run for their money in the acting department. Giulio Kukurugya plays his variety of parts with a marvellous dignity. And Susan Gudgeon was open, expressive and touching throughout. This is a Luscombe show so nobody is wasted. The five accompanists are onstage throughout, and take part in the action as actors and do so charmingly and unpretentiously.

Theatrically the show owes much to the brilliance of Luscombe's regular designer Astrid Janson. TWP's stage is formed of some kind of plastic grating through which light can shoot up from beneath, sending fractured patterns over the actors and disorienting the audience spatially.

There are failures in the show. The first act has problems and the second act bites off more than it is willing to chew, hewing, perhaps inadvertently, to the new Left rhetoric about Israel. But there is more good—even great—theatre packed into this one evening than one can really expect from a full season of the usual fare. If the Pannells keep up this kind of work and keep finding collaborators like Luscombe, they might actually succeed in pumping life into their chosen form, opera, that poor attenuated and anemic form, long since relegated to pompous experiments with only a hopeful, incompetent and condescending sense of the theatrical.

19 October 1979

32

Rain

Adapted by John Colton and Clemence Randolph from a short story by
W. Somerset Maugham, directed by Eric Steiner. Toronto Free Theatre

It's been a long time since a woman could shock an audience by
sweeping onstage in a red dress and chug-a-lugging from a whisky
bottle. This creates a big problem for any revival of *Rain*, first produced in 1922. The whole first act rides on the outrageousness of a
Sadie Thompson flouncing about in glorious technicolour and aban-
don while the affronted missionaries, who have been stranded with
her in a tropical outpost, gasp and splutter. This problem is by no
means solved in Eric Steiner's production, and the first act is a bit
boring as a result. However the play—and this production—shows
its mettle in the second and third acts. This morning the local
reviewers will have their knives out on this old warhorse, long since
retired to the remoter pastures of summer stock. But in fact, even
given the theatrical hollowness of the first act, it's a rather good
play, fully justifying a revival. The basic plot has to do with a missionary who becomes obsessed with saving the soul of a lively good-
time girl on the lam, while, all the time, sublimating the hope that
she will save his body from years of chastity. This would seem sure-
fire melodrama. But, even though it's handled much more intelligently than that outline would suggest, it's still rather dangerous
material today. The audience warmed to our Sadie right from the
beginning. Yet they were a little uneasy with her conversion. It was
perfectly logical, theatrically and psychologically, and yet it cuts
rather too sharply against our modern complacency about human
needs. Likewise they resisted sympathy with David Fox's repressed
and rigid missionary, wanting to turn him into a figure of fun. It's to
that impressive actor's credit—Fox handles dramatic language as
well as any actor I've seen onstage—that he pulled them back to
the truth of the situation by his solid playing. In fact, the climactic
confrontation between missionary and convert was charged with
sexual and moral tension and not a titter was heard, even when the
missionary, somnambulant and sexually alerted, followed the rapt
and innocently oblivious Sadie into her bedroom with no talk, for
once, of praying.
      The actors too, in the early stages of the play at least, signalled a
little uncertainty about their characters by overdrawing them. Mind

you, they never approached the cartoon effect of those ludicrous palm fronds painted on the backdrop which threatened to turn every scene into a Carmen Miranda number. But the actors' uncertainty allowed the audience the room to giggle when they felt uncomfortable. Yet I wager that the real discomfort of the audience was not with the material but with the primal clash between two psychological forces, starkly suggested in the central confrontation.

I mentioned the problem with the first act. Of course the actress playing Sadie Thompson takes the brunt of that. Wendy Thatcher's Sadie has serious drawbacks as a performance. Sadie must, at the very least, be at home with her body, and this element is lacking. The first act contrives to have the character at the centre of the action to the point of having most of the dialogue revolve around her rather mechanically. Unless the actress at the centre can fill the centre, one begins to wonder what all the fuss is about. If Thatcher's Sadie were a striding ego like Joan Crawford's or a gorgeous tabula rasa like Rita Hayworth's, perhaps the first act would make sense. But I'm not sure the rest of the play would. Wendy Thatcher's Sadie is no goddess, just an ordinary young woman, disguising her fear with bravado, and this makes her striving for an impossible purity touching and true. Her last lines, in particular, are lovely. In them we can see the generosity of Somerset Maugham who allowed this brave, lost woman one final moment of grace in understanding.

This *Rain* is an uncertain and only partially successful production, but it's one that has plenty of possibilities. Its fine cast needs to trust their material a bit more and not to worry quite so much whether every line hits the back wall. And someone needs to take a can of white spray paint to those palm fronds.

26 October 1979

Lady of the Camellias

Written by Suzanne Grossman, directed by Robin Phillips.
Theatre London

In her program notes, playwright Suzanne Grossman expresses gratitude for Theatre London's patience in working on her new play. Her gratitude seems misplaced. If, indeed, the production has been "perfected" in the sense that every curtain fall, every silence, seems timed with a stop watch, the natural crude force of melodrama (which is its only true virtue) has been subdued, muted and otherwise tamed. There could hardly be a story less suited to Robin Phillips' abilities than the old tale of a courtesan finding true love and sacrificing her life for her lover. To my knowledge Phillips has never presented a convincing love relationship on the stage. His director's hand seems to deaden the passion it should quicken. And although nothing in this show is as awkward as the young lovers' scenes in his Stratford production of A *Winter's Tale* a few seasons back, still the central love scenes are of a flatness and lack of conviction that strike to the heart of the play and kill it. It's almost perverse to have made such a cold little pageant of the old story.

Phillips has always brought a good hard intelligence to his analysis of texts. In this case, faced with the slightness of Grossman's play, he seems to have grafted on an interpretation in which Marguerite glumly trudges on to embrace her own death. Even if one grants him that interpretation—and it has severely hampered Martha Henry's Marguerite—it doesn't excuse the tight control Phillips has exerted on his actors. They move about the stage like exquisite wax figures. I have rarely seen a production so devoid of spontaneity, so carefully and ineffectively manipulated.

Perhaps nothing could have been done with Marguerite's young lover, once Stephen Russell was miscast. The actor fails to respond either to the terribly young and vulnerable suitor of the first act or the haunted and embittered wastrel of the second. But what does one make of the complacent readings of so many of this experienced cast? Their emphases and bursts of emotion could have been timed by computer. William Needles is not a crude actor. Is there any reason why he should play his scenes on such a thin and insistently hammered note?

The ensembles are marginally better than the intimate scenes. Grossman has sketched in the society milieu competently enough, and actors like Pat Galloway and Diana Leblanc handle their characters well. But even these scenes betray a mechanical rhythm, never for a moment suggesting a life of their own, and at their worst seeming merely an excuse to display exquisite period furniture and even more exquisite costumes.

Self-congratulation drips from this production. Cast and director seem insufferably proud of themselves for avoiding all that tacky melodrama at the heart of the story. Grossman, too, seems to have been a party to this case of misplaced tact. Why else would she have avoided the climactic deathbed reconciliation between the parted lovers? Ladies and gentlemen, it is no coincidence the *Lady of the Camellias* has served well as an opera. If one does not find one's artistic impulses quickened by such inherently operatic scenes as the reconciliation, then for heaven's sake, why bother rewriting the story at all? And if that is to be compounded by a director who picks up the tale fastidiously between thumb and forefinger, holding it away from his body with a moue of distaste, then that story will no longer exist. May I make the obvious comment that good art and certainly good theatre cannot be equated with good taste.

I never thought I'd fail to respond to Martha Henry. I've loved her from afar for years. I still find her every vocal inflection, her every gesture, enchanting. But I think she has failed with Marguerite. Can she have missed the irony at the heart of the character? She telegraphs tragedy from her first entrance. Where is the humour that delights in her courtesan's life, as destructive as it may be to her? Where is the hope that emerges from behind her cynicism? And—again—where is that irony that must watch as her hope effects her destruction more thoroughly than her cynicism could have?

Finally, I'm not sure Grossman was right in bringing sexuality to the surface of the story. The easy coarseness of a modern sensibility sits awkwardly beside the delicacy inherent, for instance, in Marguerite's displays of camellias, red only for a certain time of the month. Besides, it makes strange bedfellows with Phillips' corsetted rendering of human sexuality.

3 December 1979

Coming through Slaughter

Written by Michael Ondaatje, directed by Paul Thompson.
Theatre Passe Muraille

Coming through Slaughter is Michael Ondaatje's dark fantasy of turn-of-the-century New Orleans. Deriving partly from research, partly from fancy, it juggles events in the life of Buddy Bolden, a major early innovator in New Orleans jazz, and ends with his violent breakdown while playing at the centre of a Street Parade. The story takes place in short cinematic scenes, or it's told to us in monologue form by the participants, or it's simultaneously described and acted out, Story Theatre style, as when Bolden and an ex-rival go at each other in an elaborate fight with straps, belt buckles, razors, chairs and flung shards of broken glass.

Ondaatje's Bolden has spent years with his horn, tuning himself, machine-like, past the point of taste and emotional control. Ondaatje's image of the artist would be romantic were it not so bleak. Bolden has tuned an aspect of himself past humanity, but this doesn't mean he's reached a higher plane, for his tuning has nothing to do with finer awareness—it's merely a finer tuning and it makes him susceptible to fits of violence or lust, rather like static in an electronic device.

Bolden appears at a parade in New Orleans from out of nowhere, apparently having formed almost magically as a musician. But in fact he has spent years practising before making his appearance. When we first meet Bolden, he's established as a local musician, and married. It becomes clear that he needs a woman to give him stability. After his violence erupts in the fight I've described, Bolden leaves his wife, home and friends as if they never existed. He appears in another town and throws himself before a friend's wife, begging her to save him. She takes him as a lover and the three live together, the triangle forming another volatile equilibrium.

Bolden's final madness comes when his friend Webb, a detective, tracks him down in his new life and forces him back to New Orleans, where he must resume his musician's career. Bolden is tuned only for the present. When forced back into a position in which he must recognize time and change and the force of the past, he loses his hold on reality altogether.

It's a fascinating pattern that Ondaatje gives us (I can only give a cartoon outline here). And there's a lot in the stage treatment that's very fine indeed. Many of Ondaatje's monologues work very well, particularly when handled by an actor as good as Layne Coleman, who plays Webb. Coleman knows exactly how to draw an audience into the life of a bunch of words, and in the process of doing that, he gives us the outline of an intriguing character.

37

I'm not sure that Ondaatje's jigsaw approach to narrative works as well for him onstage as it did in his book. It may obscure the dramatic pattern I've talked about, without really adding enough in the way of contrast and irony to justify it. Occasionally I felt wrenched about to little effect beyond the wrench, although I suppose one could argue that such an effect mirrors the psyche of the central character. There are also some weaknesses peculiar to this production. I wasn't convinced by Ardon Bess' Buddy. As physically well-judged and precise as that actor was, his moves were calculated—his eyes aware of effect, and his voice too proud of them—and that was fatal in a character supposedly at the mercy of his own impulses.

This is a show for which atmosphere is crucial, and on the production side there was plenty of it. Jim Plaxton's set is full of corners and recesses, planks and pillars, and director Paul Thompson and his cast know exactly how to use it. They strut about it, leap over it, lean against it, huddle secretively in the alcoves, and, in general, occupy it with the proper intimacy. I do, however, have a tiresome quibble with the music, so important to the show. Thompson has put Jim Galloway and Ken Dean and a few of the Metro Stompers right up there on the stage, but as enjoyable as they were, they weren't right. Nor do I simply mean that they didn't try to reproduce some academic's idea of 1907 New Orleans' polyphony. But I defy anyone to close his eyes and listen to that band and imagine himself anywhere further back in time than in a good white Trad jazz club in the late fifties.

But there are lots of fine things in this production. Ondaatje is one of our more intriguing writers. Aside from the power of his conception, which comes through with some consistency, he and Thompson take an almost naïve delight in presenting certain marvellous sights such as Bibi Caspari climaxing a wild dance by wriggling an oyster down her pretty and unclothed body. Now *that's* worth the price of admission alone.

10 January 1980

Automatic Pilot

Written by Erika Ritter, directed by William Lane. New Theatre

Well, if New Theatre doesn't have a hit on its hands, if Erika Ritter's sore little four-person comedy isn't picked up by half the regional theatres across the country, and very soon, then there just ain't no justice in theeaytre land ladies and gentlemen.

Automatic Pilot has a standup comic at its centre. Her name is Charlie (as in Charlotte) and when we meet her she is in the process of falling in love with Nick, a successful young man with a good bank account and a liking for short-term relationships, the kind that are ended with flowers and notes that say "No blame, no regrets, just good memories." Nick's that kind of guy.

Our heroine Charlie is still getting over the breakup of her marriage to Alan, a perpetually unemployed actor who has "come out of the closet," as they say, and who isn't too sure whether he likes being gay any better than being straight. Charlie and Alan have a touchy post-marriage entanglement based on some residual affection and great sticky piles of guilt with which they torment each other.

Now in falling in love with Nick the swinger, Charlie is setting herself up for rejection and she gets it, complete with flowers and note; what she doesn't count on is the loving attention of Nick's kid brother Gene, with whom she is soon sharing her bed and her apartment.

Charlie has always used her disappointments in love to fuel her comic routines. Her marriage breakup led to some funny anti-homosexual material. Her drunken flirtations with promiscuity led to some funny anti-male jokes. But Gene is a good man, earnest, responsible, witty and intelligent. Nevertheless, he doesn't fit her ready-made categories so Charlie tries to end the relationship. She wants to be rejected—needs it, partly for her routines which cannibalize her rotten sense of herself. Gene, however, won't play ball. He won't let her down. In fact, in a very charged emotional scene he tries to make Charlie take responsibility for her rejection of the possibility of happiness with him. He fails. She insists that eventually Gene will become dissatisfied with her, largely because she is seven hears older than he is. Gene packs and leaves. When last we see Charlie she is doing a new comedy routine; this one is about

39

younger men. The lines are just as good as in the previous mono-logues, but it isn't very funny. We've seen behind this one.

Automatic Pilot is a comedy—and a good and efficient one, beautifully crafted with its climaxes in the right places, and its an-ticlimaxes very well judged. It's full of hard funny dialogue. But it's also a moving, even disturbing little play, fencing around in cavalier fashion with various contemporary obsessions such as the nature of sexual identity, the permanence or impermanence of love connec-tions. It's not a complicated play but it leaves one with very compli-cated feelings.

Ritter has also given us four fine characters, and although most of them have distinctly unlikeable aspects, she never cheapens them. Even when they are at their least engaging, Ritter looks at them with humane and forgiving eyes. And—most difficult of all—she never lets her terrific talent for the wisecrack get the better of her characters. The play never really goes soft, but I sometimes got the feeling it wore its heart on its sleeve a bit too openly. Mind you—it's a good heart. It's got nothing to be ashamed of in showing itself.

Fiona Reid may be best known as a comic actress. Fact is, her real impulse has always been toward tragedy. Did she set the tone for this production? Not that any of the strong and well-balanced cast play tragedy. But they certainly don't play comedy—at least in one accepted and unfortunate sense. They simply play characters who are blessed with witty tongues and natural comic timing. Perhaps director William Lane is responsible for that approach—the only approach to a well-written comedy. Ritter's lines can take care of themselves perfectly well without being goosed or mugged.

Well what can I say? I liked it. It makes for a fine theatrical evening. If you're in Toronto go and see it. If you're not, well, you'll just have to wait for some theatre in your region to pick up the play.

Incidentally, you might be interested in knowing that Erika Ritter did a bit of legwork for *Automatic Pilot*. Charlie must deliver three crucial comic monologues in the course of the play. Ritter wanted to be sure they worked so she betook her monologues to a local comedy cabaret and played a week there as a standup comic. A fate worse than death, I'm told.

18 January 1980

40

Rumours of our Death

Written and directed by George F. Walker. Factory Theatre Lab

I spent an hour and a half laughing myself silly on Friday night at
George Walker's *Rumours of our Death*. Y'see there's this king who
may or may not be from another planet. He's got blue wires on the
back of his hand and he talks without moving his mouth. He makes
regular public announcements such as "Civil liberties are hereby
remote" and he ends up in the woods singing a song to his father, a
red maple, after which he lies down to die for a while. There's a
beautiful queen too and she has visions about bombs which do very
particular kinds of damage. For instance, one doesn't kill anybody;
it merely evaporates all water everywhere. She ends up losing her
faith and getting addicted to cheezies, many of which end up on the
floor kinda half-chewed. Their daughter gets kidnapped by a decaying fifties rocker and becomes a punk Patti Hearst, filling in appli-
cations for government grants. She also sings great punk rock duets
with her captor cum mentor and they're just fine at cussing and
bouncing up and down all violent when they sing. Then there are
all the people who live under these shifting rumours of war and
destruction and traumatic change. There's a farmer, rooted firm in
the land, and reflecting the wisdom which no one understands, least
of all himself. When the first rumours of war hit he burns his crops
because that's what farmers do in a war. Everybody celebrates by
singing "Burn the crops down burn 'em burn 'em down" and the
farmer comes to the city where he dies from injuries incurred by a
restaurant bill. After that he gets up and walks around dead, attracting many disciples, different costumes and getting more and
more beautiful until at last he attains Travolta-hood. Then there's
the farmer's son who becomes a student and merges souls with
Raymond. Raymond is an artiste, a writer, whose main function is
to attract tourists. Under the rumours of impending disaster he
rejects art for action, discovers the monarchist under his skin, forms
a fascist party, loses an eye and an arm, is born again, hops on the
slow train comin', hops off and merges souls with the farmer's son.
But I told you about that already. You see, the country is suffering
from rumours and terminal helplessness. As a result everybody in it
is prone to unpleasant diseases such as merging souls, talking to
oneself, eating quiche, and my personable favourite—patriarch lust.

Now this poor bewildered and incompetent country is perfectly mirrored in a bumbling, stumbling, lovable and purposefully vacant production. Arnott and Elchen have designed a set of unremitting tackiness, a loving throwback to those underground theatre days of yore. George Walker's lines are of an opaqueness and blunted purpose that, after ten minutes of headscratching, become hilarious. And he's brilliantly directed his own perversely funny-in-spite-of-itself script with a spluttering coughing hiccupping rhythm which allows you to take nothing for granted. Everything seems a surprise in this show. In fact *Rumours of our Death* reminds me of nothing else on earth—except possibly one of those elaborate free-association fairytale sagas that Walt Kelly used to write for his Pogo books. Now people used to point hopeful fingers at those pieces of peripatetic nonsense, nod sagely and say "Aha! Political allegory," thereby making dull sense out of inspired chaos. But the fact is they were mere crazy house reflections of contemporary life. And trying to make a coherent political statement out of Walker's jelly punch drunk nihilism would be like trying to choreograph the Northern Lights.

I should add that Walker has designed regular breathers for us in the form of songs, mostly in various sixties and seventies modes of pop music. It's hard to know how good they are. You see it's such a shock to have something solid and structured to listen to that in context they seem just about the greatest things since Schubert. But my feeling is that they are good songs written by John Roby who grins pleasantly out on the proceedings from his upstage piano. And they are sung by some terrific people. Dianne Heatherington may deliver lines like Ma Kettle on a diet of adrenalin and phonetic records but when she sends that throaty voice out through those mikes you'd give her anything. And she's surrounded by terrific singers and performers like Susan Purdy and Pat Vanstone and Tim Wynne Jones. And then there's Steven Bush playing inspired variations on his comic mysterioso routine. And Mina E. Mina who cracks me up for some reason. And Peter Blais the King, looking like distilled minister of culture, and singing a song of his own devising which I won't attempt to describe as helpless giggles are not considered good FM listening.

Factory Theatre Lab may be the only Toronto alternate left that still has the guts to brave off-the-wall extravaganzas. Mind you they've got George Walker on their side which helps. Anyway, more power to them. *Rumours of our Death* isn't to everyone's taste. But I spent an hour and a half laughing myself silly and found it exhilarating. I hope this show gets a regular audience that will do likewise.

21 January 1980

The Mac-Paps

Adapted and directed by George Luscombe. Toronto Workshop Productions

At the end of last night's benefit performance, George Luscombe introduced those veterans of the Mac-Pap battalion who were in attendance. In front of the audience, the men mingled onstage with the young actors who, for two and a half hours, had been portraying them as they were 40 years ago and speaking their words as their own. It's no slight to the production that this sight and the wrenching sense of displaced history it entailed was as dramatic as anything in the show.

A few general remarks. The show is culled from the reminis-cences of men who served with the Mac-Paps in the Spanish Civil War. The difference between this show, however, and a production like *Ten Lost Years*, also drawn from oral history, is simply that the latter had its direct source in a book and was reshaped for the stage. In the case of the Mac-Paps, the creators were also intimately in-volved in the gathering of the histories. There is a certain close identification of actor and material and director and material which is both this show's strength and its weakness. That accounts, I think, for Luscombe's choice to suppress that extraordinary richness of invention which marks his work. There are passages of great power and dramatic explosions of violence, but only once or twice— as in a breathlessly funny sequence about a crying driver managing to save the lives of a truckload of troops—does he make the stage come alive with the wonder of his theatrical playfulness. Although he's hardly thought of as a director of musicals, no one stages a song better than Luscombe. Yet only at the opening of the second act does he really choose to let that aspect of his talent stretch itself out. For the most part he seems determined to let the men speak for themselves, being true to their words and to the tenor of their ex-

43

periences rather than placing them in their historical and social context. This is the most solemn Luscombe I've seen. His comments are very subtly placed and they are of a moral nature rather than a social one. The ironies—and there are always ironies in his work, usually very funny ones—are tragic. The first act faithfully reflects the heroic idealism of these young men. At one point reference is made to an incident in which the fascists execute several prisoners without even giving them the formality of a trial. Immediately afterwards we are involved in a tense attack by the Mac-Paps. We are pulled into the excitement of victory and find ourselves taking vicarious part in the execution of fifteen fascist prisoners who are not even given the formality of a trial. The battle and its aftermath are presented heroically by the actors—or at least they concern themselves only with the excitement of the moment—yet the placement of the incident carries with it its own unstressed but terrible irony.

I mention this partly to stress that this show celebrates the people who were prepared to die for their ideals. It doesn't celebrate war. Throughout, a dark under-current runs which asks whether killing for whatever cause can be married to idealism.

As I say, this show has a respect for its text which must have come from the direct human contact with its source. This respect sometimes muddies the theatrical clarity and may give some viewers the feeling of a show which has not quite taken the step from life into art. But that respect gives the show its own solid warmth and dignity.

Luscombe has chosen four fine actors to communicate that dignity, among them two of our best young performers, R. H. Thomson and Tom Butler. He has also—quite consciously, I suspect—chosen marvellous faces which suggest a wide range of background, class and experience. The actors deserve every credit. Their performances are detailed without being fussy, absorbing while remaining extraordinarily self-effacing. And because the director has chosen to rely so heavily on the voices to whom he owes his material, the actors are given a heavy burden. In fact Luscombe ends his show not with a piece of theatrical razzle dazzle but with a straightforward emotional speech of thanks from the Spanish people to the International Brigade—this is very nicely delivered by Seana McKenna incidentally. But again he brings us back to the men, leaving us with a quiet and haunting admission of conscience by one of the veterans. That ending, by the way, nicely demonstrates the show's juxtaposition of the heroic with the commonplace and its insistence that despite the unequivocal rightness of the men's endeavour, their job took on a heavy burden of moral responsibility.

TWP gave up its opening night's proceeds to aid in the campaign to have our government acknowledge the Mac-Pap veterans. That's no minor sacrifice for a small theatre in this period of lousy arts funding. Luscombe asked the enthusiastic audience to send friends to the show for the next couple of weeks. I hope they do. But those who plan to see it don't have to feel they're doing anyone a favour. *The Mac-Paps* is a hell of a story and TWP gives us an exciting, intelligent production in telling it. It's also an interesting departure for Luscombe in the kind of emphasis he chooses to make. I think I like it all the better for that.

1 February 1980

Maggie and Pierre

Written by Linda Griffiths and Paul Thompson,
directed by Linda Griffiths. Theatre Passe Muraille

On Friday night at Theatre Passe Muraille there was a full house made up of the kind of people who go to the theatre only when the subject matter interests them. *Maggie and Pierre* will need no word of mouth. The title does it all. Even at this point it has all the earmarks of a hit. I wouldn't be surprised if a national tour was in the offing. No doubt there are many to whom the prospect of spending an evening peeking into the scandalous marriage of our two most famous Canadians would be distasteful. I can assure those people that *Maggie and Pierre* is not a dramatized gossip column, as much as it draws on prurient interest in its subject matter. Nor has it very much to do with politics. It is, in fact, a serious attempt at analysis of a public myth. The fact that it's a pretty clear failure as theatre makes it only slightly less interesting, and won't hurt its box office at all.

In this play, besides the two eponymous characters, there is a third figure, a journalist, who represents our desire to know and to understand. All three figures are played by Linda Griffiths who also wrote the play with the help of Paul Thompson. Griffiths is alone onstage despite the fact that a fair proportion of the piece consists of dialogue scenes between two or three of the characters. Beyond a few charming moments during the courtship of Maggie and Pierre, when Griffiths takes the licence to portray her two central figures as rather charming cartoons, the awkward convention of one actor switching from character to character in mid-dialogue fails to make up in theatrical charm for what it hampers by way of rhythm and character interplay. Put bluntly, it's boring to watch the same parlour trick for two hours. Surprisingly, many of the scenes are played against the grain of the natural comic thrust of the gimmick. As an actor Griffiths is clearly more comfortable with drama, if not tragedy, and in the more serious scenes of which there are a number, the cartoon effect of role switching is distracting. At times I wondered whether Griffiths and Thompson were testing how far the central technique would stretch. The answer is not very. Yet in the second act there's a scene in which Griffiths portrays the three characters jumping about in a long and intense interchange. I was amazed at how little of it was even passably effective, judging by how it failed to carry what seemed to be a nicely written scene.

One has two responses to Griffiths the performer in this play. First of all, what guts to attempt it at all. Secondly how clear it is that as a performer she's unready to tackle such a thing. In part it's a simple question of technique. She doesn't look at home on stage. Even in her quieter scenes more tension collects in her arms and hands and shoulders and in her face than any performer can afford to carry, let alone a performer in a one-actor show. Last season director Pam Brighton attempted to use that tension, casting Griffiths as the title character in a superb production of *St. Joan of the Stockyards*. It didn't work and I don't believe tension can ever be used onstage unless the actor himself is in control of it.

But as a writer Griffiths strikes me as a potentially strong voice. Her dialogue is fine, her monologues, the sense of how to turn a line, likewise. Her writer's perception goes beyond the obvious enough times to keep one's attention at least halfway tuned. Almost as often it returns to the obvious, and she doesn't yet have the confidence to follow through, nor the craftsman's objectivity about ideas and shape, the cruel logic that must be brought to bear on talent. At one point her reporter asks what many Canadians were asking themselves during the Rolling Stones scandal; what was going on behind the admirably dignified response of the public

46

Trudeau? The reporter in a nice reference to the fact that all three characters are present in one actor—simply says, slyly, "Why don't I ask him?" and immediately switches into the Trudeau role to reply. What Griffith's Trudeau shows us—which I won't reveal—is the one thing that most Canadians might have trouble accepting, and yet it makes sense of the seeming contradictions of the man. The liberal believes that heaven can be created on earth, the Catholic that heaven is reserved for the hereafter. Might not Trudeau's apparent arrogance be based on the deeply religious man's ironic perception of how puny our endeavours are in the eye of eternity? Having given us this suggestion in a neat little *coup de théâtre*, Griffiths hedges with a joke and retreats into a conventional feminist interpretation of man locked into his own sex, none the less banal for its elements of truth and made tedious by her having just niggled around the edges of a genuine perception.

She winds up with an interestingly hard attack on the audience which has about as much artistic validity in relation to the rest as does Chaplin's plea for world peace at the end of *The Great Dictator*. Put simply, if you haven't made your meaning clear in the story don't try to tack it on in a postscript.

Maggie and Pierre may be a failure but it's an honourable one, nothing to be ashamed of, and as I say, it will have no trouble finding an audience.

18 February 1980

Fifth Business

Written by Robertson Davies, adapted and directed by Ron Hartmann.
CBC Radio

The publicity release on the Deptford Trilogy is proudly headlined "CBC Radio Drama's most ambitious project ever." I wasn't around for much of CBC's Golden Age of Radio Drama, so I can make no great historical claims on behalf of *Fifth Business*, Part I of the Trilogy. But if Ron Hartmann's adaptation of Davies' 1972 novel isn't one of the finest things CBC radio drama has ever produced then I happily submit my ignorance to the knowledge of those fortunates who know better.

I've listened to all four hours of *Fifth Business*. It seemed like thirty minutes. Davies' novel is both one of the most effective pieces of narrative in Canadian literature and a challenging creation of a complementary Canadian mythology. The radio version is absolutely faithful to the heart and core of the novel. The mythological structure is intelligently set forth and deeply moving, and the richness of incident and character constantly enlivening. Of course this is radio and richness in character must be mirrored by richness in voices, and Hartmann has amassed what amounts to an embarrassment of riches by picking from several generations of fine Canadian actors. What's more—oh world of wonders!—not one of these sharp professionals seems wasted or misused. They exist as a series of absorbing voices, every one of them speaking of a lifetime of experience and idiosyncrasy.

There's Jackie Burroughs' sexy husk bringing out the vulnerability of poor Leola Cruickshank, and Claire Coulter using her intriguing reedy voice to emphasize the unearthliness of Mrs. Dempster. Zoe Caldwell has a high old time with Liesl, one of Davies' most striking creations. And Wenna Shaw's musical trilly intelligence invokes every young man's dream of a sexy nurse. On the male side Mavor Moore creates a touching cameo, a little masterpiece of characterization, as Mahaffey, the tramp turned preacher. He employs a nasal voice and a sense of personality which assiduously avoids cliché. I will not soon forget Eric Peterson's Milo, the chatty barber, generously spilling out the unpleasant contents of his small mind, nor Hush Webster's garrulous Padre Blazon—another fine Davies' creation brought perfectly to life. All of these are beautifully contrived vocal performances. There are many more. I've tended here to mention the striking cameos which are used as counterpoint to the lives of the story's principals. The principals' less colourful work is every bit as impressive. Central to the whole endeavour is Eric House as Dunston Ramsey, who is not merely the major character but also the narrator. House cannot be praised too highly for his work here. He has been one of our finest actors for years, but too often he is thought of as a comic relief man. He is a fine comic actor of course. But in *Fifth Business* he is given the straight part of all straight parts. Davies has written the ultimate observer's role in Dunston Ramsey—and the observer is the central male figure in Canadian literature. But in doing so he has taken that character into the realm of myth and created a brilliant apologia for him.

Never has the observer seemed so interesting before. House's quiet intelligence and precisely judged neutrality of manner brings Ramsey to life. My admiration for his work here can't be overstated.

I've already spoken highly of Ron Hartmann's skill as an adapter. He also served as director and producer. As director I gather he rehearsed major dialogue scenes to be played to the microphones all of a piece as opposed to recording them in bits and editing them together. In any case the major scenes have a dramatic cohesiveness which pulls the ear into the imaginative life of the story. Hartmann has even dared to challenge radio's favourite bugaboo, dead air. In this case dead air is successfully translated into dramatic pauses. In each instance the silence is more effective than any underlining musical cues could be.

In general, *Fifth Business* is fine work of which Ron Hartmann and dozens of our best performers have every reason to be proud.

I might quibble with the decision to air *Fifth Business* in two parts, a decision probably designed to avoid frightening away potential listeners. Listening to it in one sitting, the carefully structured story reaches a truly exciting climax as the pieces fall together. Splitting it in two can only lessen the impact. And as it stands, the first section of *Fifth Business* ends on a pretty weak note. I suspect that Hartmann intended the play to be heard as one piece. But in any format, this is a major radio work.

22 February 1980

Ain't Lookin'

Written and adapted by John Craig, directed by George Luscombe.
Toronto Workshop Productions

Ain't Lookin' arrives smack at the end of a season that has contained enough good work to justify a reasonably sanguine attitude toward Toronto theatre. Yet with the exception of George Luscombe's two previous productions, there has been nothing within hailing distance of it for imagination, warmth and a shrewd sense of what the stage can render up to an artist who approaches it with an open eye.

In 1939 a kid from Trenton, Ontario joined a black baseball team which eked out a living staging coon shows on small-town diamonds across the U.S. and Canada. John Craig wrote *Chappy and Me* from his reminiscences of working with Chappy's All-Stars. In collaboration with Luscombe, he adapted the book for the stage. The kid plays blackface, learns how to coon for the white folks and falls in love with a small town vision who, like the princess in the fairytale, turns out to be under an evil spell; the spell is racism. That's all, but the show is carried along by incident, by brilliantly deployed music, and by an atmosphere so rich, so hurtfully nostalgic and full of meaning, that it is closer to film than any stage show I've seen. Yet its peculiar excitement breathes theatre.

Onstage is a set of drums which is used to give immediacy to recorded jazz and to suggest anything from thunder to the rattle of a bus droning through the night. Much of the action takes place on the bus, the interior marked off by suitcases and defined by dim subtle patches of light. The men jog along talking, playing cards or simply drifting in the mental bus fog that accrues to any group of travelling players. I've never seen this sense of aimless time connect - ing interchangeable places so beautifully conveyed. One moment, the effect of a sudden thunderstorm on the men in the bus, their minds quickly alert and the sides of the vehicle squaring themselves against the elements, goes beyond anything I thought the stage capable of by way of acuity of sensual articulation. Time adrift is counterpointed by wild routines in the ballpark. And the brother- hood of the bus is cut against regularly by racist incidents with mayors, garage mechanics and small town thugs. The climax is the All-Star's act of retaliation against a sadistic pitcher, which leads into a car chase that will amaze anyone who thinks that the stage can't handle any physical action that can't be contained in a Fey- deau farce.

I mentioned the brotherhood of the bus. But the cool acknowl- edgement of shared experience by these men has nothing in common with the soft-underbelly, rugged romanticism of male camaraderie that has tainted so much of America's literature of men without women. This is no pre-sexual dream of an uncomplicated emotional life. These men are living half lives and they know it. The intelligence with which they meet the double predicament of being both black, relegated to Stepin Fetchits, and unconnected sexually is present in every moment of the play. Luscombe's refusal to lapse into one of the biggest North American cultural catch-alls, the dream of asexual maleness, is one measure of his honesty as an artist.

It's partly this sense of half-lives that accounts for the muted, haunted atmosphere of this production. Those who have had the privilege of seeing Luscombe's version of *Les Canadiens* a few seasons back might expect a similar rowdy piece of gut-kicking, eye-popping theatre. *Ain't Lookin'* could hardly be further removed. It's true both to the leisurely summer and shirt-sleeves tang of baseball and to the lives of the men whose story it tells. There's plenty of excitement in *Ain't Lookin'* but it's not in the exuberant clash of two solitudes meeting joyously, if violently, on their one common ground. It's the excitement born of oppressed human beings finding outlets in action where they can.

I will not soon forget the climactic ball game, during which Libby Lennie writhes erotically in the bleachers, her lovely mouth deformed by a torrent of racist abuse, her lovely body twisting in an unconscious act of hate; nor the summer night in the fields when the stage is dark save for the magical illusion of starlight, the men trying to sleep while the white newcomer innocently interrupts their stoic fallings-off with questions; nor the painfully hilarious sequence when two of the players must chuck off their dignity to placate an ugly crowd, shuffling and dancing like happy niggers; nor the bus sequence in which the men groggily pick up the rhythm of the motor: "Where we goin'? Where we goin'? Saskatoon, Saskatoon. Ain't no coon in Saskatoon, Saskatoon...." and on through their whole itinerary.

There is a bittersweet sense of mortality to *Ain't Lookin'*. Chappy Johnson and his team are suspended in the fragile memory of the narrator. They are otherwise long gone. This production is a dream and a memorial.

May 1980

The Life that Jack Built

Collective creation supervised by Janet Amos and David Fox, music by John Roby. Blyth Festival

In 1972, a group of actors researched and prepared a play in the small Western Ontario town of Clinton. That was Passe Muraille's *The Farm Show*, a production that toured across Canada and Britain

51

and set the pattern for the Collective Creation in this country. Just six or seven miles north of Clinton is a village with the lovely name of Blyth. And there it was a few years ago that James Roy set up a summer festival with a strong mandate for Canadian plays. I would guess that the Blyth Festival was able to build on the audience created by Passe Muraille's work in the area. In any case, the company this season is well stocked with alumni from that theatre: David Fox, Miles Potter, Anne Anglin and new artistic director Janet Amos, to name a few.

The Life that Jack Built is very much in the Passe Muraille Collective tradition. As a show, it rarely rises above the level of earnest and amiable exploitation that is the usual province of the Collective. It moves in jerks and spasms and takes lovable pratfalls, sometimes when no pratfall is called for. It's as ragged as any under-rehearsed summer stock show could be. It folds the ideas of heroism and national identity in clumsy heartfelt embraces which sometimes leave the objects of its affection abashed and cringing. It never quite pulls itself together into a theatrical statement and leaves good intentions and kind wishes lying about like paper valentines. Yet as a piece of work or even as a theatrical experience I think as highly of it as any show I've seen this summer.

The Jack of the title is Jack McClaren, creator of the famous WWI comedy troupe, The Dumbells. Act I tells the story of the troupe and the story of the Canadian Princess Pat Regiment, using actual songs and sketch material from the Dumbells, as well as the reminiscences of McClaren (who, incidentally, was in the audience on opening night). But the show is no exercise in nostalgia. It becomes clear that the players are using the Princess Pats as a metaphor for the coming of age of an entire generation of Canadians. This generation in Act II sets out to interpret Canada to Canadians. There is a roll call of heroes—A.Y. Jackson, Lawren Harris, Fred Banting, Emily Carr—all people whom McClaren came to know and admire when he was a member of the famous Arts and Letters Club between the wars. These people provide the focus and the character of the second act.

I don't think it's presumptuous to assume that the actors who created the show (under the supervision of Janet Amos and David Fox) identify with McClaren's generation. They tried to bring Canadians out from under the psychological domination of the Empire after the first great war. The generation of Canadian artists

52

to whom the Passe Muraille group belongs is trying to effect a similar breakthrough for their time, but of course the domination is now the result of 25 years of identifying with American aspirations.

The Blyth group is a strong company of actors. In particular Fox, John Jarvis, Michel Lefebvre and Seana McKenna have exceptional moments. There was one lovely moment that captured the elusive sweetness of the show. The whole gang was singing a kind of mock-serious choral song with a number of single harmony parts. Seana McKenna, a talented and charming actress, had hit several good bum notes previously. She was having trouble finding her part now, and just when you were about to wince she did it, and the others, who were holding their own just fine thank you, reacted to her clinkers with a few furtive "if looks could kill" glances. I'll never know whether that moment was rehearsed or spontaneous or a cunning mixture of both. But I can't imagine such a thing being artfully contrived without also seeming precious. It relied on a warm and intimate relationship with the audience who repaid the actors at the end of the evening with a unanimous ovation. The whole show demonstrated that slickness and polish, while being the first qualities that the mind of the urban provincial learns to recognize, are also the cheapest and most easily achieved of theatrical virtues. An emphasis on technical flash is all too often the sign of a bankrupt imagination. The artist like George Luscombe who uses technique as embodiment and as tool is all too rare.

In the Passe Muraille group there has never been a theatrical imagination or an artistic sensibility as vital and as substantial as Luscombe's. But what we have operating at Blyth is still very special and within its limits, almost unbeatable. There is in these performers a concern for the work, a respect for the audience and a love for the culture—and these are no mean qualities to bring to theatre. Listening to the strong, skilled, unaffected voices of the actors, and watching performers as extraordinarily likeable as John Jarvis, I suddenly thought I knew why there are so few good younger actors at Stratford. Perhaps they're out doing their culture's work rather than hanging around hoping that stardust will rub off on them. Incidentally the talented John Roby wrote a good score for the show and plays a pretty fair stride piano to boot.

7 *August* 1980

53

The Tomorrow Box

Written by Anne Chislett, directed by Dennis Sweeting.
Kawartha Summer Theatre

The Kawartha Summer Theatre opened this year on July 1 and runs until August 20. Nine weeks and nine different plays, a new one running every week from Wednesday to Saturday. That's a pretty tough schedule. A friend of mine who used to work as a stage manager in Lindsay once told me that the workload on the younger cast and crew was such that, as the season was drawing to a close, every one took his turn having a minor public crack-up of tears and tantrums. (Such things are among the traditional joys of working summer stock, of course.) Director Dennis Sweeting has headed the Festival since its first summer sixteen years ago. The seasons he puts together are naturally very light, but they are interesting for the number of Canadian comedies and mysteries that pop up alongside the British and American comedies and mysteries. In the present season for instance, Peter Colley's ubiquitous *I'll Be Back for You Before Midnight* coexists with an early Agatha Christie play, and Eric Nicol has his moment in the limelight along with Neil Simon. The Kawartha Festival Foundation puts out a little brochure which carefully describes each play from the point of view of whether it's suitable family viewing. For instance, one of the plays I saw was described as "a little adult" but still "a good family show."

That was Anne Chislett's *The Tomorrow Box* which the brochure also described as "a very funny and very human play," as good and accurate a description as I could come up with. Dennis Sweeting's production of *The Tomorrow Box* was the play's premiere, and the Kawartha Festival can indeed be proud of that fact. The play tells the story of a couple who return to the husband's home town in rural Ontario where he is to take over the management of his fa-ther's farm. Alice is a law student. Joe has been a professor of agri-culture. His parents are about to retire to Florida, leaving the house and outbuildings to him. The catch is that Old Jack, the father and a patriarch of the old school, hasn't told his wife about the move, has signed the papers without consulting her, but she doesn't want to leave. Alice's sister, a tough-minded lawyer, dedicated to fighting for women's rights, arrives and initiates a lawsuit and separation on behalf of Joe's distraught mother, and the situation is in place.

Sweeting assembled a strong cast headed by Joyce Campion as the farmer's wife. The pacing was relaxed and uncertain in equal proportions. (One can expect the latter in summer stock but not necessarily the former). The action took place in a trailer home. And Sweeting, in a nice piece of theatrical opportunism, had wangled an actual trailer home display from a local dealer and used it as his set. (Mighty ugly it was too, but never mind.)

It is the play that should interest us here. It would be well worth another theatre having a look at it. Its first act is very strong in setting up the comic impasse. The second act has a lot of trouble wriggling out of the impasse without more pain than a light comedy can bear. Author Chislett avoids the pain but in the process, a believable conclusion escapes her. *The Tomorrow Box* should be rethought and reworked in its next production. But I thought very well of it on the whole. And the audience loved it, recognizing with pleasure both the conservative rural Ontario setting, and the hard-edged urban mentality that was made to intrude on it. It was a pleasurable experience just to be part of the house. It's clear that Sweeting has built up a good deal of audience trust over the years.

Sextet

Written by Michael Pertwee, directed by Dennis Sweeting.
Kawartha Summer Theatre

That same audience laughed a lot at last night's opening too. Once again the laughter had something to do with recognition. For *Sextet* belongs to the tatty but familiar old tradition of the British Sex Farce. The genre is located in a kind of pubescent Never-Never Land fixed some place just past the anal and frozen in hesitancy before the genital. At that stage of development, sex is terribly fascinating but it's also still a bit frightening, so in Sex-Farce Land coitus tends to be of the humorous interruptus variety. In any case, *Sextet* is about six people on a yacht, tripping over things, walking about in baby-doll pyjamas, getting jealous, removing their bathing-suit tops with their backs to the audience and making a lot of references to naughty things. Before last night, I don't believe I had ever seen one of these farces before. This one is by a man with the somehow appropriate name of Michael Pertwee. I must admit I had a pleasant enough time of it while it was in process. I haven't been fourteen for a long time and somehow it was much less messy this time through.

13 August 1980

La Sagouine

Written by Antoinine Maillet, directed by Mark Blandford. CBC-TV

Antoinine Maillet has written of La Sagouine, the Acadian scrub woman, that she is "all together a glossary, a race, and the other side of the coin." As the author's statement suggests, *La Sagouine* does seem to speak as the voice of a people, articulating and embodying its experience. But beyond that, *La Sagouine* belongs to the tradition in literature in which an author looks at a society through the eyes of a character who exists at an oblique angle to it. The character is usually a wise innocent, often a child or an elderly person, and the author—if he's successful—achieves a surprising empathy with the character. Perhaps the most distinguished predecessor of Maillet's charlady is Huckleberry Finn. Like young Huck, La Sagouine casts an eye on society that is not ironic, but merely free of cant. And like Mark Twain's, Maillet's imaginative projection into her character is so complete that we never feel that the character is being made to act simply as spokesman for the author.

But *La Sagouine* belongs equally to a tradition in Canadian literature in which a character, in a minority and despised position and conscious of the eyes of conventional society, nevertheless insists on the validity of her own point of view and refuses to apologize for it.

La Sagouine was presented on Radio Canada a few years back as a sixteen-week series. The producers of the CBC version weren't permitted that expanse of air space. Viewers of the English network will have to settle for one hour of excerpts comprising seven of the sixteen monologues—or rather excerpts from them, as several are severely edited. For instance, the monologue called "The Trade," in which La Sagouine describes her work as a scrubwoman, is represented only by a few introductory sentences. And "Youth," the first real monologue, in which La Sagouine talks about her first trade and her place of business under the street lamp on Main Street, is cut in such a way that the viewer might have trouble catching on to the nature of that trade. It's not that the monologue is any more explicit in its original form. It's simply that the lack of a more expansively general opening doesn't give us the space to accustom ourselves to the character before plunging into her life. And as this kind of performance relies on an intimate bonding of the audience with the performer, the astringency of the production hurts it at this point.

In any case, after the first ten minutes, the extraordinary Violet Leger casts her spell and the program takes on the rhythm of her performance. That performance has been mounted very lovingly. In Radio Canada's series Miss Leger was filmed in a studio without an audience. The CBC team on the other hand, under director Mark Blandford, had their cameras act as privileged spectators within a live audience at Montreal's Centaur Theatre. Even so, Miss Leger plays to the camera—or seems to be doing so—at all times, so that the intimacy between television viewer and performer is permitted.

Miss Leger's performance, in case you haven't heard, is a wonder to experience. She has been playing this part for nine years—in French and English—and yet the performance is as fresh and spontaneous in its effect as it must always have been. There is pleasure simply in watching her hands as she speaks, moving with a grace that her dumpy figure can't quite contradict. Or listening to the nasal scratchy voice that curls up with the lumpy rhythms of her Acadian speech patterns with a relaxed intimacy that has a very particular kind of beauty. And over the course of the hour, Miss Leger's worn face, with its mild bright eyes and its slow natural unfurling of expression, comes to seem one of the loveliest objects a TV camera could fasten on.

Director Mark Blandford's approach to the performance is satisfying because it acknowledges the nature of La Sagouine as a piece of theatre. There is no attempt to provide a realistic setting. The actress is merely discovered in a pool of hard light that's clearly theatrical in nature. The light hits her from one angle so that it etches the structure of her face in a striking manner. The monologues are formally separated by fades to black and simple titles. And the effect of all this is to keep the attention on the actress by subtly formalizing the presentation on her performance.

There's something marvellously selfless about Leger's La Sagouine. When the actress takes her bow at the end she almost seems to be acknowledging the applause on behalf of the character she has been playing, and the easy dignity in her bearing and the quiet joy in her face as she does so are wonderful things to share.

8 October 1980

Torontonians

A collective production from Theatre Passe Muraille, directed by Paul Thompson

There seems to be a general feeling in the air that the collective has reached an artistic dead end. I doubt that. If nothing else the collective approach will remain a tool for young companies to get work under their belts. But in Canada collectives have had, and may continue to have, a greater importance than that and shouldn't be dismissed as theatrical juvenilia.

One of the most important jobs a young theatre has to carry in a young culture is to find the voice of that culture—and I mean that quite literally. I think it's a fair generalization to suggest that until recently our playwrights in English Canada had not been doing an important aspect of their job, which is to take the voices around them peculiar to their experience and to put them onstage where they can be analyzed, criticized or celebrated, whichever response seems appropriate.

In English Canada—particularly in Ontario—it was the actors who went out and made the observations and gave them shape and put them onstage. And their vehicle in doing that has been the collective. A collective doesn't often have a very long life nor is it meant to. If a company of actors were to try to mount *The Farm Show* today they'd likely find that the material was too closely bound up in its time and place and the particular experience of particular actors to be feasible, except as a succession of audience-pleasing turns such as *Paper Wheat* became in its last manifestation. But longevity is not the point of the collective. Simply put, every time we see something of ourselves given weight and scope by a stage production it becomes material for the artist to build on and it sharpens the eyes and ear of the audience as well as the artist.

Paul Thompson who, along with a particularly talented cast that put together *Torontonians*, is responsible more than any one person for the collective movement in English Canada. *Torontonians* is his first collective in a couple of years. The show has a graceful and flexible set by Bob Pearson and Charles Pachter but otherwise, sad to say, it's a real mess. And one of the things it lacks is precisely that careful observation of the subject upon which the collective depends. I wasn't convinced by any of the performances. All of them struck out in different directions and most of them depended to degrees on a certain crude parody. Part of the problem arises from the subject matter. Talk to a farmer or a fisherman and chances are the man will have enough colour in his manner and enough humour in his soul to keep the actor who tries to recreate him busy and lively. But the people at the top of the hill, with whom *Torontonians* concerns itself, have little behavioural colour. It's been bred out of them. And almost no humour where it counts. They have too much to protect. And humour can't afford to protect anything. In any case the actors have come up with little that's visible by way of research. Instead they nudge into the softest parts of our intellectual anatomies where all the smug, shared assumptions accumulate.

What with having a plot and characters who remain more or less consistent throughout and identified with a particular actor, *Torontonians* would also seem to have aspirations toward being a play. Some might think it is an attempt to extend the collective approach into more conventional and sustained narrative. I would guess that the plot (which is a silly thing about the possession of an old patriarch's soul by an upstart French Canadian developer) was a desperation move when it was found that old establishment Toronto yielded up its secrets less readily than Clinton, Ontario. In any case the second act is all plot and mighty fierce to sit through. My whole body turned into Harry Cohn's butt and I didn't have enough fingers to scratch.

That second act has the effect of an extended improvisation that could happily fill five minutes. And furthermore it gets pretentious before the evening is out. I have trouble recalling now that much of the first act consisted of pleasant soft-focused satire and some good moments from the actors. So alas for good ideas. As subject matter, Toronto still remains infertile soil for the playwright or the actor. There must be something about this town's history that shrivels the creative impulse.

13 November 1980

Crackwalker

Written by Judith Thompson, directed by Clarke Rogers.
Theatre Passe Muraille

Judith Thompson's play involves four people struggling miserably with their fruitless lives in the north end of Kingston, a notoriously depressed area. A friend of mine who was a social worker there once told me that the only way he could cope with the existence of what he saw every day was by promising himself never to bring children into the world. The reaction sounds less illogical after one has had some exposure to the lives of the people of the area. Judith Thompson's reaction to the same thing seems to have been to write a play.

Let's get the controversial stuff out of the way first. *Crackwalker* is—among other things—a constant barrage of foul language of a particularly explicit variety. This is a shock at first but soon becomes to the listener's ear what it is to the characters—a normal way of communicating. The fact that this communication is pitched at a level of numbing repetitive violence says a lot about their lives. The dialogue is very well observed and written with an ear sensitive to the ragged cadences of Eastern Ontario low life. If one is in any doubt about the author's writing skill—or about the possibility of using lumpen dialect for art—that doubt might be dispelled by the monologues given to each of the characters in turn. If it sometimes seems that Thompson has used her ears like a tape recorder—not a bad way to use them for theatre by the way—these monologues have been turned to the requirements of actors with only the slightest hint of the self-consciousness that accompanies the writing of a monologue not rooted securely in observation. Monologues are inevitably the parts of a play that tempt a writer's worst instincts toward fine writing. But these are genuinely fine—theatrical and yet drawn without artifice from their source. And they are superbly delivered by Joann McIntyre, Jane Foster, Hardee Linehan and Geza Kovacs, a really effective quartet of actors in gruelling parts.

There is also a fair bit of physical explicitness regarding the sexual activities of the characters. It is of a kind with the language: brutal and communicative on only the roughest levels. There is a sexual encounter in both acts. Both are tied in intimately with violence and frustration, and both cue the blind frustration that these people live with beyond hope of change.

It should be apparent by now that *Crackwalker* is not the kind of play that everyone will want to go and see. It's a pretty grim little evening of theatre. Mind you it is often funny in a hideous and twisted way. But the laughter it provokes is of the kind that might emerge from the middle of the pit where laughter seems as sane a response as any. Watching the play one eventually has the feeling that no response is appropriate to these lives except perhaps horror and pity, and even in that the monstrous triviality of the language demands release in laughter—as uncomfortable as that response may be.

Laughter or no, this play is black at its core. Poor simple Alan, who alone among the characters makes concerted gropings toward love, tries to be a decent and responsible human being—in his case following good instincts toward fatherhood—actually precipitates the final disaster by his fear and ignorance and is left imprisoned and very possibly mad. His wife, the retarded Theresa, the closest thing *Crackwalker* can offer to a life force—is returned to her moment to moment existence of servicing old men for dollars and donuts.

The first act of *Crackwalker* is very fine. Individual scenes are vividly and cleanly fashioned and quite self-sufficient. The characters are placed squarely in their fiercely circumscribed world. These scenes give the impression of being so unconnected to anything resembling order or plan that it seems almost irrelevant in which sequence they happen to fall. The second act, which is largely given over to relating the grisly events surrounding Alan and Theresa's attempt at parenthood, struck me as less successful. Even though the tragedy is clearly the idea around which the play was worked, it nevertheless dwindles the events to a kind of melodrama by giving them a point to aim for, and thus subtly trivializing the whole effort. It's at this point that the author reaches for larger and more conventional reactions from the audience and loses that awful knife balance between horror and laughter so well achieved in Act I.

Where *Crackwalker* retains its interest and integrity is in the success Judith Thompson has had in turning a regional way of speaking to which she's had some exposure into good hard clear theatrical language. This sort of effort is perhaps the most needed work to be done in English Canadian theatre today. On that level alone I tend to think of *Crackwalker* as a very promising first play.

Fall 1980

The State of Toronto Theatre

Right now in Toronto we are witnessing the slow death of our theatre. It isn't a dramatic death. It's a gradual falling away of excitement and of new work. And one day we will turn around and notice that the theatre we have been building for fifteen years is gone. The theatre community in Toronto is in a state of stasis, just holding on. It has to live with the likelihood that grants from local and federal agencies will rise at best by 4% to 6% annually over the next few years. And in the meantime production costs grow at the rate of inflation, now 12% and rising. What this means is less and less new work. New work is risk work, and a theatre in financial trouble can't afford risks. Bob White, artistic director of Factory Theatre Lab, one of Toronto's major sources of new work and new talent, told me that unless things change, Factory Lab will be gone within two years. And he is not alone.

On one hand NDWT, an important touring company which did only new plays, was closed last month by the banks. On the other, Toronto Free Theatre, which began ten years ago as a lab theatre dedicated to new work has presented no new plays this year. Instead it's steered a survival course and done very well thank you with proven successes: Tom Stoppard, Joe Orton and Canadian revivals. There have been only a few new productions from Theatre Passe Muraille, another important lab. Of the major Toronto theatres, only Tarragon has been able to present a full season of new and interesting work. But Mallory Gilbert, Tarragon's general manager, doubts that the theatre can continue taking as many chances unless the situation improves.

There is simply not enough money to go around. The factions of Toronto's theatre community, never a mutually supportive bunch anyway, are quietly at each other's throats. Jealous and quick to detract from each other's work, they hold their individual grounds uneasily. The first wave of theatre artists who created Passe Muraille, Tarragon and Factory Theatre Lab, is exhausted from the constant battle. Part of the attack comes from the second wave of younger artists who form the fringe companies. Many of the companies work from the Theatre Centre. But the Theatre Centre itself was closed for two months this winter for lack of money. The younger artists feel frustrated and look with resentment on the older companies that have fit into the grant structure more securely.

A general negative feeling in the air about Toronto theatre is reinforced by the newspapers. Neither of Toronto's major newspaper reviewers has shown interest in writing about the forces at work in the theatre scene. They have long been feeding back to the public simple indifference or even hostility toward Toronto theatre. It was reported in Sid Adilman's Toronto *Star* column that the first string reviewer of the *Globe and Mail* gave priority to a scuba diving lesson over attendance at the Dora Mavor Moore Awards. The story, true or not, capsulizes the breakdown in trust and communication between the critics and the theatre community in this city.

There is a peculiar nostalgia floating around about the Golden Age of Toronto Theatre. This so-called Golden Age began only yesterday in 1971, partly because a lot of young writers and actors and directors plugged into the Opportunities For Youth and Local Initiative Programs instituted that year. The three years of the Make-Work-for-the-Baby-Boom schemes saw the creation of what we now generally refer to as Canadian Theatre. They were incredibly active years. In 1974 the programs were cut off, but the government kept the theatres chugging along for a year or so through various arts agencies. But in 1976 the whole thing was stalled. The budget of the Canada Council was frozen that year. It was only thawed last year, and then only slightly.

Lots of Canadian plays are still being produced. But just how vulnerable they are can be demonstrated by a few figures. In 1978/79, 53% of attendance at all theatres in this country was for Canadian plays. In 1979/80, that figure fell to 20%. It fell because the number of Canadian plays produced had dropped from 48% to 29%. Recent pressure from the Canada Council and the appearance of a spate of hit Canadian plays has helped to raise that figure once again. But the question is not how many productions of *Nurse Jane Goes to Hawaii* there have been, but how many new plays are being mounted.

So this is the dilemma. Without a scene bustling with a variety of new work, we will not long have a distinctive theatre here. And we cannot have this variety without more government funding. Private donors tend to be attracted to high profile endeavours like Stratford where a corporation's philanthropy will be better spotlighted. And as far as commercial theatre is concerned, Toronto, alas, is still a Royal Alexandra town. It's there that the touring shows with the television stars and Tony awards go Independent. Producers like

Peter Peroff (who funds Toronto Truck without government grants) will struggle along and good luck to them. But the important new work is going to come from funded companies, directors and writers plugging away without fear of commercial failure.

Public funding is not the solution to all of Toronto theatre's problems. But a commitment to public funding was our starting point, and we must reconfirm that commitment. Without funding, and a lot more of it, the theatre as a whole will sink into its premature middle age before its artists have even reached maturity. Toronto's theatrical life will crumble away morsel by morsel, leaving, perhaps, only those imposing theatrical edifices, Stratford, Shaw and the St. Lawrence Centre. As far as theatre is concerned it will be 1969 all over again. And once again it will be just like starting over.

Late 1980

The Summer of 1980

THE STRATFORD FESTIVAL

Twelfth Night

Written by William Shakespeare, directed by Robin Phillips.

A wise writer once pointed out that Shakespeare actually over-
stepped the bounds of his chosen comedic form in writing *Twelfth
Night*. By imagining such intense and convincing love speeches for
Olivia and Viola, he threw his conventional mistaken identity plot
under the shadow of human emotion. Because of the onstage existence of real passion, the conventional climax of happy pairings runs
the risk of being unconvincing. We can't help but find Viola's twin
Sebastian—for instance—almost contemptible for marrying Olivia,
when they have just met at the end of the play. Only Shakespeare's
wonderful ritualistic handling of the final disclosure scene allows us
to ignore the jarring of the real world against the conventional one.

The last scene of Robin Phillips' production of *Twelfth Night*
handles the light ritual of the ending rather nicely. But beyond that
and aside from some affecting moments with Patricia Conolly's
Viola, this is a *Twelfth Night* without wit, irony, joy, without even
much theatrical interest beyond the most tired professional effect.

Another wise writer once said of a performer that he had ideas
but not insight. In other words his inventions didn't necessarily
stem from the text itself, and therefore tended to distort the work.
There are several such ideas in this *Twelfth Night*. Maria is in love
with Sir Toby Belch to the point that every word she utters, every
scheme she concocts, is directed toward gaining his admiration and
finally his love. Even beyond the question of whether this idea's a
good one or not, the production applies it without shading or subtlety. As a result, Kate Reid's Maria loses much of what makes the
character an actress' plum. She becomes a weak and supplicating
woman living only to impress a drunken old sot. Reid was pleased
with the interpretation—presumably suggested by Phillips. It does
give her something strong to play, even if it's only one note. But
I'm completely at a loss to account for Brain Bedford's Malvolio.
Ineffectuality is the idea around which Bedford builds *Twelfth
Night's* most famous character. This Malvolio can't rise to any occasion. And, believe me, the double entendre in that phrase is nothing
compared to the genital puns nudged out of Malvolio's speeches.

Even Malvolio's pride is ineffectual. We are asked to laugh at him for his weakness, not for his presumption. He is not capable of real presumption. This Malvolio carries a Teddy Bear. Honest.

This interpretation of Malvolio is without a doubt the least persuasive idea that I've ever seen inflicted on Shakespeare. Against this wispy Malvolio Phillips poses a sad quartet of comics—pallid beyond comprehension—who hollow out the comic heart of this production so that what should impart violent life to the play merely keeps the plot cranking along on machinery that was ancient when the Bard resuscitated it.

I've always enjoyed William Hutt in whatever role, but I had trouble adjusting to his Fool. A middle-aged Feste is—of course—another idea. There is a reference to him someplace in the play as the Fool who once belonged to Olivia's father. Why not make him much older than anyone else in the cast? On the other hand, why bother? Of course the implication in making the Fool the most dignified character onstage is there for anyone to see. But much of that dignity is invisible and merely seems dull—for want of energetic vulgarity from his cohorts to highlight it.

There are still other ideas. Some of them—as with Jim McQueen's Mortimer Snerd of a Duke Orsino—are simply a case of making all too apparent what is beautifully suggestive in the poetry.

Which brings us back to what should be the real core of any production of *Twelfth Night*—the poetry. The magic and beauty of the play is still there waiting to be brought forth. It won't be done by the commonplace pedantic distortions of directors who approach it only by reducing its multiple levels of meaning and response to textbook summaries. The company which successfully renders this play will approach it not only as a demonstration of their invention but as something whole and mysterious to be illuminated.

10 June 1980

Virginia

Written by Edna O'Brien, directed by Robin Phillips.

Phillip Silver's lovely set for *Virginia* consists of a few pieces of period furniture and walls of white rice paper through which can be

dimly seen the outlines of trees and foliage or a section of Bloomsbury Square. It neatly suggests the cloistered mind of the heroine
and the indirect manner in which the outside world made its presence felt on her consciousness.

I would guess that Edna O'Brien has invented little in her theatrical rendering of Woolf's adult life. Certainly the presently fashionable Bloomsbury industry has provided enough primary source
material by way of letters and diaries, and what have you, to fuel
dozens of plays. In her own private way, Woolf was one of the great
wits of our century. Any reader of Woolf's writings, published or
unpublished, will have imagined a voice to fit the author. I would
be surprised if the voice in the mind's ear of many readers wasn't
very close to the voice Maggie Smith brings to her role as Virginia.
Smith even looks enough like Woolf to clinch the illusion. But even
beyond that, it's a superb performance, full of intelligence and spon-
taneously probing sensibility. For me, however, the real revelation of
the evening was in Nicholas Pennell's Leonard. The greying, thick-
ening figure of Virginia's latter-day saint, protector, doctor, jailer,
psychiatrist and literary supporter formed a solid human centre
around which Smith's peripatetic genius flitted and took bearings.
Pennell's selfless and spare performance helped to focus the entire
production. There's a third figure too. But in the play, Vita Sack-
ville West—even when played by an actress with Patricia Conolly's
ability to express intelligence—really has no existence outside of
Woolf's intense fantasy life. Virginia herself says at some point that
her own friends sometimes seem no more real to her than her
dreams. Vita's major importance for Woolf might have been as a
screen for the fantasies which she wouldn't let herself project onto
the opposite sex. *Orlando* resulted from this concentration of fantasy.

Orlando is mentioned, but none of Woolf's other works are referred to. The bulk of the play deals one way or another with her
married years, but we don't see her at work as a teacher or writer.
We see her only as a rather high-strung social animal and as a rare
creature captured in the institution of marriage. Thus her infatua-
tion with the bold and unconventional Vita comes to seem only a bit
of vicarious living.

As theatre, *Virginia* approaches the one-actor play stylistically,
but doesn't quite ask for the intimacy between audience and performer which that form demands. Besides, there are scenes—effective scenes—between Virginia and Leonard which work nicely as

straight drama. These are powerful enough that they become the emotional centre of the piece—particularly with the distance maintained between the central character and the audience. It's easy to imagine another play about Virginia and Leonard Woolf, one that would deal directly with the dozens of problems and questions only implied in this one. But such a play would have to run the risk of being more thoroughly imagined, less based on document.

Finally as drama, *Virginia* is constricted by its brilliant subject's overwhelming point of view. By the end, we long to be able to see outside the very particular viewpoint of Virginia Woolf. If we were permitted to do so, then her particular social and psychological situation might carry with it an interest beyond the prurient, the merely titillating. As it stands we rummage through her pockets, callously perusing her love letters, and enjoying her turns of phrase as one might sip a fine brandy.

But then this is the Stratford Festival, after all. People will be going to *Virginia* to see Star Theatre, and Maggie Smith is Stratford's biggest star. No one will feel let down.

11 June 1980

The Servant of Two Masters

Written by Carlo Goldoni, translated by Tom Cone,
directed by Peter Moss.

Being a pleasant way to spend a few hours isn't the highest praise that one can apply to a piece of theatre. But after having spent several hours this week witnessing the flattening and eviscerating of great plays, I'm forced to acknowledge that pleasantness isn't such a bad thing to have achieved. The Stratford production of *The Servant of Two Masters* never warms up above chuckle level, even when the scenes are clearly structured for guffaws. The director, Peter Moss, may have a pleasing eye for style, but he gives no evidence of a talented grasp of rhythm or dramatic pacing. Yet so relaxed is this production and so unassuming in its effects, that I can't bring myself to think ill of it.

I should mention that Stratford's production is the premiere of a new version of Goldoni's farce by Vancouver playwright Tom Cone.

Cone has taken the liberty of moving the action from the eighteenth century to Venice just prior to the First World War. But in spirit the characters are still one step removed from Commedia dell'arte. Our cultural referent becomes the period of classic American film comedy that began with Sennett and ended with the Marx Brothers. In fact Graeme Campbell's Pantalone, in pin stripe and bowler, looks like Billy Gilbert and occasionally lopes about in a Groucho crouch.

There's an interesting point of comparison here. The Shaw Festival is now presenting a radical stylization of that vile old Feydeau sex farce *A Flea in her Ear*. But director Derek Goldby took as his determining stylistic model the animated cartoon. He did this even to the point of quoting in the curtain call the opening and closing of the old Bugs Bunny show. Now, one of the better things about a Bugs Bunny cartoon is that its casual violence and choreographed frenzy blow over in ten minutes. The major problem with *A Flea in her Ear*—as brilliant as it was—was that it left its audience after two hours bruised and harassed well beyond comic stimulation and in need of a few stiff drinks. Nevertheless Goldby's approach was entirely logical, pushing as it did the mechanical nature of farce to its extreme, wherein the characters are at the total mercy of plot and staging. Like any successful farce, the show demonstrated that the genre must have style if it is to have anything at all.

The Servant of Two Masters has style. But director Moss takes a very different approach from Goldby's staccato pacing. He has cast the familiar *commedia* figures of clever servant, hotheaded soldier, pompous merchant, spoiled daughter with competent actors and encouraged them to flesh out the outlines with wit and warmth, all within the framework of certain flexible stylistic modes. The actors impart to their characters a behavioural charm which would be sacrificed for speed in a production such as Goldby's.

This is the kind of acting situation in which an old hand can find the tiller while a young one risks being embarrassed by freedom. Graeme Campbell as Pantalone and Lewis Gordon as the central schemer Truffaldino give us cleanly funny reactions to stock situations. And Jennifer Phipps as Smeraldina, the sarcastic servant, comments lazily on the action, her weight slouched on one hip and her eye on the main chance.

The youngsters, Brent Carver and Goldie Semple as the lovers for instance, are talented, bright, charming as puppies, but markedly less clued in theatrically. Nevertheless the company creates a better ensemble than one can usually expect at Stratford where the pecking order is often all too obvious.

It's a good enough ensemble that it's a pity that it wasn't directed with more theatrical snap. This is a production full of charming inventions, some of them , no doubt, courtesy of Mr. Cone, others I would expect, due to the actors and director. Everything is in place save for those climaxes of exhilarating frenzy which good farce must build to. Michael Egan's clever and attractive set waits expectantly for them but in vain. Perhaps if one could combine the best aspects of the production by Goldby and the one by Moss one would have a satisfying evening in the theatre.

12 June 1980

The Gin Game

Written by D. I. Coburn, directed by Mel Shapiro.

Card games played before an audience carry with them a dramatic tension that's as close to abstract as that quality gets. Perhaps that's why they make good theatrical centrepieces. The dramatic focus is provided almost automatically by the game and a playwright or actor can use that focus to his own ends. A card game onstage makes an audience more tractable, more submissive to the theatrical moment. In *The Gin Game* playwright D.I. Coburn extends that rule to his onstage card players. In an old-folks home two elderly people, fond of each other, but by no means intimate, play a regular game of two-handed Gin, and the tension that collects around the extended game works to break down their own false self-images, forcing them to face some kind of limited truth about themselves.

Coburn has written a good popular play with more theatrical awareness than one has a right to expect from a novice playwright. With its running gags and easy flowing dialogue, it's very much in the mode of the American sitcom—and that's not intended as a sneer. At its best, the American sitcom, as developed, say, by Norman Lear, is good popular theatre and demands the fine and elaborate timing of comic stage acting to win its best effects. *The Gin Game* is as neatly balanced, as sure of its best steps and aware of

71

its own limits as a good tap dance. What it sets out to do it does without excess and without posturing.

And like the sitcom, it's dependent on the charm and skill of its players if it's to have any dramatic weight at all. It's no slight on Coburn's play to suggest that there would be no point in doing it were there not two players on the level of Douglas Rain and Kate Reid to act it. In their hands, it becomes a demonstration of what it means to have honed a craft past competence and into the realm of artistry. As the Old Groaner used to say, "These two will get it when the gettin's gone."

Believe me, Stratford can use a demonstration of something like that this year. This rep company has a serious problem in the middle range. Young actors with neither the technique nor the authority of experience are failing to fill the boots of that great crowd of Shakespearian clowns and characters that peoples the plays, leaving the productions sorely deficient in acting weight.

What a relief it is then to deliver oneself up to two actors who are more than capable of shouldering that trust. Kate Reid has developed an arthritic hobble for her character, a bit reminiscent of Edith Bunker's muddled waddle, but ironically so, as Reid's character eventually reveals herself to be a hard, unforgiving Methodist, protecting her self-righteousness by her very loneliness. Similarly Douglas Rain's blustery cynical retired businessman comes to be seen as a man protecting a soft centre.

These two argue incessantly—ostensibly about cards, but really about the nature of their self-deceptions. Coburn's play hangs on a simple conceit. She, who presents a meek and confused face to the world, consistently wins the games. He, who presents the face of a man who knows the rules and has the sense to live by them, can't win. Of course the truth is that she wins not by dumb luck but by skill and intuition, and her winning, because it contradicts both of their cherished self-deceptions, is the lever which pries away their masks.

Reid and Rain bring out even more from the interaction of their two characters. These two people, well past the age when sexuality is the most important link between man and woman, genuinely share liking and respect. Yet finally their separate ways of coping with felt inadequacies threaten and cause them to do violence to each other. There's a further resonance in the fact that both have taken refuge in the classic social postures of the sexes. Nor is the facing of their own true natures invested with any special meaning. At the end, the man staggers offstage, perhaps to die, while the woman stands alone, confused and paralyzed with indecision.

I felt momentarily cheated by the inconclusive ending. But I'm sure I was merely expecting that a play that so often had the easy charm of a situation comedy should end like a situation comedy, with both characters fixed in the attitudes that define and limit them. At the end of *The Gin Game*, that cosy circle is broken and life asserts its dominance over formula.

13 June 1980

Much Ado about Nothing

Written by William Shakespeare, directed by Robin Phillips.

I now know where all the lightness and gaiety that was denied Stratford's *Twelfth Night* went. Phillips was saving it for *Much Ado about Nothing*. Good spirits fairly wash over the apron of the stage, conquering even the muffled acoustics of the Festival Theatre — which acoustics, incidentally, demand that you must either have at least a passing familiarity with the lines or be prepared to forego the good portion of them which are not directed straight at you.

This is a fine *Much Ado*. The presumptuous tinkerer who threw several monkey wrenches into *Twelfth Night* is nowhere in evidence. In fact, at their best, Phillips and his actors come up with alive readings of the speeches which seem to have sprung—not from some bright half-baked interpretation, but directly from the heart of Shakespeare's great romance. Further, where Phillips has placed the interpretive emphasis—on Maggie Smith's and Brian Bedford's brilliant star turns—makes good and interesting sense, not just from the point of view of pleasing the tourists, but from the standpoint of textual reading. Beatrice and Benedick are the only really sane people in this Messina. They are governed by their hearts as well as by their sense of convention. They stand by the wronged Hero after she has suffered great calumny when even her father is all too ready to believe the crude evidence against her.

Look at how this reading of the characters affects their wonderful sparring matches. They are in love right from the beginning of

73

course. We know that, even if they don't. And their wit is the means both by which they keep the human contact open between themselves and by which they deny their mutual attractions. There's nothing new in this interpretation; nor should we look for novelty in the handling of Shakespeare—the freshness is in the actors' intelligent exploration of a situation that is immediately comprehensible.

Maggie Smith—even in Beatrice's most shrewish lines—keeps an element of hope and excitement alive in her character's heart. When she eavesdrops on the conversation in which her friends plant the idea that Benedick is in love with her, her reaction has little of the comic in it. It's a deeply touching confusion of hope and terror. If we didn't realize it before, we know now that she's been protecting with her sharp tongue a heart too good, too pure and too vulnerable for Messina. Our concern now is that Bedford's rather more callow Benedick will be worthy of her love. One of the more impressive aspects of Bedford's performance is the way in which he suggests a growth in moral stature during the course of the play. It's right that his Benedick should begin by preening himself before the audience, a little removed from the action of the play. And there's a subtle tension in the way he's slowly pulled—as a result of his love for Beatrice and the near tragedy that befalls Hero—away from the audience's eye and into the inner life of the community.

Incidentally—a rare achievement for a Stratford production — there really is a sense of community created here. When Don John disrupts its pleasant life with his plot, we feel the shock—as we should—as being an affront to the community, as much as an assault on the heroine's honour. This emphasis helps to make sense of the problematic Hero/Claudio affair. Hero is rebuked for her apparent lack of chastity because she has broken a community ideal.

Another indication that this production found the right track is Nicholas Pennell's superb rendering of Don John, the worm in the apple. He's not conceived as a bundle of modern neuroses but, properly, as a negative inversion of the community's ideals so that he makes sense only in relation to the community. The actor's malicious torpor is just right. Pennell has surprised me twice this season with evidence of a substantial artistic growth. His performances have had an impressive sense of scale and thus of integrity.

For the main this production shares that sense of integrity while managing not to skimp on its tourist attractions. Occasionally it goes too far in its desire to ingratiate, clutching the pant leg like an untrained puppy. At other times it oversteps the bounds of inven- tion, as when it burlesques the song "Sigh No More Ladies" in a manner that's funny in itself, but which does violence to the func- tion music has in the comedies. On the other hand Louis Apple- baum's incidental music is quite unaccountably banal, so much so that I was almost relieved that the production cheated by denying the community the affirmation of the final dance.

I was happy to see one of Shakespeare's romances properly costumed. I've had enough of tight-ass Edwardian, Victorian and eighteenth-century costumes which often serve merely as excuses to do violence to the comedies, replacing convention with repression and swamping joy with the darker undercurrents which exist in anything Shakespeare ever wrote and should never be made the meat of the banquet.

16 June 1980

Henry V

Written by William Shakespeare, directed by Peter Moss.

Well, what can I say about Stratford's *Henry V*? If, like the preten- tious school teacher in the sketch by Sears and Switzer, you are of the mind that Stratford is "theatre in decay" then by all means get you to *Henry V*, for there you will have evidence enow of every negative quality necessary to mew up your cherished bad opinion of the place. Flaccidity is an apt word. And incompetence. But finally dullness conquers all.

Who would have thought that Shakespeare's great folk drama should fall such easy prey to the dictates of lousy theatre? I've seen high school productions with more sense of what they were about.

Now, you may think I'm reacting a bit vehemently. The fact is that I had to sit through this damn puppet show twice. The first time I sat meekly and obediently among the note-takers and the hungry-eyed actors and the stuffed tuxedos, breathing in the stale intimidating air of officially sanctioned culture, and fleshing out the prosaic doodlings of the production with a willing imagination. I was pitifully grateful when an experienced performer like Mervyn

75

Blake or Amelia Hall made something of his few paltry moments, or when an enthusiastic young actor like Diana LeBlanc or Barry McGregor managed to wriggle out from under the clammy hand of director Peter Moss. But second time through—oh monstrous!

The single most distressing thing about this production is that neither Richard Monette nor Jack Wetherall can speak a Shakespeare line to save his soul. Monette has a vocal pattern wherein his light voice catches on a key word for emphasis and breaks the line right there. And he repeats that pattern as unconsciously and as mercilessly as a metronome. His idea of varying his delivery is to jerk off little swatches of a speech in sudden spurts of interchangeable fury, joy or despair: choose one. At least Monette's approach carries with it a faint recognition that there's music to be had in Harry's orations. Wetherall runs pell mell away from Shakespeare covering his head and hunching his back as if afraid that the grandeur of the language will crush him like a gnat. And it does. At no matter what arbitrary pace Wetherall chooses he vindictively chops the bard into little bitty pieces of speech, taking his revenge on the poetry which eludes him. When the speech seems to demand a build he has one technique to apply. He starts fast and quiet, white of face and ends fast and loud and red of face.

In the past Monette and Wetherall have acquitted themselves well in contemporary roles. But Shakespeare is another world and requires another technique. Neither are within hailing distance of the great parts. The fact that they are getting them says appalling things about Canada's largest and richest rep company.

These Henrys have no connection to their courts, their Lords, their situations in time. "Once more unto the breach," they holler to no one, and clumps of unenthusiastic soldiers follow them as if they've been at Cowboys and Indians too long. It seems as if the background characters and situations have been willfully flattened, the better to set off these desperate non-performances. The English Lords are given no life of their own. Exeter, for example, is not uncle to Harry, but merely one of several uncurious onlookers. The distinction between the French and English courts is blurred as if the director was embarrassed by Shakespeare's vigorous folk chauvinism. And the two Harrys stride about their no-courts, making their no-speeches, and entering into their no-battles, treating eloquence like a bawd. As they have no production and no cast around them, they fill up the void with bits of business too contrived, too self-serving and too isolated to be called interpretations. Wetherall is particularly shameless with his business, clasping Lord Scroop the betrayer to his bosom and wincing back his tears in full view of his soldiers as if recalling Christ's treatment of Judas. Monette is mostly satisfied with strutting up and down all kingly and such, applying the hill-and-dale cadences of his voice and leaving the more aggressive tricks to his rival.

Both actors are victims. They have been put into a situation before they were ready and given not a jot of intelligent direction to guide them. Because of Stratford being what it is, and because they've been breathing its air for a long time, they know they have to deliver the goods and impress the crowds by putting on a show. Neither of them puts on a show, but they do put on a show of putting on a show.

In a recent N.A.C. production Neil Munro gave us a King Harry which was close enough to definitive to please me. But sitting in the Festival theatre after seeing Peter Moss' production for a second time and watching Jack Wetherall take his bow, I could have sworn I heard a little child's voice saying insistently; "But the King has no clothes."

16 June 1980

Brief Lives

Adapted from the writings of John Aubrey, directed by Martha Henry.

Saturday evening in Stratford was brutally hot and muggy. The Third Stage interior didn't have even the benefit of the moist breeze which blew over the Avon tantalizing the senses if only with the idea of coolness. In the bleachers the fanning of programs in front of tired, wet faces took on a rhythm as steady as a metronome. And at the centre of the audience's soggy attention was Douglas Rain cooking pieces of kidney over a real hearth fire, lifting out a red hot poker with which to heat his various drinks, rolling from the coals a hot brick and wrapping it in heavy cloth to warm his bed. Mr. Rain was dressed for a winter's day in seventeenth-century London — hefty feisty robes, thick and warm, but ragged enough to seem an extension of the unruly white hair which covered his face and

77

straggled well below his shoulders.

Little room to feel sorry for the audience in the presence of an actor so burdened with gear and business inappropriate to the temperature and the humidity.

Except: there was no actor there to feel sorry for. Only an old man dressed for winter, talking and going about his business—some of it very elaborate business indeed. Come to think of it, talking would seem to *be* his business. From where I sat I swear I could see no signs of perspiration on that man's face. I wouldn't be surprised if Mr. Rain was capable of *willing* the retention of his own sweat.

Now it may seem a trifle naïve to go on about an actor's absorption in his role. After all, isn't that an actor's job? Well, yes and no. Since the revolt against classical acting effected by the generation of American actors led by Brando, there has been a large change in our expectation of what an actor is, or should be. It's widely misunderstood that that generation made stage acting more naturalistic. If that was all they had to do, the earlier group of great Hollywood actors—Spencer Tracy, say, or James Stewart—had already cleared the way for naturalistic acting, but there was not a clear enough acknowledgment of craft to make that kind of acting flexible enough for the stage. Stage acting must by its very nature contain artifice in its playing style. In fact, if anything, Brando and the others encouraged at least as much artifice as they took away. What they really did was to make the actor's personal sensibility as much a focus for the audience as the part they were playing. Thus the actor now fits comfortably into the role of Romantic artist rather than that of the classical disciple of an exacting craft.

Douglas Rain is a truly fine Classical actor—a master of his art, and a genuine source of theatrical wisdom. We all realize this, I think. Nevertheless it helps never to take the best for granted. I'm happy to have the privilege of praising Douglas Rain. But I'd also like to point out how the presence of a classical actor affects the presentation of the one-man play. First of all there is little of the person-to-person intimacy which is often the main appeal of the genre. Three of the four walls of *Brief Lives'* set may be open to the audience, but Mr. Rain (in character) stays within four walls, for the most part, creating his role and creating relationships to his stage environment. No naked mime and bare stages for this actor. Daphne Dare and Co. have had a great deal of fun putting together one of the most elaborate and brilliantly cluttered sets you can imagine. But as full of props and pieces as it is, Mr. Rain uses that set and what is in it to its fullest. When the evening is done, there is not one bedpan, one utensil, one candlestick, one curious toy, one goblet, one crutch, one stack of books or papers that he has not made a part of his performance in some way. The character he creates is there in the way he handles these things. A sound system suggests the slightly unruly world surrounding the walls—babies crying, voices singing, the chants of the town crier—and Mr. Rain uses these aural intrusions as well, even when it's not scripted that he do so.

You can enjoy *Brief Lives* as a demonstration of his craft by a fine actor. You can enjoy it as an amateur antiquary would, drinking in the homely details of another age. You may not want to see it as theatre in its fullest sense. The play is a compilation of writings by John Aubrey, a British gossip and antiquary who was born in the Jacobean period, lived through the reign of Cromwell, saw the restoration of Charles II, and died with the century. Its purpose is to recreate the age, not in historical detail, but by invoking the spirit of a man intimate with its trivialities and its day to day life. Aubrey's gossip incidentally is very often of a scurrilous nature— even to the point of reporting the cries of a serving girl being swiven against a tree by Sir Walter Raleigh. We know very little more of Aubrey at the end of the evening than we did when it began. This is as it should be, perhaps. The main character is clearly the century itself. From the actor's practical point of view, the main character to play against is a cluttered room. I'm sure that much of the credit for the pleasing details of the performance, both with regard to business and to speeches, should go to the play's director, Martha Henry.

21 July 1980

Bosoms and Neglect

Written by John Guare, directed by Mel Shapiro.

Bosoms and Neglect opened in Chicago in 1979. It gathered fine reviews until it hit New York in the spring of that year where it was panned and expired after a few performances. Despite its fate many people consider it one of the finest of recent American plays.

John Guare's play is about parents and children and the way in which unresolved tensions between them affect the child long after he has become an adult, even to the point of arresting his development. In particular the play is about the attempt of a 40-year-old computer analyst with the nickname of Scooper, to get to the root of a problematic relationship with Henny, his blind and conveniently crazy old mother. Scooper is a confused individual, hooked equally on analysis and the world of literature, where life, as he says, is held in order by nice straight white margins. Both obsessions have kept him from facing the true source of his problems and that is, of course, rooted in his childhood and in his mother's unlived emotional life.

There is a short prologue to the play during which Scooper discovers that his mother has had breast cancer for years. He quickly sees her to the hospital for a mastectomy. But most of the first act centres on his new-found relationship with a woman named Deirdre whom he has picked up in a bookstore, and who mirrors his obsession with literature and shares a fixation on the same psychiatrist and an inability to handle a guilt-ridden relationship with a parent—in her case the father.

Act I ends with bursts of pathological violence from both characters and an incident with a knife that sends the two of them to the hospital. So when Act II begins all three major characters are in the same hospital and proceed to batter through to their own particular self-revelations.

I feel I should confess that this play totally perplexes me. And I wish to emphasize that it's the play that does so. The production, in every respect, struck me as a distinguished one. Kate Reid's Henny is as hard and as funny as report had her to be. In particular the actress has lots of room to work with that brilliant skill she has developed of projecting the thought patterns of an instinctive half-aware consciousness. Pat Collins is well on her way to centering her very difficult part. And Ray Jewers as the central character Scooper does a fine job in a demanding and, for me at least, a very unsympathetic role. As he showed in this season's *The Gin Game*, director Mel Shapiro has a talented grasp of the American mode I call Neurotic Sit-Com, and that grasp lies in the difficult knack of keeping the humour accessible while giving the underlying teeth-gritting an intelligent focus. And Phillip Silver's sets are of the rare kind that justify big-budget set design—they are evocative (I especially liked Henny's shabby living room), visually spare, and cleverly designed for fast changes.

But about the play—and I would be happy to be challenged on this—I found it schematic in its intellectual underpinnings, pat in its resolutions and ambitious in its execution—ambitious, that is, in the wrong way, by which I mean that I sense the ambition to have been the propelling force rather than something that sprang out of the author's attempt to get at a situation, or even simply to tell a story.

The long first-act scene between Deirdre and Scooper is written in a heightened literary style from which metaphors and unconversational adjectives stick out at odd angles. Having seen some of the piece in print, I realize that this reads better than it plays. I also realize that it's arguable that such a style is proper to two book-obsessed people. Nonetheless, I'm still uneasy with it. It even reminded me on occasion of the pretty awful "high-tone" writing which surfaced in ABC-TV's recent attempt at dramatic art, the series about marriage called *United States*. I was interested too in the rhythmically stylized swapping of short lines between the two characters—again something that looks good on the page, but in this case sounds artificial to the ear. I don't feel that the writing goes far enough in its stylization to allow for the artifice; it hews in other respects to the unpretentious manner of the American sit-com as developed, for instance, by *All in the Family*.

Act II, largely taken up with spirited and funny interplay between the pretentious and self-involved Scooper and his wily undercutting mother, is much better—at times it's really fine stage writing. But I'm still left uneasy with the patness of the Freudian resolutions proposed for Deirdre and Scooper, and with the calculated irony of Henny's final monologue. And I feel that most of them are there to protect the writer from his own creation and to answer the kind of objections I've raised.

For instance, given the play's satirizing of analysis and analysands, how are we to take the climactic psychiatric breakthroughs of Scooper and Deirdre? It's made clear that they happen without the presence of the doctor, but they are experienced very much in the implied framework of psychoanalysis.

Nevertheless it's an interesting production and, as for the play, I would particularly suggest that you make up your own mind about it if you get the chance. One of the things that made me most uncomfortable about the piece was my own response to it. I suspect that I'm not very sympathetic to recent trends in serious American playwriting.

21 July 1980

Foxfire

Written by Susan Cooper and Hume Cronyn,
directed by Robin Phillips and Peter Moss.

Foxfire was suggested by a magazine of Appalachian folk culture anthologized under the same name. The story which carries the play along its rickety road turns out to be the old one, beloved by Americans, about the ageing widow stubbornly holding onto the family farm in the face of Progress, which force wants to turn her land into a valuable development. No doubt this story has appeared on the American stage before. I know it best from the movies. The most distinguished example that comes to mind is Elia Kazan's *Wild River*. The most interestingly irrational example is John Ford's film version of *Tobacco Road*, the visual style of which Daphne Dare's elaborate set actually brings to mind. There's the same pretty heightening of a natural setting using light and shade and a Disney animator's idealization of the rustic.

I'm afraid the same cleaning-up process has been at work on the characterizations and the accents employed by the actors. Hume Cronyn and Jessica Tandy do skilful actors' approximations of dialect—no more than once-over-lightly suggestions of hillbilly rhythms. *Foxfire*'s lack of well-observed characterization wouldn't matter much if the production had less of a documentary purpose. Without purpose, it would just be a bad commercial play. With it, it's a silly play as well.

In the middle of both acts the plot stops dead and, on the baldest of pretexts, Mr. Cronyn holds forth on how they planted crops or delivered babies or what have you in the old days. He does this in character and sounds for all the world like some rustic Helen Creighton giving a lecture on Appalachian folkways to a gathering of the Ladies Home, Tea and Humanitarian Action Committee.

It's clear that while the Foxfire books were the basis of the play, Mr. Cronyn and his collaborator Susan Cooper had no idea how to make documentary material work on stage. Their solution was to fall back on a particularly tired tradition of American playwriting. Sitting side by side with recitations from the *Foxfire* books is a great deal of folksy whimsy, mostly centred on the Cronyn character, the old patriarch. Shortly into the play we are told that this character, whom we have been watching for some time, is actually a ghost. Only Miss Tandy can see or hear him, but sometimes he can affect the actions of others by his invisible presence.

We can also recognize that *Foxfire* is an old-fashioned American play because it can't bear to face the implications of its story. The old ways, *Foxfire* tells us, were quaint and sweet and the new ways may look soulless beside them, but the new ways do constitute progress; progress means better education and money and the end of superstition and this is all good and necessary. So finally we are merely asked to shed a sentimental tear for what has been and to meet the future with gratitude. *Foxfire* finally doesn't question or illuminate either the old ways or the new ways. Can this play have been written in 1980 after Sam Shephard's assaults both on the rural myth and on the liberal myth of progress?

More to the point, can this play actually have been produced in 1980 at Stratford, Ontario, Canada? Canadian theatre on this very subject matter has done work that makes this play look pale indeed. The good Canadian work on the subject usually has a harder political framework than this play could approach (and I'm using the word political in its broadest sense). American theatre fears the discussion of politics. Even post-Vietnam film-makers and dramatists—Shephard again or Coppola in *Apocalypse Now*—refrain from looking at the nightmare structures they show in their works, preferring instead to glory in the melodramatic chaos which they have created.

And of course Canadian theatre, like British theatre before it, has long since perfected ways of using documentary material that is both moving and theatrically dynamic. Has Robin Phillips, who presumably chose *Foxfire* for this season, managed to see any of this?

The time is past that Stratford can afford to ignore the culture upon which it floats. But then there is really only one reason that *Foxfire* was produced, and that was to insure the presence of Cronyn and Tandy on the glittering star bill of Stratford's brochures. When a theatre begins to rely on stars rather than on the quality of its productions, it's well on its way to irrelevance.

11 August 1980

The Seagull

Written by Anton Chekhov, directed by Robin Phillips.

Stratford's production of *The Seagull* has an extraordinary cast of well-known actors. I hardly know how to begin talking about their performances without going through the tedious charade of saying that this actor was good but that actor was bad. It's a charade because observations of that sort when unconnected to a larger sense of the play really come down to personal reaction or lack of it. So let's go to the interpretation behind Robin Phillips' production. It has to do with the perception, more or less justifiable from the text, that everyone in the play is a tragically self-centred person incapable of imagining the suffering of another human being.

That's only the beginning of the interpretation, but even so it might account for the disconnected reading of the dialogue, the indulgent pauses, staging in which the characters are given to turning their backs on the action and staring out over the audience, and even the well-judged sense of casual cruelty in the characters' dismissals of each other. Does the interpretation justify the fact that so many of the actors seem to be fighting for their part to be heard and seen as central above all the others? For instance, take the clever offender William Hutt, who plays the debonair and emotionally remote Doctor. Can we justify his habit of waiting when he's due to deliver a line until the audience's attention settles on him like a robe, and his way of preening in that robe as he speaks, using the arsenal of tricks available to a skilled actor? And Mr. Hutt is a very skilled actor. But let's take Jack Wetherall who plays young Konstantin and who is not a very skilled actor. There are Mr. Wetherall's usual habits of fidgeting like a schoolboy and parsing his every speech into identically timed breathily punctuated phrases that have no connection to the meaning.

No, I think whatever relationship these approaches have to the interpretation, they amount to bad performances. But was interpretation behind the stilted nature of the first act, as tedious a ninety minutes as I've experienced in the theatre?

In Chekhov, the onstage impulse flows from person to person, rarely remaining with one character for long; themes and motifs appear and reappear, and this flow, this sense of processes unfolding in time, is much more important then the characters' individual moments of awareness. Phillips has directed with his customary deployment of actors' business—simple striking gestures or oddly accented responses which are intended to clarify the movement of the action. When Maggie Smith as Madam Arkadina turns very suddenly to look at the young girl who is beginning to rival her for Trigorin's love, that moment of recognition is so strong it's as if a spotlight were placed on the actress. Yet in the text, Chekhov gives us the character's dawning awareness of the situation in subtle ways, revealing it over time by inflection and passing remarks. If Phillips had found the proper rhythm for the play he wouldn't have needed to rely on such accented moments. As it is the action seems to stop and start as the audience's attention is jerked from the speech of one character to that of another. And as a character in Chekhov rarely says anything conclusive if divorced from the flow of things, the effect is wearing.

The highlight of the evening was a highly charged scene between Smith and Brian Bedford in which Madame Arkadina begs her lover to forego his attraction to young Nina. In fact, the whole section of the play that dealt with the triangle was good theatre, if not good Chekhov. For one thing Roberta Maxwell gave an affecting performance as Nina. For another, Bedford and Smith seem to bring out each other's best instincts.

But my favourite performances in *The Seagull* were those by the less central actors. Lewis Gordon as old Sorin, for example, knew his own weight and place within each scene and balanced his acting accordingly. He would have fit well into a good production of *The Seagull*. It's true that the play is arguably the bleakest of all Chekhov major works, yet I can't help feeling that the sensibility of the director rather meanly circumscribed the writer's vision which depends on a double focus of warmth and severity. But if the direction hampered it, Stratford's characteristic lack of a decent ensemble style defeated it.

11 August 1980

Henry VI

Written by William Shakespeare, adapted and directed by Pam Brighton.

Pam Brighton has adapted the three *Henry VI* plays to allow them to fit into a single evening, but don't imagine it's a short evening. Fours hours top to tail as they say in the radio business. (I should get some sort of award being here today.)

The condensed version sometimes degenerates to Musical Thrones as various Yorks take the crown away from Henry, are defeated and die horrible deaths before the King is returned. These deposings and restorations are punctuated by battles with real swords and a lot of leaping about. Audiences should be advised to sit way back. Not only are swords swung about like towels in a locker room, but heavy head gear, grisly looking decapitated heads and bits of fabricated intestine are flung or spattered in the general vicinity of the audience.

But I'm running ahead of myself here. I was going to say something more about the adaptation. What Brighton has done is to cut away whatever doesn't focus directly on the War of the Roses. *Henry VI*, *Part I* for instance is represented only by three or four scenes. Gone are La Pucelle (or Joan of Arc), Talbot and all of the French sequences. As I say, the cutting leaves us with an awful lot of gruesome narrative to get through. And as Pam Brighton is no believer in restraint, the experience is exhausting. I enjoyed the first act very much. I'm a sap for swift and witty stage narrative and for the use of melodrama to get across the idea of the thing. I'm aware that the language was given short shrift by most of the actors, who hollered and spat and grimaced their way through it. (The main exception was Nicholas Pennell who is incapable of overlooking language no matter how *Stürm und Drang*.) But even with the language diminished, and even with one perverse and unfair bit of casting in a major role, for which Brighton must take full responsibility, the nobility's maggoty ferment around the saintly boy king was sharply created. Nobody has ever understood the corruption that surrounds power better than Shakespeare. Certainly no one has ever given it such terrifying theatrical clarity. And it's Shakespeare's particular genius to put at the centre of a cruel drama of power a human being wholly incapable of understanding the workings of same.

Stephen Russell played Henry VI quite satisfactorily. But

Nicholas Pennell as the two main villains really took the honours. When his Suffolk died, the production followed suit, reviving only near the end when his Richard Crookback came to prominence. Two superb performances.

Brighton's rendering of the central idea developed no further after the first act. As if to compensate, she lets loose an outrageous arsenal of gimmicks and shock techniques in the second and third. York's youngest son has his belly slit open by Clifford and out burble his intestines in glorious Technicolor. A goodly number of soldiers are gored. Blood spurts from their wounds and splatters to the floor. A soldier enters at the top of one of Michael Eagen's impressive ramps carrying a body. He lets it drop and it rolls all the way to the bottom. By the end of the second act the audience was giggling whenever more gore and massacree made an appearance.

Part of me was pleased to see an attempt at Stratford to make Shakespeare more physical, and to see some of the less familiar younger players getting a chance to set up a good holler. One can get more than a bit sick of the prevailing effete Stratford aesthetic of pretty, tasteful, controlled productions, with pretty sets and pretty pre-recorded music. People walk out of *Henry VI* occasionally. It's almost Stratford's answer to the Shaw Festival's *A Respectable Wedding*. But whereas I would argue that the latter more than justified its obstreperous approach, *Henry VI* is really little more than an example of The Theatre of Excess.

14 August 1980

The Grand Hunt

Written by Gyula Hernady, adapted by John Hirsch and Suzanne Grossman, directed by John Hirsch.

John Hirsch's production of *The Grand Hunt* is an efficient piece of narrative with a satirical edge that slices rather too quickly for the cuts to register, and a secondhand sensibility derived from Ernst Lubitsch, but leaning toward Billy Wilder, his postwar disciple. The plot is a fantasy rewoven around the historical events that accompanied the fall of the Hapsburgs. Hungarian playwright Gyula Hernady imagines the deaths of Charles, joint ruler of both Austria and Hungary, and of his queen Zita, several years before their historical deaths in 1922. Hernady fills in the intervening gap with a wild story of deception and political manœuvring. A Hungarian nobleman with a taste for power engineers a grand hoax: he takes a courtesan and a naïve law student and independently coaches them to take the place of the dead King and Queen. Each of the rulers-in-training believes the other to be genuine.

Whatever the effect of the original play, Hirsch and collaborating adapter Suzanne Grossman have made *The Grand Hunt* an old Paramount movie of the sophisticated European émigré school. Rowland Hewgill plays the count with the speedy gleeful manœuvrings of James Cagney's amoral Coca Cola magnate loose in Russia in Wilder's cold war comedy *One, Two, Three.* The count has three comically inept sidekicks played by Gillie Fenwick, Sandy Webster and Al Kozlik who behave exactly like the three commissars in Paris in the Lubitsch movie *Ninotchka*, a movie, incidentally, written by Wilder. More generally, the production casually mixes humour and violence rather like a lightweight version of Lubistch's *To Be or Not to Be*, an astonishing black comedy about a troupe of actors in Nazi-occupied Germany. Carole Shelley's beautifully timed rendition of the courtesan-turned-queen is reminiscent of the lovely Carole Lombard, and Jan Triska's wonderful version of a likeable boob has dozens of precedents in Wilder and Sturges films.

Hirsch uses the Festival's talented stock company well, whipping them through their paces to be sure, but leaving room for them to work easily and efficiently. One of the most pleasurable aspects of the evening was the cast's enjoyment in stirring up the frothy style Hirsch seems to favour.

Despite a narrative structure based on paranoia and power manipulation, little that is disturbing sticks as it flies past. Hirsch reserves his gut effects for tricks like sudden murders and gunshots which startle but pass immediately, leaving the watcher free to enjoy the clever unravelling of plot.

I haven't got a lot to say about *The Grand Hunt* beyond noting its efficiency. Maybe I can round things off with a few Reviewer's wrap-ups. Ready? First: The Reviewer as Consumer Reporter. "*The Grand Hunt* is as spicy as Hungarian goulash and as refreshing as cold Austrian beer, a perfect recipe for an evening's entertainment." How was that? If you prefer, I could mix a few metaphors, or rather shuffle a few similes. This one is called The Reviewer Has Reserva-

tions! Ready? *"The Grand Hunt* tears along like a freight train out of
control but it never quite gets off the ground." How was that? I
have more, but perhaps you'd better go to some music.

18 August 1980

Long Day's Journey into Night

Written by Eugene O'Neill, directed by Robin Phillips.

Those people who endured Stratford's production of *Long Day's Journey into Night* last Saturday evening might be forgiven for thinking
that the play is one of those verbose masterpieces best left on the
printed page where it can be absorbed in small doses. Those people
who love and respect the play might simply be wondering what
went wrong. Of course it's a notoriously difficult play to do, lengthy
and obsessive in its repetitions, and verbally explicit in the fashion
of the American Family Melodrama in its heyday. But even so,
O'Neill's masterpiece—and it is that—is written with such close
and genuine observation that 90% of the of the job of the director is
in the casting of the four main roles. Get them right—it's not
easy—and the play unfolds itself with a little conducting from the
pit. Fail in that and nobody will be able to help it. Not the costume
designer who provided subtly co-ordinated outfits in Stratford's
favourite colours—beige and blue-grey (the beige for the father and
the father-dominated son, the blue-grey for the mother and the
mother-dominated son). Not the scenic designer who provided a
picturesquely scruffy living-room from O'Neill's detailed notes. And
not the actors whose roles are written in such intimate interdepen-
dence that one false performance can crumble the works.

Robin Phillips has made two serious casting mistakes. The obvious one is in the choice of Graeme Campbell as Jamie, the elder son.
Campbell is a fine and enjoyable performer with many strengths as
an actor. It's unfortunate that he should be made to struggle—no
matter how skilfully and sincerely—with a young part that is wholly
wrong for his foghorn voice, his man-mountain physique, and his
robust middle age. Jamie is meant to wilt beside his father's natural
presence. As it is, Campbell has to do some fancy squirming to seem
ill at ease. He has a stance that naturally dominates any scene. This

89

is the kind of arrogant casting that a director makes when he wants to demonstrate that he—Svengali-like—can bring out aspects of an actor overlooked by others. It should be left for workshops.

The other mistake in casting is perhaps more serious but less obvious and tied up with the overall approach to the play. Jessica Tandy as Mary, the mother, the "mad ghost" as her husband's terrible phrase describes her, gives a performance that illustrates the limits of Phillips' characteristic and muddle-headed romantic empathy with suffering, and kills whatever chance the production had to grapple with O'Neill's savage liberating irony. Not much of a mind for irony has our boy Phillips.

Tragedy without irony is usually little more than self-pity. Looked at in a certain way, there is little but suffering to the part of Mary. Yet there are distinctions in the way she experiences that suffering and they are clearly marked by O'Neill. In several instances there are passages that require a sense of girlish enjoyment from Mary, even in her maunderings through the past. There are other passages of genuine tenderness which are to be kept distinct from her mechanical expressions of maternal concern when she is under the influence of the drug to which she's addicted. These distinctions were blurred in Miss Tandy's performance. I very much missed the clarity with which one should be permitted to perceive the shift in her mental state. Miss Tandy hits, instead, a similar oppressive note of suffering throughout.

On the part of the director there may have been a misguided attempt at subtlety here as if following the dramatic shifts in the character's state of mind might tempt the excess of melodrama. That may be what's at work with William Hutt's James Tyrone, which performance avoids the theatrical posturing that might well be prominent in the technique of an oppressive patriarch who also happens to be an actor. Yet Hutt's almost casual reading of the part is persuasive. But then very few actors are better at handling high irony than Hutt, so he at least is in tune with O'Neill.

I have some quarrels with Brent Carver's Jamie but for the most part I thought the actor managed a remarkable performance in what is probably the most difficult part in the play.

6 October 1980

THE SHAW FESTIVAL

Misalliance

Written by G. B. Shaw, directed by Christopher Newton.

Misalliance was written in 1909 as Shaw was approaching the peak years of his career as a playwright. It's written very much in the style of *Heartbreak House* and can be looked on as a warmup for that extraordinary play. Our focus is split among a large and varied cast of characters representing different classes and attitudes. As in *Heartbreak House*, a group of family members is the focus of our attention but in this case the idea of the family actually becomes the subject matter. The relationships are too complicated to go into any detail. They centre around the bourgeois family of a successful underwear manufacturer. Tarleton may be a businessman but he has the soul of a poet and the morals of a philanderer. His son has embraced the businessman role, but his daughter reflects the other side of his personality. She's stifled by the role of well-bred young lady and she's hungry for life. Nevertheless when the play opens she has resigned herself to marrying the bright but insufferable son of a well-known member of the upper class. At the end of the first act, however, an aviator and a female acrobat literally drop from the sky into the midst of this little group of people. He is a well-bred young man for whom the daughter immediately sets her cap. She is a Shavian projection of the fully liberated woman, given an exotic quality by virtue of the Polish nationality. With the intrusion of a member of the lower classes, weaned on a diet of socialism and melodrama and determined to have his revenge on Tarleton for having seduced his mother years before, the elements of the Shavian world are in place—or rather in battle.

In part *Misalliance* is comedy of manners. A good deal of its humour derives from the spectacle of people who will not abide by their classes' rules of good conduct. The daughter, for instance, pursues her young man in a way that good middle-class daughters simply don't and this causes him grave discomfort. But it's also a problem play in that it sets out to question the kind of relationships that families impose on human beings. However, its method of dealing with the problem derives again from the comedy of manners. The play is structured around a series of revelations regarding the sexual indiscretions of the characters, and at its climax the daughter insists that such acts should be acknowledged freely even among the family members. She does so in defiance of the traditional discretion between parents and children—a discretion which, Shaw suggests, prevents them from responding to each other as full human beings.

Misalliance is a long play, a bit bulky and unwieldy. The longueurs locate themselves mostly in the first act in which Shaw sets his themes in place. His characteristic verbal arias and duets are a bit thin and abstract and stick out at odd angles until the characters have established themselves in our imaginations.

But if it hasn't the richness of feeling and atmosphere that characterizes *Heartbreak House*, if its ideas are comparatively haphazard, it's a damn fine play and—I think—a good choice for Shaw's new artistic director Christopher Newton to open his first season with. It's rich enough to test the mettle of a new artistic regime and yet it allows a certain amount of enjoyable tomfoolery to please the Shaw's summer stock patrons.

Newton has made a couple of crucial errors in casting. Deborah Kipp is too settled, hasn't got the edge of danger that a Shaw ingenue requires (of course she is an ingenue in name only) and Geraint Wyn-Davies as her chosen mate lacks the fire of Shavian contradiction. Further, I think I detect some general uncertainties in acting style. Sandy Webster comes just short of mugging his way through the central role of the underwear king—mind you he mugs with great skill and I enjoyed his performance on that level. David Dodimead as the aristocratic father heads upriver in the opposite direction. His is an understatement of the West End blithe school, not without subtlety but a bit stiff. Then there is Andrew Gillies whose wired-up Gunner, the clerk as avenging angel, manages Shaw's lower class dialect brilliantly well, and who, along with Carole Shelley as the female acrobat, really picks up the show and shakes it to life. Both actors are more emotionally tuned to their characters than most of the rest of the cast, and this points to the problem with the production as a whole.

At his best Shaw is performed with an edge and lightness that can slip over into emotion and out again like quicksilver. This production catches that quality in spots but just as often it turns Shaw's wit against him, heading straight for the laugh with tricks and cleverness rather than riding the words to theatrical glory.

But I must add that James Rankin's climactic second act out-burst was the single finest example of the temper tantrum, man and boy, that this reviewer has ever had the privilege of witnessing. A thing of beauty. Spare, but telling. And real loud.

30 May 1980

The Cherry Orchard

Written by Anton Chekhov, directed by Radu Penciulescu.

Strange things happen in a repertoire company. Last night in *The Cherry Orchard* I watched virtually the same cast as I saw Wednes-day night in *Misalliance*. The same actors who in the former play seemed a bit ill-assorted became a real company of actors in *The Cherry Orchard*, achieving a first rate ensemble style. This was partly a matter of different, more focused direction, and partly a matter of a more achieved play in the case of Chekhov's masterpiece. But I can't help thinking that there's something about Shaw that stymies nine out of ten productions. For one thing there's the problem of his rhetoric. No actor can play Shaw without somehow grappling with that wonderful extravagant language. He can't go around it, it's there and it requires a technique that no natural precociousness can muster. Further, the conventions which Shaw used—or rather abused—the conventions of the stage of his time, are close to cer-tain types of popular theatre which have never really died—the drawing-room comedy for instance. Of course Shaw went to great pains to parody the theatrical conventions of his day. Yet that hasn't stopped producers from presenting *The Devil's Disciple*, for example, as the straight melodrama it is intended to mock. In the case of his comedies the temptation to play them as farce by manhandling the theatrical hooks which Shaw carefully put into place has been too great for many directors. *Misalliance* fell between two stools in that respect. It will be interesting to see which stool Christopher New-ton will finally choose to sit on. For the moment I reserve judgment.

With Chekhov there are fewer pitfalls in the way of a good pro-duction. His language avoids extravagance, and he is a genre unto himself. Besides, contemporary theatre has many fine examples of how to approach his work. Which is not to underestimate the work of director Radu Penciulescu with *The Cherry Orchard*. First of all his touch with actors is impeccable. David Dodimead as Gayev is a case in point. The performance is built around a simple idea. Everything Gayev says and does works on some level to protect his hurting pride around which he wraps the tattered remnants of his debonair youth. At any point in which Dodimead is onstage one can see on his face his character's particular response to the peculiar moment in time. A remarkable performance. And I point it out when several others could have illustrated my point almost as well. The actors are focused not on the laughter or pathos suggested by the scene they are playing but on the moment in time. As a result the audience doesn't wait passively to be entertained by the next pratfall, but actively seeks the centre of even the quietest scene.

What the production imparts so well is an impression of life. And I hasten to add that this production doesn't give a fig for the mechanical illusion of life. Its designer is Astrid Jansen, long respected for her brilliant work with George Luscombe, and she is not the type of designer whose secret ambition it is to reproduce the Taj Mahal with matchsticks. Hers is a non-representational set, consisting of a riser on which sits some furniture and a few painstakingly chosen props, surrounded not by walls but by layers of hanging lace. It's a design which is a concept in itself. And it sets things up for a final coup de théâtre which is extravagant and close to silly but perfect for all that.

The theatrical impression of life may have nothing to do with physical verisimilitude but it has a lot to do with emotional reality. This production is a fine one because it has that quality. And it has that quality because fine actors have been given the room to be fine actors, not encouraged to perform for applause like dancing bears. From what I've seen of The Shaw Festival's productions over the years there's something to learn from that.

There's no time to mention all of the fine work here. Carole Shelley's Mme Ranevsky and Gillie Fenwick's faithful old servant should be mentioned. But all of the company conspires successfully to make Chekhov's great comedy of frustrated passions, lost hopes and trailing impulses something to cherish. In this production, the sense—so central to the play—of time slipping away, is palpable. The characters for the most part are helpless before it, but we the audience are permitted to witness it with understanding and compassion through the kind of clarity in articulation that only good theatre has. Time is given shape and form for us and therefore its own kind of permanence. It's a privilege only art can give us.

29 May 1980

The Philanderer

Written by G. B. Shaw, directed by Paul Reynolds.

At the end of all three of Shaw's *Plays Unpleasant* we are given happy endings true to the theatrical sentiments of the era. But Shaw so presents his plots that we can't help seeing that his characters are living out sentimental shams plastered imperfectly over moral capitulation and social despair. *The Philanderer* is the subtlest of the three in that it employs no social muckraking to subvert the plot, but simply brings to bear on the action the hardest and most uncompromising eye we're likely to be blessed with in this century.

Shaw's accusing eye is all the more impressive in *The Philanderer* by virtue of its focusing on a character very like a certain aspect of himself, and a social milieu a bit like that proposed by the more advanced social thinkers of his time. The philanderer of the title is Leonard Charteris, a fortyish philosopher in love with the self-possessed widow Grace Tranfield, and hounded by Julia Craven, his wilful ex-mistress who is determined to capture him in marriage. All three belong to the Ibsen Club, a haven for advanced thought, but whereas Leonard and Grace actually follow the rules of the club, in which men must guarantee their unmanliness and women their unwomanliness—that is to say they must renounce their adherence to the sentimental fantasies of the male sex—Julia is really a formidable womanly woman, posing as an Ibsenite merely to corner Leonard.

That's the situation as Shaw presents it. And in doing so he follows closely the outline of a well made comedy. The audience is encouraged to participate in the cat-and-mouse game between Leonard and Julia, she turning the full force of her womanly wiles on him, and he desperately breaking the rules of social intercourse in shaking her. The first act could be simple farce. The second act could still pass for farce with allowances made for several astrin-

95

gent Shavian asides about vivisection and quackery, and for a sharply written speech in which Grace, the true Ibsenite, roundly chews out Julia the impostor. But in the third act, even with everything still falling beautifully into place, and laughter still being provoked regularly, it becomes apparent that the conventional happy ending is close to tragedy. Small wonder Shaw couldn't get the play produced.

One of the many pleasures of Paul Reynolds' production is that it manages to sustain a light playing style while still delivering the goods in the final scene—which should quite simply be emotionally devastating, even while it's funny. There is still a lot of nonsense being parroted about Shaw. One line involves variations on the idea that he couldn't deal with passion. In fact there has rarely been an artist who valued it higher. In *The Philanderer* he presents us with a group whose views are rather like the popular conception of Shaw's own. Yet finally we are made to see these witty people as juiceless and unfeeling. And, interestingly, the only real life-force of the play comes from Julia Craven, the apparently contemptible spoiled coquette. It's her tragedy and her thwarted passion which we feel so keenly at the final curtain. And the charming philanderer Leonard, whose advanced ideas fuel the play, comes to seem callow and detestable.

I was much impressed by Dana Ivey's Julia. Angling for advantage, changing with the prevailing winds, her eye on the final goal of attaining her quarry, Ivey physically embodied the instinctual nature of her character, her body shifting like a weathercock and her eyes flashing momentary sensation. Without a strong Julia this play would be impossible to perform.

One could almost make the same claim about Leonard Charteris. In the ideal cast of my imagination Charteris is played by Fred Astaire 30 years ago, but in the absence of Astaire, Christopher Newton will do fine. He plays Charteris like an ageing boy and in him the charm that goes with irresponsibility never really overpowers our sense of moral unease with him. And this is as it should be.

Well, I've spent too much time talking about the play again. It's hard not to do that with Shaw because his works are endlessly fascinating and yet they're so rarely approached with real intelligence and understanding. But in this case I regret not having the room to discuss the production more fully. It follows a strong theatrical line on every level you'd care to examine. The actors lounge about Guido

Tondino's warm sets as if they lived there. And each performer, from Jack Medley's sentimental manly man, to Francine Volker's posturing new woman, to Michael Fawkes' doctor and clumsy paramour, makes his mark in a clear and respectful interpretation.

There's one thing I feel I should bring up. Susan Wright's Grace Tranfield, so fine in the first half of the play, becomes in the later stages rather more an idea of an independent woman than a character. We need her to be more than this—as it stands, the character's inadvertent smugness affects Shaw's marvellous balance. I'm fairly sure that this fault is merely due to a miscalculation of effect and not to a misinterpretation. Susan Wright is too fine a performer to stay hampered for long by one of the most common pitfalls for any contemporary actress playing a strong woman.

In any event, *The Philanderer* with *The Cherry Orchard*, the other Festival highlight, demonstrates a kind of solid cheerful ensemble work which bodes well for the Shaw Festival.

27 June 1980

A Respectable Wedding

Written by Bertold Brecht, directed by Derek Goldby.

This has been a terrifically interesting season at Niagara-on-the-Lake. New artistic director Christopher Newton has set some wonderful theatrical forces in motion. There are three first-rate pieces of theatre running now. Chekhov's *The Cherry Orchard*, Shaw's *The Philanderer*, and now Brecht's *A Respectable Wedding*. You know that the Festival is doing something right because of the wild polarized reactions the shows have been kicking up. (Of course uniform raves are always a sure sign of mediocrity.) Radu Penciulescu's lovely and subtle approach to *The Cherry Orchard* has been hollered down by some reviewers as Marxist propaganda, a hilarious reaction which goes to show the truth of the old adage that a little knowledge is a dangerous thing in certain minds. The little knowledge has to do with the well-known political affiliations of translator Trevor Griffiths; it has nothing to do with his translation. The reaction to *The Philanderer* was even funnier in an ironic way, for the local reviewers reacted to it in precisely the way critics did 70 years ago when the play was a calculated Shavian assault on the sentimental theatre of the time. How little things change. Critics still tend to be bold champions of orthodoxy.

Now *A Respectable Wedding* is a different thing altogether. It really is an assault and one of the damnedest things I've ever seen on stage. I suspect that the people who walked out during the previews and flooded the Shaw offices with complaints about its coarseness were really upset about the sustained visual and aural assault contrived by director Derek Goldby and his brave and talented cast—an assault that blew apart the nice safe fourth wall like so much wet tissue paper, and brought the play's thoroughly unpleasant people into uncomfortably close proximity with an almost unbearable familiarity of manner. There were moments, watching it, that I simply wanted to get the devil out of the theatre; my nerves were popping, but the fact that it kept being funny and, more importantly, the sense that this cacophony was actually going somewhere kept me tight in my seat, and I don't regret it.

Briefly, the show is a one-act piece in the German folk play tradition, in which Brecht presents us with a bunch of nasty mannerless low bourgeoisie at a wedding party. Whatever veneer of civilization they begin with breaks down until they have emptied their lightly repressed vileness all over each other, and depart, some of them thoroughly refreshed by the experience, leaving the bride and groom staring at each other in disgust and loathing.

As I've mentioned in an earlier piece, director Goldby's major stylistic referent is clearly the anarchic American animated cartoon of the forties. This piece has periods of sustained violent slapstick that I would have thought impossible on the stage. They are brilliantly choreographed, although I don't want to give away any of the surprising effects with which this show is crammed. I merely want to raise aspects to watch for. First of all, every actor on the stage—although cartoon-like in his or her ferocity of manner—is a carefully observed and clearly defined character. One actor, Al Kozlik, is so painfully real in his humiliation that I don't think I'll ever forget his performance, much as a part of me would like to. It's a brilliant piece of work, and Kozlik can be proud of it.

The second point is this: I would find this production contemptible were it merely a piece of stylistic excess at the cheap expense of its petty characters. But its excess has a life of its own. It drives you right past the sneering reaction that might otherwise hold the play's terrible image of bourgeois life at arm's length. In a way excess is the point of it. The action of the play is redeemed when the new husband and wife, alone at the end, go beyond humiliation, go beyond anger and contempt and, joyously drunk on cheap wine, play with the leftover food, pushing it into each other's faces, licking it off and toying joyfully with each other's bodies. It's a liberation of the spirit and after so much meanness and vileness it brings us a kind of spiritual relief. That relief is earned by the production, and it's proof that it has its heart and its talent in the right place. The actors who perform this climax, Nora McLellan and Joe Ziegler, do so while carrying on two virtuoso laughing fits—one of the hardest things for an actor to sustain. It beats me how they brought it off, but they did. And so does the production in general.

1 July 1980

Overruled

Written by G. B. Shaw, directed by Paul Reynolds.

Paul Reynolds' production of *Overruled* is very bad theatre. However, it's bad in such a guileless and transparent way that it would make a good textbook case for those interested.

The play is a witty précis of Shaw's attitudes on love, marriage and that strange entity known as the couple. The plot is simple. Two men, who have never met, fall in love with each other's wives. The four people involved meet unexpectedly at a seaside resort and a half-hour comic discussion of marriage ensues. The basic comic method is in the pricking of conventional systems of morality and myths of romantic love by placing against them the possibility of simple, natural affection between people. The basic mode is farce.

Now this is a one-act lunchtime theatre production and more casual than an evening's entertainment. Well and good. After all, Shaw's one-act plays tend to be talented doodlings in the margins of his major works. But even so it can't help a play to ignore whatever substance there might be in it and to slap on an approach completely at odds with that substance. Before the performance began I was already a bit uncomfortable when the mood music was that of a good twenties jazz band. I was more uncomfortable when that band gave way to one of those repulsive British dance records of the period, cute as wet toffee dropped down your collar and twice as sticky. In this case a bunch of windup Betty Boops with British shopgirl accents were singing about the sea oh the sea tra la tee hee, when a chorus of men, armed with a single gonad between them, came on to chant about girlies in striped bathing-suits or some such fancy.

I couldn't imagine that Shaw had written anything that might suit this strange display of the depraved state of British pop music in 1930. He hadn't. The performance began—Susan Cox and Hayward Morse appeared wearing cute bathing-suits. Mr. Morse should sue. A man looks silly enough in one of those ridiculous two-piece jobs without having to mope and mush and moon and mince like the juvenile in the awful musical comedies that never were. The juvenile mould from which the performance was cast was hopelessly at odds with his intelligent and witty lines about fidelity. Miss Cox, for her part, gaped and dallied and gawked like a schoolgirl. Both characters were meant to be mature adults.

If it was not clear before, it was then that the only approach director Reynolds brought to the piece was a misguided attempt at period. Once again the audience was asked to indulge an inept performance as a piece of nostalgia. By five minutes into the show we had been signalled in broad gestures to laugh at the quaintness of the characters. We were not signalled to hear a word they said.

As to a practical demonstration of how this ruined the piece, one example will suffice. Leon Pownall's character has been unsuccessfully attempting to woo another man's wife, unaware that her husband is nearby. He turns around to see her embracing an unfamiliar man. Outraged, he denounces her for brazenly making love to another man in front of him. "This," says the lady, designating the man she has embraced, "is my husband." Pownall turns his shocked face quickly to the audience. By this time the audience has been trained to laugh at big unsubtle gestures, and it does so now, anticipating Pownall's embarrassed comeuppance. But he is not embarrassed and their laugh goes right over his line, a clever Shaw reversal to the effect that if the stranger is her husband she has committed a double offence, as it's not proper for a married couple to show affection in public. Now this is funny—and it has a point—for Pownall's character is that of a man who puts convention before morality. But all of this is lost on the audience who must take only what is delivered by way of the lumpish, faggy approximation of twenties' musical comedy. I'd wager that the audience came away from the play with no more than a vaguely pleasing sense of cute manners and silly bathing-suits.

I am disappointed largely because Reynolds and a fine cast did such a hard and intelligent job on another intellectual farce, *The Philanderer*.

I admit that I had many distractions watching *Overruled*. There were the latecomers creaking into their seats and munching sandwiches. There was the critic sitting in front of me who arrived late and sat hunched over his pad scrawling down quotations and looking up only once or twice. Clearly a man used to reviewing radio plays.

Some of the distractions were onstage too. Twice during the performance Paul Whiteman's concert version of "Sweet Sue" was played as background music. It is not background music. Ferde Grofé's arrangement is grotesque to a degree rarely known to music. What with the strange combination of woodwinds and tuba evoking pastoral, elephantine dances by hefty nymphs and dryads, what with the lugubrious whinings of a dozen muted brass instruments harmonizing the verse, what with Jack Fulton's sappy falsetto vocal, a marvel to hear, it was very hard to take one's attention away. In real life the record redeems itself by following the vocal with 32 magical bars of muted jazz cornet by Bix Beiderbecke. On stage the record was allowed to fade before Bix blew it to shreds. However Bix did appear at the piano playing "In A Mist" behind a later section. That's typical, I'm afraid. A director who could imagine that Bix's sweet yearning composition could ever be suitable as background music at a seaside hotel—well, words fail me.

18 July 1980

Canuck

Written by John Bruce Cowan, directed by Christopher Newton.

Canuck was written by John Bruce Cowan in the late twenties, but until Christopher Newton discovered it and introduced it into this summer's festival season it was unperformed. It turns out to fit very comfortably in some respects into the Shaw Festival. The period is right, if not the continent (*Canuck* takes place in BC). But, more interestingly, *Canuck* belongs to the school of discussion drama which Shaw, inspired by Ibsen, pioneered in England. Cowan's discussion centres on the need for English Canadians to cut colonial ties with Britain in order to develop as individuals and as a people. This was a debate that much concerned the generation who had lived through the first world war, just as the concern about postwar American domination of our cultural life has obsessed the present generation.

It's interesting that *Canuck* came out of BC. Recently Tarragon produced Margaret Hollingsworth's *Mother Country*, a distinguished play which, like *Canuck*, dealt with a family in Vancouver irrationally ruled by British assumptions. *Mother Country*, in dealing with the identical phenomenon 50 years later, is much more despairing about the effects of the colonial mentality on the present generation. Cowan's play is the optimistic work of a young country and a young intellectual who had spent countless evenings arguing with friends about the nature of his land.

The Canuck of the title is Paul Ecclestone, an intelligent young farmer in love with Ruth Ormsby Grey. She is a talented pianist and the daughter of a well-connected British-Canadian family and her parents want her to marry a "dash-it-all," "jolly-good" sort of chap with the proper background. Ruth wants to marry Paul and take her chances with life. Ruth's main ally is her uncle Richard, a prospector, and a rough closet socialist of the Western individualist school. He rather looks down on his brother, Ruth's father, for marrying into a rich British family and not rolling up his sleeves and joining in the work of a new country. It's Uncle Richard who carries the main burden of argument in favour of Canada and he has great fun at the expense of transplanted castes and the Orange mentality that forgets that the French settled the country.

No one is likely to mistake *Canuck* for a great play. It's funny without being witty, touching without being profound, earnest without being searching. Yet I feel very warmly toward it. I found it interesting on several levels. First of all, as a cultural artifact it's fascinating and speaks perfectly of a period of intellectual ferment that I'm sure many of us were unaware of. It's the same ferment that gave us the great flowering of Canadian painting in the twenties, even now arguably the single most important cultural achieve-ment of this country. Secondly, I found it intriguing as a Canadian theatrical experience, one that I've had recently in other circumstances and which I'm coming to value more and more. Simply put, the people in the audience seemed to me almost eager to take in the arguments put forth in the play and I'm sure this alertness came from the simple fact that the play spoke directly to them about their lives, and forces which affect them. It must be remembered that the Shaw audience is not privy to much Canadian work.

Canuck is sometimes dull, never really clumsy, certainly not slick. Yet the audience, I felt, time and time again, gave the play a lot, let it have its slips and responded warmly to its humour and its good nature. Once or twice you could hear the knowing laugh of the urban provincial striving to demonstrate superiority to the material. But this completely died for want of nourishment. The audience applauded hard at the end, wanting the actors to return for an ovation. They didn't: I wonder whether the enthusiasm took them by surprise.

I'm not sure whether *Canuck* will be so warmly received by every audience. If it is, all credit must go to Christopher Newton and the cast. They approached the material openly and honestly without a touch of condescension or that dreadful disease which afflicts the theatrically second-rate called camp. They even took chances with silence, trusting both the material and the audience's ability to respect it. Strangely enough, both *Canuck* and *Misalliance*, Newton's other directorial effort of the season, end with young people making hopeful breakthroughs. Whereas I wasn't comfortable with his handling of the theme in the Shaw play, I thought *Canuck's* last moment perfect in its understatement. There is a very sweet-natured quality to Newton's work that I might very soon tire of but at the moment find appealing.

Once again I've given short shrift to the actors. James Rankin was everyone's idea of the perfect kid brother. Barney O'Sullivan had a good time as the philosophical prospector. John Gardiner as the father had an impressively judged aura of half-defeated grace. I liked everyone else too, and I must add that I find Martha Burns quite irresistible.

15 August 1980

EDITORIALS

All for You

A common reaction to recent announcements of a peculiarly complex and ambiguous restructuring on the part of the Stratford artistic management was that Robin Phillips had finally got everything
he wanted from Stratford's Board of Directors. Be that as it may, I
think it's pertinent to ask whether we are getting everything we
want from Stratford. Now I think it's quite likely that the greater
part of Stratford's audience would answer yes without hesitation to
that question. For much of Stratford's audience is made up of people
who don't necessarily like theatre, almost certainly know little of
what kind of work is being done in other companies, and who yet
make a pilgrimage to Stratford every season to see a new batch of
frozen culture slightly thawed. Even so, I'd like to point out, in my
understated way, just what kind of theatre Stratford offers us.

It's the custom of reviewers—and I'm no exception, for it comes
with the territory—to look at an individual production as a product
(let's use that loaded little word) to be consumed quite independently of other products prepared by the same theatre. So it never
seems to occur to anyone that Stratford's wispy, pretty sets and its
pretty picturesque costumes and the round, pretty faces of the
younger actors, all form an aesthetic of pristine decadence quite as
pervasive as the bright plastics, the neat expendable containers, and
the cheery cartoon statuary that successfully embody that international secular cult called McDonald's. And as McDonald's temples
vary from town to town while yet remaining reassuringly the same,
so the Stratford aesthetic flexibly adapts itself to the individual
production, whether it be a great Shakespeare romance or a modern
piece-built wimpery like *Foxfire*. Against the bland matrix of this
corporate style, the director will have calculated a mildly novel interpretation to satisfy the Shakespeare connoisseur and the major
actors will have strained to create little detachable pieces of fine
acting to satisfy the acting connoisseur.

Every now and then a moment of power breaks loose from it—
even a sustained scene, occasionally the better part of a play (Shakespeare is a hard man to keep in check). And there are of course
several performers whose love of language and sense of theatre are
incorruptible. But these are exceptions.

As with McDonald's, the assumption communicated by Stratford to the consumer is that the product offered him is the Best; the best hamburger or the best playwright interpreted by the best actors. Of course, the real selling point of neither is the product. McDonald's is a quasi-religious celebration of the consumer way of life. Doing it all for you involves bright surfaces, expendable dishes and expendable nourishment celebrated because they are expendable. And at Stratford the high priest, Robin Phillips, intercedes on behalf of supplicants for whom art is a terrifying mystery and for him alone the gods appear to us, made visible by the wonderful medium of abstract culture. The gods of course have names like Smith and Bedford and Ustinov.

A well-known Stratford actor, familiar with the Festival from the beginning, recently complained to me that the level of attention to language on the part of the audiences at Stratford has fallen drastically in the last decade. He blames television. I rather think it's simply a case of Stratford attracting larger audiences. The increase, particularly if the actor's sense of deterioration is correct, is hardly attributable to a growing taste for classical drama. The increase derives from marketing. And the selling point at Stratford is not the play. Whatever pretence it cherishes of being a Rep Company, Stratford is very much Star Theatre—of a tasteful variety to be sure. Tourists, like those who make a trip to Disneyland when they're in the vicinity, come to Shakespeareland in the summer. And they come to consume Maggie or Brian. On a slightly more refined level, the more sophisticated patron may come for the equally demoralizing motive of consuming a particular performance by Maggie. In either instance the impact and meaning of a work is abstracted and diluted for both audience and artist. Rather than a participant with an involved mind, the spectator becomes a mechanical consumer of culture or, worse, a connoisseur. And the work of the Stratford actors and designers and directors—quite unconsciously I'm sure— becomes that of a service industry.

How demoralizing this can be to artists who haven't been worn down over the years by the crushing job of making a steady living in the theatre, or those who are work rather than career-oriented, can be judged by the appalling scarcity of good actors under the age of 40 in a company popularly considered the finest in North America.

I'm reminded of a young actor friend of mine who spent the final two weeks of his Stratford contract sitting in the Green Room singing "I ain't gonna work on Maggie's farm no more."

As I've said, we must ask ourselves whether this is the kind of theatre we want from Stratford. And I've suggested that most people are quite happy with the way Stratford operates. After all it's nice to have an internationally respected theatre museum in Canada. Yet now it seems Stratford is going to be taking productions to New York and London on a regular basis. And just as the London critics come to Stratford and believe that what they are seeing is the cream of Canadian theatre, Stratford will come to represent Canadian theatre abroad. This is silly, because Stratford has no connection with Canadian Theatre. Like McDonald's and the creations of the Walt Disney Organization, it is international in style. Stratford operates on a self-defined lofty plane that rarely sullies itself with Canadian Theatre, and is more likely to connect with London and New York than Toronto and Vancouver. The new plays it chooses to do are picked because they conform to the international style of detachable performances by interchangeable stars. Even a moderately successful production at Stratford seems to float in an undefined matrix where there is no colour, no vitality, no real sense of life.

I can't ask Stratford to face these problems, for the problems are what make Stratford Stratford and, like the defence that a neurotic sets around the sources of his neurosis, cannot be dealt with without the real danger of breaking down the entire personality. No, Stratford will be Stratford. And of course it's a nice luxury to have an annual festival of Shakespeare plays even in a diluted form. But I can suggest that the people who dish out funds for arts institutions take a look at where the real work in our theatre is coming from. Having done that, I suggest the Canada Council and like bodies leave the responsibility for funding Stratford where it belongs—in the laps of those Ministries responsible for tourism.

1 September 1980

Do Fury Honour

Yesterday I said some very reasonable things about the Stratford Festival. Unfortunately many people are likely to feel that I've been rude rather than reasonable. Nothing could be farther from the truth. McDonald's and the Disney Organization are very successful international endeavours. The minds that conceived them and the energetic entrepreneurs who cemented their success deserve our recognition. And such is the case with Stratford.

My only point of contention was with the way we view Stratford. It is not now, nor has it ever been, an expression of our cultural life. And this is clearly demonstrated by the way in which it has no connection with our homegrown theatre. When Stratford was founded there was little professional Canadian theatre to speak of. Since then there has been a great flurry of activity on all levels, some of it encouraged, to be sure, by the Stratford example. However, that example led only to the plunking down of huge national or regional theatre centres, fuelled by the same tired old colonial assumptions that have hung on in our theatre long after they drained away in our political and social life. It's significant the Dora Mavor Moore's New Play Society lost impetus after Stratford was formed. It's even more significant that the creative activity of dozens of small theatres across the country has had to survive in the shadow of institutions such as the laughably named National Arts Centre and Stratford itself, which siphon off funding from those who are doing the real work of artists in this society.

The work of the small theatres is, of course, variable. Some of it is bad, some of it is brilliant. But at its best it is connected to the pulse of life, the pulse of the community, the pulse of the region, the nation, and, through the wonderful ability of art to make such leaps, the pulse of the world.

It is from those very connections that work which is truly international comes and will come. Is it too obvious to point out that even when Shakespeare, the greatest international dramatist in the English language, wrote about ancient Rome or some fairytale Italy, he wrote as an Elizabethan Englishman, from an Elizabethan point of view, using Elizabethan language as it was understood by other Elizabethans. If one removed the physical and verbal particularity from Shakespeare, that which made him part of a living culture, one might be left with a conventional or an unconventional philosopher, an accurate or an inaccurate historian, but one would not likely be left with a great poet, and certainly not a great dramatist.

There is—and there should be—room for museum theatre in Canada. But if that theatre becomes our national theatre, we're in trouble. And if that theatre cuts itself off from its society with wan ideas of internationalism and smug assumptions about the superiority of what it is doing, then it's small wonder that its vitality is replaced by tastefulness, invention by cleverness, and passion by virtuosity. This is hard to do with Shakespeare, but all too often our Stratford has managed it.

The Shaw Festival has been for years a place where one might expect some pleasantly hammy approaches to Shavian language, but rarely satisfying theatre. But if we look at what has happened at the Shaw Festival this season we can see an interesting phenomenon. New artistic director Christopher Newton brought with him from the west coast a whole group of actors, designers and directors while keeping a certain continuity with the previous regime. Some of the directors who worked at Shaw this season were international heavyweights. As a result the audience was presented with a variety of theatrical conceptions—and I mean good hard conceptions—of the different plays.

Stratford's production of *The Seagull* dwindled Chekhov to what we have been trained to expect and applaud from Stratford, a vehicle for several high-powered performances strung together by an obvious directorial concept—in this case a literal-minded sense of alienation. For Shaw, Radu Pencilescu directed *The Cherry Orchard* with a subtle and moving ensemble approach that respected the dignity of the actors and the playwright. On the other hand, when Derek Goldby directed two plays at Shaw, the result was an imposition of style so complete, so wrenching, so unconcerned about good taste, that there were people who ran from the theatre in indignation. There were others, myself included, who would defend Goldby's version of *A Respectable Wedding* to the death. Put simply, there was no corporate stamp on the Shaw Festival's season. It was not Chris Newton's Show the way that Stratford is Robin Phillips' Show. And that is all to the good.

Now this may well change. When Phillips first came to Canada, he made an effort to incorporate some of the better younger actors into Stratford. But under the Stratford corporate mentality, these young actors who were offered the good parts and found the situation amenable were groomed to be stars rather than set to work at their craft. The results can be seen in this season's doubly miserable *Henry V*.

Success will probably bring expansion to the Shaw Festival, but I doubt whether we shall see it becoming a vehicle for one man's career—at least for a while. Newton's regime has a healthy air of openness, both to its surroundings and to the work at hand. And it has a fine smallish company of actors who seem truly excited and who have not yet made a career out of one Festival.

However, the combined effect of the natural airlessness of Museum theatre and the tendency of success to seek an institutional form and thus be turned into a corporate entity with a corporate image with which tourists can become reassuringly familiar will almost certainly squeeze the life from the Shaw Festival in time.

Until then, however, good luck to the Shaw Festival. And let it be remembered that it provided a miraculously lively season of theatre in the summer of 1980.

> Every fury on earth has been absorbed in time, as art, or as religion, or as authority in one form or another. The deadliest blow the enemy of the human soul can strike is to do fury honour—James Agee, *Let Us Now Praise Famous Men* (1937)

2 September 1980

Fall 1980

The present wrangle over Stratford may yet be the best thing that has happened in Canadian Theatre since Tyrone Guthrie set the place in operation. During the recent reign of young Robin, trends that had been emerging before were confirmed and Stratford became a slick classy commercial operation still rooted in the classics but aimed at the tourist audience who could afford the inflated ticket prices that went with the inflated seasons. And if the quality of the theatre experience was diluted, who could notice something so trivial with all those high-powered international stars being trotted out like expensive horseflesh. But because Stratford was originally plunked down in a theatrical wilderness, it was well established as the major theatrical operation in Canada by the time an indigenous theatre had begun to thrive across the country. And it took on, rather uncomfortably, the role of the senior commercial theatre. Stratford is as close to Broadway as Canada gets. What this means in terms of the financial structuring of Canadian theatre is that the salaries negotiated at Stratford set the levels for the whole theatre community. This is an important function and one the layman tends to forget. But in other ways the analogy with Broadway points out what's so strange about Stratford's position in Canadian theatre. Along with the big musicals and spectacles, Broadway serves as a showcase for the more commercial shows of the regional theatres outside New York. One might expect Stratford to do the same with the contemporary side of her repertoire. Well, look at this last season. When the works of Canadian playwrights such as John Gray and David French were doing very nicely thank you, in New York, what was old Stratford presenting by way of contemporary theatre? Three not very exceptional American comedies and a nice little hothouse star turn for Maggie Smith as Virginia Woolf. And as for the Third Stage, originally set up in part for new Canadian work, there was Doug Rain delivering eighteenth-century English gossip and Pam Brighton's crude experiment in Shakespeare.

To add to the irony, two of Stratford's American comedies had already played Broadway and they had been originally developed in regional theatres in the States. The seekers of material at Stratford had somehow overlooked the regional theatres in Canada and gone straight to Broadway. If David French becomes visible enough, perhaps he'll actually make it to Stratford.

Now a director is a busy man. And a director like our young Robin was permitted only a few short weeks on his arrival to case Canadian talent and to snatch up a few promising young actors to fill out his company before starting his first season. After that, he had to rely on his international contacts to seek new works and new talent—and on the senior actors at Stratford (and no one who hasn't actually talked to the more established actors at Stratford would believe how cloistered and out of touch with Canadian theatre they tend to be). As a result the festival has been an all but closed shop to our best directors and to our writers as well. And no one but a doughhead can really expect it to have been different under John Dexter. This is what is so bizarre about Stratford's position as the grand old duchess of Canadian theatre. It sets salaries, standards of production and yet barely breathes the same atmosphere as the genuine—if poverty-stricken—mainstream theatre of Canada, above which it haughtily holds its head.

There are over 90 professional theatre companies in Ontario alone. Of all the money provided by the Ontario Arts Council for theatre, 12% goes to Stratford. Of the many more French and

English theatres which the Canada Council funds, Stratford takes a bite of 8%. Think of it, 8% from the whole budget of Canada Theatre funding. It's a question of priorities. And those who really think that Stratford in any significant way helps theatre as a whole in Canada had better start clapping their hands and chanting "I believe in fairies" over and over again. No, Stratford, slowly, has become a highbrow Disneyland, providing cheap trips to England for tourists. And Disneyland is a far more interesting institution because it truly reflects the nature of the society that has given birth to it.

One of the most amazing pieces of confusion to emerge over the last month or so is the peculiar idea that Stratford is our national theatre. A national theatre that turns its back on the artists of the nation whose work it represents? No, forget it. Stratford is a rich fat old dowager who can afford to pay her own bills. None of us should have any cause to resent the old dear as long as she does so. Let's not burden her with any such responsibility as having to pose as our national theatre. She was not made for that. And as for the rest of us, let's please get the stardust out of our eyes and grow up.

And perhaps we are doing that. Mr. Axworthy's decision not to grant John Dexter a work permit is an important precedent. In the States, the Immigration people have long acted as the heavy for American Equity. But in Canada our Immigration Department has generally rubber-stamped entries of American artists as if flattered that anyone might want to work in poor little Canada. As a result, Equity has always had to do the dirty work and take the flak.

So this is an extraordinary development. I still can't quite believe it. Yet if it holds good we'll have made an important step toward maturity. It's more than time we took responsibility for our own artists. Then, by all means, let us meet the world and welcome artists from other countries on a proud and equal footing.

As for old Auntie Stratford, my guess is that Hicks and Co. will resign, blustering all the way. And what then? Why young Robin will be back of course. Back to save the day and to rebuild his nest.

Part Bloody IV

I suppose it's possible to argue—and I've come close to arguing it on several occasions—that whatever transpires at the end of the current crisis at Stratford, it won't have much effect in the long run on the real work being done in Canadian Theatre. Despite the fact that Robin Phillips' star remains untarnished in the minds of some well-meaning but credulous people (many of them Stratford citizens, some of them artists), I think it's clear that the direction he took the Festival was a disastrous one. And I do not accept the opinion held by a good many intelligent people—again some of them artists—that Phillips was a genius to whom it was our privilege to play host for half a decade. I have never seen evidence of more than a very facile talent from the man, with little sign even of artistry—unless that word can be extended to a man who, given the privilege of staging a steady stream of works of almost unreachable exuberance and subtlety, typically corsetted them into the tightly circumscribed sensibility of an Art Nouveau Decorator. But questions of artistry aside, Phillips is in many respects the author of the mess at the core of that national obsession we call Stratford. His astonishing expansion of the Festival—an achievement of epic dimension which impresses as much as it appalls me—alone created more problems than any successor could easily deal with, even if that successor had been properly prepared for the job. (And I should make it clear that I am speaking of artistic problems rather than financial ones.) Even in the case of the Board, that terminally befuddled group of would-be mandarins, on whom so much accumulated frustration and wrath has been disgorged, even they are naught but feckless victims—albeit semi-scrupulous ones—blundering about and trying to cope with the problems that Phillips left in their playpen.

So, having registered the floating disembodied quality of the Festival's recent productions, and having noted the simple fact that Stratford has made little or no connection with living theatre in Canada, either generically or on the simple level of professional community interchange, and having noticed the barely concealed and perhaps unconscious contempt for all art, for artists and for living culture at the centre of the organization (nor am I speaking only of the Board of Directors)—a contempt that is no less crippling for the misguided loyalty that many good and sincere artists who work there feel for the place. Having registered all that, I'm surprised to find a stirring of something very like interest in my breast at the possibility of John Hirsch being accepted as artistic director.

At the very least I think Hirsch is the best of the choices that we could realistically expect the present Board at Stratford to make. Whether he will have any real long-term effect on the place, it's hard to tell. New Stratford regimes have a way of starting with energy and bright intention which quickly get squashed by the weight of the institution or by the awareness of career possibilities that such a place affords. But Hirsch has stated—and I think that we can believe him—that he will not use Stratford as a power base. His main priority would seem to be finding an institutionally fixed way of training people to take over when an artistic director leaves. Perhaps the Hirsch regime will be an interim one. And perhaps calling the sojourn of an artistic director a regime is merely a holdover from Phillips. A more hopeful example would seem to lie in Christopher Newton's first season at Shaw last summer. Newton directed only two plays, one of them actually a bit of a risk by the standards of museum theatre. The rest of the season was farmed out to other directors including some first-rate people—directors, I might add, of an international standing rarely to be seen at Stratford when Phillips was there. One of these directors was John Hirsch himself. So let's not hope for a John Hirsch regime. Let's hope for an intelligently managed Museum Theatre that is, however, open to Canadian as well as so-called international artists. The longer Stratford keeps itself sealed off from the hundreds of interesting artists in the Canadian scene, the larger the handwriting on the wall will become. And I like to think that John Hirsch realizes this.

16 December 1980

Tempest in a Chamber Pot:
A Stratford Tempest by Martin Knelman

In the fall of 1980, the Board of Directors of the Stratford Shakespeare Festival summarily fired a four-person directorate that had replaced the one-man rule of Robin Phillips and hired British director John Dexter in its place. The action set off a dramatic series of events including a militant near-boycott of the Festival by Canadian Actors' Equity, and a decision by Lloyd Axworthy, Minister of Employment and Immigration, to deny Dexter a work permit.

In a recent column in the Toronto *Star*, author Martin Knelman wrote that "the Stratford saga...seemed to embody and symbolize all the issues and conflicts that had been bubbling away beneath the surface of Canadian culture for decades." Whether or not this point of view is valid, Knelman's book *A Stratford Tempest* does little to explore or illuminate the issues and conflicts to which he refers.

A Stratford Tempest is hardly a book at all. It seems to be little more than a couple of articles stitched together and padded out by a cursory prehistory of the affair, along with a grouping of tired reviews and insubstantial aesthetic opinions. The two articles (and presumably the reviews) have appeared before in the pages of *Saturday Night* and *Toronto Life*. Even at the time of their appearance, right on the heels of the Stratford crisis, the heat of the events was cooling and the particular details on which Knelman's narrative relies seemed trivial.

The reader who is familiar enough with the minutiae of recent Toronto and Stratford theatre history to follow the story might enjoy elements of Knelman's narrative to a limited extent, but he might also find the experience a bit unpleasant. Knelman treats the details of the affair in *Saturday Night* fashion; like a voyeur squatting in the alcoves of power with his pencil in his hand. For instance, Knelman tells us that John Dexter, on learning that his work permit had been denied, wrote in his diary: "Axworthy is a cunt." Where did Knelman get this information? Why does he pass it on to us? Is it meant to be titillating? Or is it meant to tell us something about the character of John Dexter?

Knelman makes no intelligible picture from the chaos of events with which he presents us. He has stated that he wanted to organize the material in such a way that it takes on the urgency of a detective novel. But this is a poor organizing principle unless the author finds a way to make the story important to the reader. I can't imagine anyone who was not involved, at least tangentially, in the Stratford crisis wanting to wade through the undigested mass of reportage, however skilful, that makes up *A Stratford Tempest*. Knelman answers trivial questions, such as, "What did John Dexter write in his diary after being barred?" He doesn't even *ask* the important ones. What did the Stratford debacle mean in terms of our cultural life? It isn't enough to juggle journalistic clichés about art vs. commerce or nationalism vs. internationalism. Nor is it enough to present gossip as if it were history.

The "detective" format allows Knelman to maintain a pose of objectivity. His objectivity is in manner, not in substance. His two major sources of information would seem to be actor Hume Cronyn, then a member of the Stratford Board, and Urjo Kareda, Festival dramaturge under Robin Phillips, and one of the four-person directorate fired by the Board. Not surprisingly these men appear as selfless and disinterested in the affair. I don't blame Kareda and Cronyn for this, but I do blame a reporter who does not question his sources. Knelman's villains are clear, and relatively safe: the members of the Board, and Peter Stevens, executive general manager of the festival, now back in England.

But try to "draw your own conclusions" (as Knelman apparently wants us to do) about the ambiguous role of Robin Phillips in the whole affair. Knelman simply presents us with accusation and counter-accusation and does an elaborate tippy-toe around the subject, looking to the sky, and whistling with rare ingenuousness.

As a prefatory quotation to *A Stratford Tempest* Knelman uses Octave's famous statement from Jean Renoir's *La Règle du Jeu.*

"In this world, the worst part is—everyone has his reasons."

Knelman could hardly have chosen a less appropriate quotation. Renoir's character used the phrase in reference to actions of the heart. In *A Stratford Tempest* the reason for virtually everyone's actions appears to lie in personal ambition. Everyone seems to want to use Stratford to further his own ends. If Knelman had had control of his material, *A Stratford Tempest* might have been an interesting if mean-spirited little book. As it is, it seems only a further instance of what it chronicles.

The Canadian Forum, Summer 1982

At the CBC in 1982

The Politics of Entertainment
George Luscombe and TWP

There was a time when actors
With a gesture of the hand
Could play a drum or play a fife
Or be a German band—*Hey Rube*

George Luscombe has been making plays for over twenty years.
Since 1959 he has been offering his theatrical inventions to the city
of Toronto (occasionally to the rest of Canada, more occasionally to
Europe, Britain or New York), first from a tiny cellar on Fraser
Avenue, then from an old warehouse nattily repainted and rede-
signed, on Alexander Street two blocks above Yonge and Carlton,
smack in the downtown core of Toronto.

It's clear that Luscombe likes the location of Toronto Workshop
Productions (or TWP as it's commonly known). It seems appropriate to his conviction that theatre should be at the centre of any
city's community activity, ready to take part in the debates of the
day as well as scrambling for entry into the precincts of Art.

It's appropriate too that past the doors of TWP every weekend
pours the stream of ragged humanity that floods Yonge Street's
tatty downtown stretch from King north to Bloor, gawking, hus-
tling, looking for cheap thrills, spare change, a good lay or record
bargains. For no Canadian artist, surely, has taken more delight in
the sometimes glorious impurity of the human race. And, certainly,
no one has used that delight to more interesting ends. His joy in
humanity vies with the anger that is so much a part of his work, and
often wins.

George Luscombe grew up in a working-class family in East
York during the great depression. His reaction to the school system
is best expressed in his repeated threat to sue the Board of Education. Associative thinking patterns—still evident in Luscombe's
conversation and his work—don't adapt well to systems. After he
failed a grade, his parents decided that his older brother would be
the one to crack university and the professions. George was enrolled
in East York Technical School. This was a heavily regimented school
with mandatory uniforms and marching bands. Luscombe's only
ambition there was to become a drummer for the East York Cadets.
When he failed in that he wangled a transfer to Danforth Colle-
giate, a more informal school where old comfortable clothes were
the order of the day.

At that time a working-class kid at a technical school had a year to decide on a trade. Luscombe developed an aversion to bandsaws and a horror of the 6 am rising which came with a trade. Nevertheless, as a lad who'd been witness to the depression and whose father had just managed to hang onto his job as a CNR lineman in the thirties, he had a healthy respect for trades. He might have become an electrician had he not discovered a four-year reprieve by way of the arts program.

Several times in his early career Luscombe had reason to be thankful for his training as a commercial artist. Work in that field put him through school and saw him through several patches of rough water during his acting career.

Music served him well too. He whacked skins in an amateur swing band as a kid. Later he billed himself as "The Shortest Piano Player in the World" (he was self-taught) and played for food and drink during his acting apprenticeship in England.

Theatre, although it was eventually to absorb all of his skills, was barely present in Luscombe's upbringing. He remembers being dressed in a sailor-suit and performing a tap dance for his family when he was a tyke, but aside from that auspicious debut he had no experience of theatre until the war years during which he was involved with the CCF and the workers' movement.

A group of CCF members under the direction of Anne Marshall committed themselves to making theatre part of the movement. It must have been Luscombe's first exposure to the idea that theatre should have a place in the life of any civilized community. In any case, Anne Marshall was the first of two women who filled the role of mentor in Luscombe's artistic life. He credits her, for instance, with first making clear to him Stanislavski's distinction between creative ego and vanity, instilling in him a concern for the quality of the work rather than the advance of his own career.

Luscombe seems not to have seen any of the productions of the workers' theatre that was active during the depression years. And the fare of Anne Marshall's group was hardly radical: Noel Coward was one of the authors whose plays were frequently performed. But his work with Marshall's company constituted Luscombe's first exposure to the craft of acting, which was to remain his major focus for twenty years. His feel for the craft and his sense of its possibilities was to be the single most important impetus for his work as a director.

After a postwar period sustained by commercial art, radio work and the odd theatre tour (Luscombe worked with the generation of performers that includes Don Harron, Alfie Scopp and Lorne Greene), he realized that the kind of work available to an actor in Canada didn't allow him the scope to develop. He completed a tour with the Museum Players and, on the urging of Marshall, left for England where he was to live from 1950 to 1957.

Among the many auditions was one with Noel Coward. In an effort to stand out from the huge flock of hopefuls George prepared a sketch about an American coming to England. The sketch done, Coward stood up and said graciously, "Thank you very much George. That was very nice. You understand of course that we can't use an American at this time." Luscombe was already halfway across the stage. "Okay. Would you like to see me play the piano?"

His first work as an actor in England was in many ways a perfect training ground for the director he was to become. He took a position with a rep company, meaning that the actors were expected to "fit up" the stage and scenery or whatever else was necessary for getting a show on the boards. Members of the company bunked with the family who ran the theatre. The father was a former comedian who acted as director, the mother was a dramatic actress and the family's life centred around the operation of the company. It would descend on a small community in Wales and run shows until the audience stopped attending. As the villages were small enough that one evening's performance would use up the audience for one show, this entailed fitting up a different play every night and the company's run, barring disaster, would last as long as the stock of plays held out—eight to ten weeks on the average.

Luscombe never forgot this experience. Aside from the daunting task of setting up a new play and learning a new part every night, there was also his first close contact with the pleasing vulgarity of debased popular culture, its pantomimes and melodramas. An affection for this kind of theatre was to touch his work at Toronto Workshop Productions.

In 1953, back in London and on the loose again, Luscombe saw a production of Ewan McColl's *The Travellers*. The production was the work of Joan Littlewood's company. Seeing it Luscombe knew he was home.

There was a long list of actors eager to become part of Littlewood's company—this despite the fact that an actor wasn't paid, slept illegally in the theatre and ate cracked eggs, bruised tomatoes and bacon rinds from Angel Lane. (Littlewood refused arts funding on principle.) It may have been a communal living situation but Luscombe is at pains to point out that above everything else there was a hard eye on the work at hand.

The company managed a new production every two weeks, alternating, as Luscombe was to do later at TWP, classics with new work. Luscombe acted in *Le Malade imaginaire*, played Pistol in *Henry V* and Sebastian in *Twelfth Night*. As in a rep company the actors were called the black squad in reference to their appearance after they had emerged from the basements where the props were stored.

Luscombe calls his three tough years with Littlewood the best artistic training he can imagine. If his work with Marshall in Canada had given him an idea of what theatre should be and the respect an actor must bring to the text, and his work with the rep company had given him a healthy respect for getting the show on the road, Littlewood's company showed him that the two approaches were not incompatible. After Littlewood, Luscombe's first question when faced with a play became not "How should I do it?" but "Why should I do it?" The first question answered, his talent and imagination would take care of the rest. Luscombe had finished his apprenticeship. By 1957 he had had enough of living with no address but his suitcase. He felt it was time to come home.

Home was a much altered Toronto where nobody gave a damn about what George Luscombe had done in England. He had to fall back on his training as a commercial artist until he had re-established himself as an actor, now mostly for CBC television. It wasn't long before he felt once again the limited nature of the work being done in Canadian theatre. Neither the Crest nor Stratford could have satisfied his ambitions.

A determination to broaden theatrical possibilities in Canada led Luscombe to join forces with actor Powys Thomas and teacher and writer Anthony Ferry to form the Theatre Centre, a combined theatre and practical training school. They shared the conviction that the school should be run for artists by artists and—an extraordinary step for 1958—they intended a bilingual school that would develop productions in both English and French. Luscombe felt strongly that a conventional theatre school would be of little point when there were so few places for a graduate to take his skills in Canada. For that reason the Theatre Centre was to provide work for the actor as an extension of his training.

The problem was finding the money. Even that seemed to be solved when Thomas came up with what he assured Luscombe was as much money as they needed. However, with the money came a board of directors and the stipulations of well-meaning cultural forces in Montreal. Among the inevitable compromises and provisos was the scrapping of the practical theatre aspect of the project. Luscombe and Ferry wished Thomas good luck, formed the Theatre Centre, and quickly went broke. Thomas went to Montreal and formed the National Theatre School. It's typical of this country's approach to the arts that a theatre school should be given precedence over the work of creating an actual theatrical life.

In 1959 the Theatre Centre rose again on a very tiny scale and on an amateur level when Luscombe acquired the use of a basement on Fraser Avenue and began working with a small group of actors. This was the original Toronto Workshop Productions. Luscombe took upon himself the training of actors who would be prepared to do the kind of work he was interested in pursuing. He also took upon himself for the first time the role of director, simply to see to it that his kind of theatre was being done.

Clearly TWP was set up with Littlewood's company as some sort of model. The first production was an adaptation of a CBC radio play by Len Petersen. It formed half of a double bill with a play by Lorca, thus establishing the initial pattern of alternating new work with neglected work from established writers. On opening night, when the stage lights came up for the first time, Herbert Whittaker was heard to exclaim, "My God! They've got dimmers!"

Early TWP fare included the work of Brecht and an interpretation of *The Tempest*, but as time went by there was more and more emphasis on new work.

The first original production in the style that has become associated with Luscombe was *Hey Rube!* Its script was by Luscombe and Jack Winter, dramaturge and script collaborator during TWP's formative years. There are longtime theatregoers in Toronto who still insist that *Hey Rube!* is the best show Luscombe has ever done. I would guess that this has mostly to do with the way a dynamic theatrical style hit Toronto in 1961 when little else of theatrical interest was happening. Be that as it may, *Hey Rube!* didn't find its audience immediately. Arnold Edinborough remembers that on opening night he was one of four people in the audience. Luscombe's wife Mona, who has worked front of house for TWP from the beginning, quickly got out some handbills and the audience built, mostly by word of mouth.

If there is anything of the sentimental populist in Luscombe it shows itself in his attitude toward publicity. He still frustrates the actors who work with him by not allotting enough of his budget for publicity. TWP has the talented graphic artist Theo Dimson creating the most striking posters in Toronto, yet in many respects TWP's publicity still works on the optimistic assumption that good shows and good word of mouth, nudged along by buttons, banners and handbills, will bring in the people. What this tends to mean is an initial three or four weeks of small houses, and in a theatre like TWP, scheduled in advance for a season, that amounts to a good portion of a play's run.

In 1963 TWP became a professional company of six actors with Luscombe as director and Winter as official dramaturge. At that time Luscombe found an important supporter in Nathan Cohen, drama critic, nemesis of the Crest Theatre and in general the most respected theatrical commentator of the period. Cohen recognized the importance of what Luscombe was doing in the thin air of Canadian theatre.

For a short time in the sixties Luscombe seemed to have found his audience. The director identified strongly with the protest movement in the United States. For a while TWP was part of the underground railway for deserters and dodgers and put to work as many of the expatriate youths as possible. *Faces*, a light satire on middle America, was actually put together in collaboration with many of these young people and produced at TWP.

In response to the black power movement Luscombe put together *Mr. Bones*, a satirical rendering of events leading up to Lincoln's assassination, placing the work of the radical black writers of the sixties in the ironic framework of a minstrel show. Nathan Cohen praised Luscombe's production of Mario Fratii's *Che* when it opened in 1970. But perhaps the peak of Luscombe's identification with the counter culture was reached when *Chicago 70* went to New York in that year. Observers of the strange ways of fashion might be interested to note that the *New York Times'* Clive Barnes ended his enthusiastic review with an uncharacteristic "Right On!".

During that period Luscombe was briefly considered in the vanguard of theatre in Canada. From the point of view of most

123

popular journalism, this had more to do with the impression his theatre gave of being at one with the fashionable movements of the day than with any formal advances he was making. There were great successes in the seventies too, but more and more the press (and, indeed, the theatrical community) has been taking Luscombe for granted in a way that reflects its disillusionment with the idealism of the previous decade and its mechanical identification of Luscombe with that period. The trend was partly due to the death of Nathan Cohen and the subsequent deterioration of theatrical comment and debate in the Toronto papers. It was partly a question of a highly talented and prickly individual working steadily for twenty years and thus making more enemies than anyone else in the volatile theatre community. And it was partly a question for an artist pursuing his own lights and ignoring the question of what is fashionable, a pursuit which is an implied affront to the journalist whose secret function it is to reflect fashion. There is too the shifting of political fashion to the right. But all these considerations aside, I have an idea that Luscombe's insistence on remaining something of a maverick, long after the natural order of things would suggest that he should have faded from the picture or become an institution open to attack, secretly infuriated those of the younger generation of theatre professionals whose rebellious attitudes were thus threatened.

The irony in all this is that Luscombe's work has never been less doctrinaire, more searching—political in the broad sense of the term—than it has been in the last decade. Yet, because of his reputation as a socialist, whatever he presents is categorized as political and didactic and is kept safely on the fringes. Luscombe matured into a major artist in the seventies. It's disturbing that this should be the period in which he was most ignored.

I have been seeing George Luscombe's work for ten years now. As an arts student in 1970, relatively ignorant of the theatre, I found it interesting and lively at the very least. I was next exposed to his work during a period when I was earning a living toiling for a small theatre company in Kingston. This time it seemed a revelation (I saw *Ten Lost Years* and a brilliant adaptation of *Good Soldier Schweik*.) What struck me most about it were its stylistic and formal aspects. It seemed as if the bare stage could offer anything to the artist who approached it with imagination and an open eye.

I cherished, in particular, moments such as the one in which the actors created a wild coach ride through the streets of Prague, Schweik an unwilling passenger but helpless, as the major, drunk on wine and words, spurred on the horses. And in *Ten Lost Years* a brilliant sequence in which the men ran for the train, hopped the boxcars and grappled the air for their balance as the train rattled west.

Sequences such as these proclaimed to my impressionable eye that there was no action that the stage might not articulate, no physical idea it might not approach, no metaphor for which it might not stretch, using only the basic tool of the stage, the actor—his body and voice—and the honed skills of stagecraft, lighting and set design to serve the actor in imaginative ways. Even then it was clear to me that Luscombe's shows were anything but "workshop productions." They were finely and elaborately designed pieces of theatrical entertainment.

It was about this time that James Reaney, working with Keith Turnbull and what was to become the NDWT Company, initiated his ambitious Donnelly Trilogy with *Sticks and Bones*. I remember having the opportunity to compare two theatrical approaches to the rendering of a similar incident. In *Sticks and Bones* there was an elaborate fight sequence that ended in death. Turnbull had his actors wrestle about the stage, panting, sprawling and raising welts on each other's naked backs, pausing only to deliver dialogue. The literal translation of the action on stage served only to make me notice how unsuited were the actors' bodies to that kind of rough and tumble, how unconvincing was violence when literally acted out onstage and how needlessly the two actors were suffering. In addition the speeches were all but lost in the fury.

In *Ten Lost Years* a speaker tells of a particularly chilling incident of violence, and Luscombe's actors described with their bodies one simple stylized action. It was presented in slow motion. From a kick to the head to a fall that ended in death the action uncoiled itself in one smooth and inevitable arc that imprinted its horror on the spectator's mind like an indelible image. It was a case of embracing the artificiality of the stage and using it as a lever on reality to achieve your theatrical ends. I was sold on the work of George Luscombe.

The stagecoach and train sequences were as completely and satisfyingly simple. The stagecoach was suggested by two actors on painted wooden boxes facing the audience and lurching about as if shaken by the motion of the coach. An illusion of forward momentum was created by the other actors who appeared downstage facing the audience, striking stationary poses close to the imaginary wheels and moving rapidly backwards, still holding their stances, as if they were townspeople going about their business and left behind in the wake of the stagecoach's forward rush. Each of the townspeople was wittily characterized by visual shorthand; a change of hats, a newspaper, two women chatting, another splattered with mud and shaking her fist, and as an actor reappeared he had changed props, hats or attitude so that a constant stream of interesting extras was left behind as the coach rattled through the town.

In *Ten Lost Years* the boxcars were merely delineated by cleanly demarcated squares of light on which the men jiggled and held their balance. As a new arrival raced—in a stationary mime run—to catch the car, one of the riders stretched out, grabbed his hand and hauled him aboard where he spread his legs and groped for his balance until he got the feel of it.

In both instances the actors were busy giving speeches or—in the case of the train sequence—speaking narrative. Yet I never felt distracted from what they were saying by the visual liveliness of the presentation. In fact, the effect of the overlay of the verbal and physical action was to widen the senses by way of the imagination so that the speeches seemed extraordinarily alive. I can recall now, with vividness, the story of two brothers meeting from boxcars headed in opposite directions, their precise inflections as they hail each other across the tracks, and the edges of surprise and joy in their voices as they greet each other.

In productions such as *Esmeralda and the Hunchback of Notre Dame* (1978) *Refugees* (1979) and *The Mac-Paps* (1980), Luscombe was to extend his mastery of stage space past the merely physical and into the realm of poetry.

During his mature period Luscombe has had the good fortune of working with and nurturing the career of Astrid Janson, perhaps the most brilliant designer at work in this country. The physical concept of the set is more important for Luscombe, whose art is centred in physical expression, than for any other stage artist I know. Furthermore he uses his sets like no-one else. For *Refugees* Janson had the entire floor of the stage covered in what looked to be some kind of plastic grating but which turned out to be milk cartons. At key moments in the play Luscombe lit the performers from below through the grating and this violation of normal stage lighting had an extraordinarily disorienting effect. The actors seemed about to float loose from the pull of gravity, while the shadowy bars thrown across their bodies fragmented their physical presences. All of this was eerily appropriate to a play about uprooted refugees from Hitler's Germany. More than a mere illustration, Luscombe's use of such visual motifs was an element of the play as important as the words and, indeed, the music. For *Refugees* was an opera designed for the kind of stage narrative that Luscombe pioneered in Canada.

Produced in collaboration with the Opera Workshop and the composers Beverly and Ray Pannell, *Refugees* was a brilliant production. Typically, I'm afraid, it was killed by a combination of a blind and tone-deaf press reaction and a lack of funding with which to keep the show running until it found its audience. This last is ironic, for *Refugees* pointed the way for genuine operas within the most important tradition of Canadian theatre. And, of course, that tradition frees opera from the killing rigidity and expense of properties, sets and costumes which tends to keep full-scale operas beyond the reach of most contemporary composers.

Luscombe first became important to me for the cavalier imagination which he brought to the stage, freeing it, as I thought, from the artificial limitations accepted by most of the theatre available even today. It didn't occur to me to ask more of him as an artist than that. Yet after I stopped toiling on the outskirts of professional theatre, I began to see that he was also a genuine voice speaking to the world I lived in, and by that act defining it. When I moved to Toronto in late 1975 Luscombe was on a year's sabbatical, his first in the fifteen years since TWP was formed. When he returned in 1976 he initiated a series of productions of astonishing quality. It was seeing these shows that demonstrated to me that Luscombe was more than his hard-won technique, as brilliant as that technique was.

Even as I write those last words I'm aware of feeling the pressure to answer the thoughtless criticisms that have been levelled at Luscombe over the last few years. The most serious one is also the one most easily answered, and the one most unthinkingly parroted. This is the old story of Luscombe's having only one "style."

There is no doubt that Luscombe places his stamp on every show he undertakes. Consequently every Luscombe show has a recognizable feel to it. Yet that feel has less to do with Luscombe's "style" — it is actually a hard-won technique of considerable power, subtlety and flexibility—than it does with the pervading warmth and generosity of spirit that counters the fury of any Luscombe work. In fact I would argue that Luscombe, who calls himself "no writer," differs from most theatre directors in that he is a creative rather than an interpretive artist.

It is true that a technique that reduces every subject matter to a similar theatrical experience would be a tyrannical one. Yet who could have confused the slashing, ironic, violent and tender comedy Luscombe made of Rick Salutin's *Les Canadiens* with the quiet, tragic and introspective ironies of *The Mac-Paps?* To do so would be to confuse a technique with the experience of a play. It would be not to experience the play at all.

And even if Luscombe's style can be suggested by reference to his magical transformations of stage space such as the ones I've described, it must be acknowledged that he applies this technique differently in every instance. Luscombe himself insists that he seeks a different rhythm suitable for every story he tells. And the proof of the claim is there for anyone who cares to look. *Ten Lost Years* (a collaboration with Cedric Smith) counterpointed vivid stage action and invention (the train sequence, a Shirley Temple dance poised against a silver screen) and the haunted stillness of personal narrative remembered through time. *Les Canadiens* was presented in a swirl of action that reflected both the experience of a hockey game and the joyous clash of two cultures meeting on their one common ground—the hockey arena. *Ain't Lookin'* was true both to the rhythm of a baseball game (a slow winding of tension released periodically into action) and to the lives of the men it depicted (stoic periods of helpless waiting relieved by occasional instances of humour or violence). *Esmeralda*, an admirable failure of a production, was perhaps most dependent on Luscombe's physical conception. With a cast of ten actors Luscombe created a world in flux, in which no fixed points of reference existed. Religion, the monarchy, art, all seemed on the verge of being swept away in the torrent of ideas released by the invention of the printing press. The dialogue and speeches followed hard on the heels of Victor Hugo's plot, but the real meaning of the play was in Luscombe's restless, fidgety staging. His actors scrabbled over the many levels of Janson's set like so many ants—ants that have lost their centre as a colony, left to fend for themselves.

Even at a distance of three years I'm amused by the outrageous things that production attempted. On the level of sweeping action there was the scene in which the beggars swarmed the cathedral, at the climax of which they took a massive battering ram to the door while the Hunchback high above in a bell tower tossed boulders (or whatever) down on them and scalded them with boiling oil. (I won't attempt to describe how this action was articulated.) On another level altogether there was a wrenching moment in which Esmeralda's death throes on the gallows were seen from a distance and translated into one last tiny dance in slow motion.

The *Globe and Mail* reviewer managed to write off this extraordinary exercise in shoestring spectacle as a "sociopolitical tract." Judged as drama the play *was* a failure. Luscombe was determined to present Esmeralda as the central character, yet she was such only in that she existed as a focus for the projections of the other characters. He created a pretty good anima figure, but hardly a character. However, if the play failed, it had nothing to do with the cheap sneer of the reviewer, which had more to do with currently fashionable dismissals of the man's work than anything else.

The reviewer's irrational objection, however, does serve to raise the second accusation brought against Luscombe. The assumption is that Luscombe twists every production to make political points. Behind this is the unexamined thought that politics in entertainment is merely an excuse for didacticism. Much of what is written about Luscombe in the press reflects these assumptions.

In fact, political convictions are as good a fuel as any for an artist. Yet the tendency of the urban provincial, in Toronto at least, is to shoot peas at whatever banner they have heard may be flying rather than really looking at the work itself.

The idea of revolution might have been a common subject matter of Luscombe's work in the sixties. But where can one see it in his work of the last decade? In *Les Canadiens?* Maurice Richard has been quoted as commenting on the TWP production that he "didn't like politics in a play about hockey." And there were the odd program notes written by Miles Potter for his production of the play at Theatre Passe Muraille the season after Luscombe's:

Politics? Not really. National Unity? No thank you, not today.
No, this play is about hockey and the greatest hockey team in the world.

Mr. Potter is strangely ingenuous. The play is certainly not about National Unity. (Is anything ever really about National Unity?) But unless one defines politics as specific action having to do with a specific political theory, *Les Canadiens*—as clearly in the original Centaur version as in the TWP re-working—is about the development of a mythology in the lives of two peoples, and the way in which that mythology finds expression, first in sport, where it is an indirect and veiled protest, and then in political action. If the play doesn't deal directly with the rise of the separatist movement in Quebec, it certainly uses the hockey team as a metaphor for that phenomenon. But the political action of the play is rooted in Salutin, not in the direction of George Luscombe.

Further, the extraordinary emotional effect that Luscombe's production had on Toronto audiences was in part because the play addressed itself directly to the trauma suffered by English Canada in general, and southwestern Ontario in particular, in November 1976. I very much doubt that many people found the play didactic, but I'm sure that many found it challenging and searching, perhaps even a crucial step in coming to understand the human basis of otherwise impersonal political events.

In *Ten Lost Years* there is a strong undercurrent of anger that implies the possibility of revolution. Few would suggest that it was out of place in a play about the suffering inflicted by the great depression. Luscombe ends the play by expressing the idea—indeed it's almost a truism—that the system only managed to pull itself out of the depression by throwing itself behind another war. If I were to object to Luscombe's climax—and I'd have to work at it—it would be that Luscombe used a less than startling idea to provide a big finish, and that finish was less than sensitive to the human lives at the centre of the play up to that point. But one could just as easily argue that the sudden intrusion of a large impersonal political event into the world of people whose lives had been made personal to us was a very precise formal point.

In only one other Luscombe production of the last six or seven years was politics a central aspect of the subject matter. *The Mac-Paps* (written in collaboration with Mac Reynolds) told the story of Canadians who went to fight in the Spanish Civil War. Some of the men were deeply committed politically; others were merely seeking adventure. Because of the nature of the subject matter there were lots of political banners out on the line to shoot at. And, indeed, *The Mac-Paps* brought the pea shooters out from under the table. The Toronto *Star* reviewer spent the bulk of her column explaining that the Mackenzie-Papineau Battalion and the International Brigade were mere dupes for Stalinist Russia. By extension Luscombe and his talented coworkers were dupes as well.

The Mac-Paps was as frightening an exploration of war as were any of Luscombe's previous plays on the subject (notably *Good Soldier Schweik*), yet the mode he chose was not his customary high irony but a grim tragic irony that could hardly be further removed from flag waving. The play was simultaneously a celebration of personal heroism and a severe questioning of the efficacy—or even the possibility—of heroism in the modern world.

I want to discuss one scene from *The Mac-Paps* by way of supporting my contentions and to demonstrate how easily preconception can distort the impact of a work. *The Mac-Paps* used oral history in the manner developed by Luscombe for *Ten Lost Years*. Near the end of the first act we are told that fascist forces had occupied a village, rounded up a group of villagers and shot them without (it is stressed) benefit of a trial.

Immediately we are plunged into the thick of a battle. Smoke drifts across the stage. The Mac-Paps are advancing on a village held by fascist forces. After a tense battle the village is all but taken. The only remaining resistance is from a group of snipers who have refused to surrender and are picking off the Canadian soldiers one by one. The snipers are captured only at great cost, so that by that time the Canadians are frustrated beyond reason. So great is their tension that it can be relieved only by executing the captive snipers on the spot (without benefit of a trial). Immediately after the shots are fired the men turn to the audience and sing the "Internationale."

These are the bones of the action. But the effect of the sequence is very charged and complex. Throughout the play these men have had our complete sympathy—even when we have been nudged to question their naïvete. In the scene under consideration, we have shared with them the strain of the battle to the extent that when they shoot the snipers the narrative tug is so insistent, and the act so quickly done, that we have no time to consider anything as abstract as morality. As with the climax of any strong narrative pull, the outcome seems inevitable. Indeed the release that the men seek is sought by the audience as well.

If we are uneasy with the event it is only for an instant. But Luscombe stages the singing which follows the act in such a way as to take that unease and draw it out. The soldiers sing the "Inter-nationale" fervently, staring out over the audience with dead fanatic eyes as if their lusty voicing might smother any lingering moral unease. From offstage other voices echo the song, and this echo is in a minor key and discordant like an imperfectly suppressed qualm. It is hard not to think back on the story of the fascist execution which preceded this episode and which creates a disturbing parallel to the event.

The crucial thing to note here is that this parallel—central as it is to the experience of the play—is not made in the actual dialogue. An audience with a literary bias, say, or with an eye untrained to the visual and aural levels of narrative as Luscombe has developed them for the stage, might well experience the sequence under consideration as a piece of thoughtless flagwaving.

The Mac-Paps seriously questioned political idealism no matter what flag it operated under. By extension it sought the limits and strengths of Canada's peculiar national innocence. This last theme has run through Luscombe's work in a fascinating way in the last few years. It has found particular expression in characters played by Tom Butler and R.H. Thomson (*The Mac-Paps*), Bill Lake and Jonathan Welsh (*Les Canadiens*) and Paul Hubbard (Joe Giffen in *Ain't Lookin'*).

Luscombe's use of music is always interesting. In the above scene from *The Mac-Paps* he uses martial music in such a way as to emphasize the role it plays in encouraging men to step past their moral boundaries. As I've suggested, the actual script of the play offers relatively little of the kind of philosophical musing that Luscombe drew out of the material. Luscombe has said that he originally envisaged the show as a much more dynamic stage piece, more on the level of *Ten Lost Years,* but found as he went along that the material kept demanding a more thoughtful approach. It should have been clear to anyone watching the show that Luscombe the artist came before Luscombe the popularly imagined proselytizer.

It should be equally clear that Luscombe's relation to his material is that of a primary creator rather than an interpreter. He is capable of taking a script of very little literary distinction (*Ain't Lookin'*, say, which reads like a barely sketched film script) and making it into a rich work of art. A misunderstanding of the basis of Luscombe's art is at the root of the critical misapprehension of it. To the person with a traditional sense of theatre the words that an actor speaks carry most of the meaning to be derived from a play.

After the critic has seized on several quotable lines of speeches from a play in process and written them down in his notebook, he proceeds to give a connoisseur's once-over to the actors (mostly to decide whom he finds appealing and whom he doesn't). After that he has a cursory look at such things as pacing, costumes, set design—all of these things pretty well abstracted from their particular context. This piecemeal approach is not all that inappropriate to the bulk of conventional theatrical productions. It's murder on an artist like Luscombe. In an atmosphere so stifling and so hostile to good art it's not surprising that Luscombe, who uses stagecraft in fresh and unconventional ways, and who approaches his audience with a healthy respect for its intelligence, should be so undervalued.

In *Ain't Lookin'* there is a scene that demonstrates Luscombe's complex relationship to his material and to his audience as well as any I can think of. The black ball team of the story makes its living playing local white teams in small towns across the United States and Canada. (The story takes place during the depression.) They generally win because they are very good ball players. They get away with being good because in the process of whipping the local boys they put on a fine coon show, tumblin' about and clownin' fit to kill. They are allowed the status of good athletes because their "natural" ability is perceived as compensation for belonging to a clownish inferior race.

When it is discovered during a game that one of the team is a white man in blackface the crowd starts to get ugly. There is only one way to placate it and that is to reaffirm the crowd's sense of racial superiority. Two of the team members hop to the fore and address the crowd as happy shuffling niggers, going through illustrations of common stereotypes (natural rhythm, shoe-shining, southern-fried dialogue, rituals of glad abasement), finally climaxing their lightning routine with a rousing version of "Li'l Liza Jane" in which the rest of the team joins, tap dancing, plucking banjos and waving their arms. Just when the number is approaching a peak of exhilaration a sheriff appears and arrests the white player for "fraud, cheatin' the public and impersonatin' a nigger."

For the spectator the scene carries a rare wallop. Until this incident he has been sympathizing with the ballplayers' plight and innocently enjoying their imaginative ballpark routines without necessarily being aware of a contradiction. But here the connection between those wonderful routines and the plight of the men is too clear to ignore. Yet even as he fully realizes how humiliating the ritual must be for the men, the routine they are presenting at that very moment is still very funny. The contradictory pull between two responses is painful. By the time they are halfway through "L'il Liza Jane," which number is in reality a harshly ironic celebration of the "act" of being a nigger, it's impossible to fight it anymore. Nervous giggles are washed away by the infectious rhythm. In fact it is apparent that the ballplayers themselves have taken the number past irony and are letting themselves go with the sheer pleasure of the release. The act of joining in the celebration by clapping time is getting harder and harder to resist. But before all consciousness of the situation can be lost—and the timing is uncanny—the sheriff interrupts the proceedings and we're back to reality—as insane as that reality might be.

Most directors would never have cut off a successful musical number until every last drop of audience enthusiasm had been milked from it. And yet the willingness to interrupt the flow of—let's call it pure entertainment—is what makes *Ain't Lookin'* a rich and moving experience for an audience who will remember it long after *Eight to the Bar* has been forgotten.

Let it be noted that Luscombe's approach is never punitive toward his audience. In this case, although the audience is implicated in the action, no one is made to suffer for enjoying *Ain't Lookin'*'s ballpark routines. Rudy Webb has spoken about how painful it was initially for the black actors to recreate oppressive black stereotypes for no matter what purpose. Yet it's clear that the actors onstage have gone past the discomfort of having to present a cultural embarrassment and are able to communicate a certain amount of unguarded pleasure, trusting that the audience will accept the entertainment while coming to terms with the social implications. Neither is the audience left with the feeling of complacency with which campiness loves to nuzzle. (Camp merely encourages an audience to congratulate itself for being superior to a less "progressive" age.) There is an honest feeling of respect between audience and performers. This is characteristic of Luscombe's shows and one of the things that makes his work such a rich experience.

Luscombe's approach to narrative has been touched on throughout this essay. Let's take an unexceptional example of how it operates by examining the opening of *Ain't Lookin'*, a rather more straightforward narrative than that usually favoured by the director.

Chappie Johnson, owner and manger of Chappie's All Stars, the black baseball team, is talking tensely to his players (the team is represented by four men in bright orange uniforms). A key player has skipped town without notice, leaving Johnson short a first baseman. Joe Giffen, a white kid on the bum, drifts onto the playing-field (a sweet and evocative set by Terry Gunvordahl). Giffen and Johnson have met years before in small-town Ontario where the manager offered the kid some tips on playing the base. Johnson works his way around to asking Giffen to take the place of the missing player. Giffen protests. Johnson does an easygoing job of fast-talking him. As he does so the team, who up to now have been practising their "reams" (comic routines that are worked into a game on signals from Johnson), begin to circle Giffen, pulling off his shirt (he is wearing an All Stars sweater underneath), helping him to step out of his pants (he is wearing All Star pants). During this activity Giffen has been resisting ineffectively. He finally gets to the point.

"But you're coloured!"

"Ain't everybody?" Johnson counters. "Don't recall meetin' anyone you could see through."

As he says this he slaps black goop all over the kid's face.

WHAM! the lights come up hard and bright. Wild music is playing (an old Fletcher Henderson recording given immediacy by an onstage drummer and keyboard player who play along with the record) and the team is in the middle of a crazy routine in the ballpark, a hapless blackfaced Giffen bobbing around on the fringes of the action with a worried look on his face.

No one in the audience is likely to wonder why the ball players are removing the kid's shirt or why Giffen should be wearing an All Star uniform under his clothes. It's clear that we're being presented with a kind of theatrical shorthand that covers three or four links in the narrative at once (a chance meeting, an offer, an argument, the preparation for the game and the first game itself). In turn the spectator experiences a pleasurable sense of events in a story whipping him along and taking him somewhere interesting. As a consequence the abrupt change in scene and situation doesn't confuse him but delivers something he's been encouraged to anticipate.

But in the same scene we've had several other points established that may have escaped the watcher's conscious notice. We've been told, for instance, what a "ream" is; we've registered the careful preparation that precedes "natural" cooning; and we've had Mr. Johnson's place set as the central figure of the story.

Now this is very fine storytelling. But it works for the director and his cast in other ways as well. The sequence I've described springs out of the first few moments of the play. It's a simple one, easy to follow and pleasurable, and it's crucially placed to gain the audience's confidence in the story and the storytellers. It signals clearly the kind of story it will be, and the method the show will pursue (for instance, music has been established as a central structural motif, and it's been made clear that more than one action may be presented at once).

It also sets precedents that will allow Luscombe to present more difficult scenes. Some of them are of a narrative excitement that one might think impossible for the stage. Others are of a quiet and leisurely nature that most stage artists would hesitate to attempt.

Before the evening is through the audience will have been whipped into a frenzy of suspense. In a climactic car chase the team in their (imagined) bus is pursued by a group of (imagined) louts in their (imagined) car around imagined curves, over imagined hills and across imagined fields. Without describing how the audience was prodded to imagine such unlikely stage action I want to assure the reader that this scene and its brilliant denouement, in which the team draws together in a dark field, tensely awaiting an attack, and silently passing out baseball bats, brought audiences to peaks of excitement and fear for the safety of the characters that would be an achievement in any medium.

There are other sequences, equally impressive, in which nothing at all is happening on the narrative level. In one such scene the men are falling asleep in an open field under the lovely illusion of summer starlight, while the newcomer Joe Giffen interrupts them with innocent questions. (In Luscombe's remounting of *Ain't Lookin'* in the fall of 1980, he filled many of these *temps morts* with business and dialogue. Although I respect his decision to bolster these scenes so they wouldn't suffer too much in the low energy of an "off" night, I still regret it.)

But Luscombe used his technique in *Ain't Lookin'* to more subtle and beautiful ends. Much of the action takes place on the bus—that vehicle being no more than an area marked off by suitcases (which double as seats) and dim, subtly delineated patches of light. The passengers jog along, talking, playing cards or simply drifting in the mental bus-fog that accrues to any group of travelling players. (I've never seen this sense of aimless time connecting interchangeable places so beautifully conveyed.) Accompanying these sequences is the instrumental work of the two onstage actors who keep the rhythm of the vehicle quietly rattling along. The instruments are also used to suggest sounds such as a clap of thunder. One mo-ment—the effect of a thunderstorm on the men in the bus, their minds suddenly alert and the sides of the vehicle squaring them-selves against the elements—goes beyond anything I had thought the stage capable of by way of acuity of sensual articulation.

If the play managed to evoke specific atmospheres startlingly well, it went just as far in the opposite direction. There were dream sequences in which a character suddenly left the objective literal rendering of a scene and transformed the stage space into a subjec-tive medium for his own imagination. Most impressive of all there were sequences in which the working of time and memory became almost palpable and deeply and mysteriously moving.

At the end of the play Chappie Johnson suffers an attack of angina while travelling on the bus at night. Following this he has a dream. The All Stars slowly rise from their seats and circle about him tossing slow-motion balls and swapping playful dialogue with him. As he has been through the play, Chappie is still the centre of their activity, but he is also a man on speaking terms with his own death and surveying his life's work from a point of rest and accep-tance. A sequence such as this is haunting in ways that the specta-tor cannot pin down while in the process of watching it. (At such moments one can sense a certain poetic identification of Luscombe with his central figure who, in the performance by Ed Smith, be-came one of the most dignified characters on the contemporary stage.)

Perhaps the single most impressive aspect of *Ain't Lookin'* was the way in which the entire narrative was subtly but precisely sit-uated in the working of one man's mind (Joe Giffen, stand-in for John Craig who wrote the original book from his actual experiences) and suspended in fragile memory, like a stage production itself. This imparted to the show a curiously bittersweet quality that haunts anyone who has responded to its gentle, hurtful poetry.

Much of what I've been discussing belongs more properly to a discussion of Luscombe's technique. Yet it is Luscombe's flexible approach to narrative that permits such moments to detach themselves from the story and comment on it in a lyrical way. Of course I've been discussing Luscombe's technique one way or another from the beginning of this essay. And as flexibility is the basis of his narrative approach it's hardly surprising that it should be the thrust of his technique. Luscombe's most basic impulse as a director, it seems to me, has always been to see how far he can push theatre past its accepted boundaries.

I sometimes think that writers and directors who accept the boundaries of conventional stage technique are living on borrowed time. Among Canadian writers, only James Reaney is really given a chance to work steadily along similar lines. Rick Salutin, trained in Passe Muraille's collective school, may yet go the distance with it. Reaney seems to have found in Keith Turnbull a collaborator willing to serve as a creative interpreter, and this kind of collaboration may well be the way of the future. Certainly if new theatrical forms that can yet remain widely accessible are developed in this country then writers must stop thinking of their work as a fixed entity such as a poem or a novel and throw themselves behind the plasticity of the stage space and the flexibility required to develop work with actors.

As for Luscombe, until he finds an equitable working situation with a writer as accomplished as Reaney, it will still be appropriate to think of him as the primary creator behind the bulk of his productions. The fact is that the quality of a Luscombe show has little correlation to the quality of a script. *Ain't Lookin'* is as rich a theatrical experience as was *Les Canadiens*, yet the latter has a life outside of TWP while the former could exist only as a Luscombe production. (I'd be happy to be proved wrong on that point.)

In Luscombe's adaptation of *The Hunchback of Notre Dame* there is a fine instance of the way Luscombe's technique springs from pressing against the limitations of the stage. First let's state the problem.

At the climax of the play Frodo, the evil priest, is to fall to his death from a great height. The problem is how to give that moment the dramatic impact it requires. There is little height to play with and, even if there were, the director would have no wish to replace a leading actor every night. However, if Luscombe lacked height he did have depth. Janson's set borrowed from restoration set design with painted black squares disappearing into an illusory horizon. As a result, the TWP stage thrust back from the audience in a striking manner. In a simple but daring ploy Luscombe had the actor (Jeff Braunstein) dangle from the highest level, drop to the floor, and fall *back* into the set in slow motion, a spot catching his terrified expression as he fell screaming into theatrical space.

I was there and I can testify that it was a stunning moment, both dramatically, and as a bravura demonstration of the nature of stage reality. On one level all Luscombe did was to trade one kind of theatrical space for another. Yet this suggests what is most important about the man's work on the technical level. Apart from all considerations of style, he is simply one of the most brilliant manipulators of theatrical space there is or has been. His is the rarest and yet the most basic of the talents necessary to a stage artist— whether he be actor, designer or director—the ability to recognize that theatrical space, all by itself, is a metaphor waiting to be used.

Most productions of mainstream theatre work against the basic strength of theatre, simply by accepting that stage action must approximate reality with only the gentlest kneading around or fiddling against that idea. If theatre is conceived as a naturalistic medium, tractable to verbal and illustrative approaches, then it is hampered severely by limitations in scope and flexibility. But Luscombe takes those limitations and turns them into the virtues they should be and must be if the stage is to retain—or rather regain— its vitality. At this point in the development of theatre in Canada this kind of work must take precedence over the work of the writer, for artists like Luscombe are redefining the medium in which writers will be inspired to work.

But I don't want to end on a technical note. I want to look at a scene in *Ain't Lookin'* that suggests as well as any the rich flavour of George Luscombe's theatre.

The All Stars have been granted a night on the town thanks to a stubborn rain. Joe Giffen meets his fairy princess in a small-town joint and dances with her to the music of a local band. The band takes a break, but Joe and his princess linger. Time goes into suspension. The musicians set a hypnotic interrupted rhythm, a record with a crack in it; she hands him a coin; Joe—his eyes still tight on hers—reaches slowly over to an imaginary jukebox. As he does so the All Stars, not otherwise part of this scene, slide noiselessly into place to form the jukebox; the coin drops (a light rim smack from the drummer); the music begins (a leisurely six-to-the-bar from the musicians) and, as Joe and his princess dance, the All Stars/jukebox gives out with the Ink Spots record "If I Didn't Care" (Rudy Webb doing a pretty fair Bill Kenny).

That established, Luscombe takes things a step farther. The All Stars/Ink Spots, still singing, break formation and gently, rhythmically, hands in pockets, toes scuffling (no one's in a hurry), circle the lovers as they dance, enclosing them in the music and creating around them a spell of intimacy. The music ends (with the bass' sweetly parodic "Oh baby if I cared for you"—ping!), the All Stars are gone, and the two lovers are left staring at each other, abashed and breathless.

In context, this sequence was as disturbing as it was charming, for it quietly but precisely pointed to the role of the black entertainer/athlete as a source of vitality tapped for the benefit of white society. (The Ink Spots were a black singing group, perfecting a sweet style for the commercial mainstream. The All Stars/Ink Spots are de-sexed onlookers to the love scene in process.) Yet this is balanced on an edge of such lightness, such theatrical stillness— holding there a recognition of black servitude, a charged ambivalence regarding popular culture, a genuine empathy with the lovers, a sadness for their innocence and an astonishing openness to both the evil and the charm of the situation—that I know of no contemporary theatre more affecting on so many levels, more aware of—but less weighted by—preconception or conventional morality.

There is a grace and delicacy of sensibility at work in this scene that I value as highly as I do Luscombe's magic wealth of invention. A stage production disappears after each performance to be recreated again the next evening. When its run is completed, it may well disappear forever. Luscombe has not given us artifacts by way of scripts to be reworked by future generations. What he has done is to put his talent and his heart and soul into moment after moment of stage time. I regret that his work will someday be available only indirectly through inspiration or memory. Yet to say that his particular ongoing achievement is not fully as important as the work of those who carve on stone is to value the artifact over art.

Theatre Reviews
1981-82

Escape Entertainment

Written by Carol Bolt, directed by Timothy Bond. Tarragon Theatre

Carol Bolt's new play takes place in a Kleinburg soundstage where a young Canadian producer is having trouble getting the money to finish his new film. The film was originally about political trouble in Quebec. Investors have altered it so that it's now about Cuban Refugees in Miami. As a result the crew has to stick palm trees in downtown Toronto and the hero has become a CIA agent played by a spectacularly alcoholic second-string Hollywood star. The star is fixated on the memory of his ex-wife. She, in turn, is a film reviewer who has recreated his minor acting career by bludgeoning his work and his personality in print. In any case she arrives on the sound stage, ostensibly to do an interview with him, but actually to slash at him in person. The situation is in place.

The situation involves ironic reflections on Canada, its culture and its relation to the big guns down South. These ironies arrive naturally enough in a story about Hollywood North. Even though irony is the characteristic mode of Canadian theatre, Bolt's ironies do spread themselves a bit thickly over the characters and ideas in the play. They threaten to smother things that are potentially most alive and interesting in her writing. Occasionally the irony shrinks to the level of sarcasm and the characters become trapped in the author's particular—and no doubt perfectly justified—angers. There are dangers, as well, in the fact that at least two of the characters are clearly inspired—if that's the word—by actual figures in the world of Canadian film and theatre. But for the most part that's just playful decoration.

Actually the more I think about *Escape Entertainment* the more it interests me, both as a piece of writing and as an example of the curious turns a good creative mind can take in order to speak about hurtful things that are embarrassing in the present climate of the arts in Canada. Toronto yearns to be New York and wants to stifle the earnest voice of nationalism that in its various manifestations encouraged the only real culture Toronto or Canada has ever known. Bolt places onstage a shrill, repellent figure—an American critic based in Toronto who hates Canada in general and Toronto in particular because it fails to reflect back to her the self-image after which she lusts and which will forever elude her. She repeats over and over how much she loves New York, which amounts to saying how much she hates herself. She takes out her self-hatred on every-thing around her living, dead or in-between. Opposite her is the Canadian Producer, soft-edged, stubborn, uselessly nationalistic, well-meaning and hopelessly compromised by his inability to stand up and be defined. The Canadian has a sentimental respect for the film star who has long since covered his neuroses in alcoholic be-fuddlement, a machismo and acceptance of the American way. If he stands up and defines himself, it is in terms of the false, funny, tough romanticism that he learned from the movies.

Those who enjoy wallowing in America-phobia—a much more defensible pastime since the last election—will find nice reflections of same in *Escape Entertainment*. Mind you, Bolt goes and spoils it all with that ironic mind of hers. The final irony is saved for the end when the producer decides to salvage his film by reverting to the most tried and true Canadian avoidance of reality—that selfsame America-phobia. Miami reverts to Toronto-hood, the palm trees are chopped down on University Avenue, and the CIA agent is given scenes to play in which he growls—in all sincerity—to the Canadi-ans around him; "We're gonna take you over. We're gonna take you over."

In effect—and not necessarily for its own good—*Escape Enter-tainment* is a hybrid of David French's *Jitters* and Bolt's own *One Night Stand*. Like *Jitters* it's full of vicious dialogue centred around the particular nature of the creative endeavour in which the charac-ters are involved and, like the earlier play, it places that endeavour under the shadow of the entertainment monopoly south of the bor-der. But it's like *One Night Stand* in its claustrophobia. *Jitters* had a cast of seven or eight actors while *Escape Entertainment* gloms onto its three characters and gives them or us very little breathing space. That closed-in quality was terrific for creating tension in *One Night Stand*. I wonder whether it doesn't cut against the spirit of comedy in Bolt's new play. I wonder further why characters who sounded interesting—such as the writer and the producer's wife—weren't brought onstage. I sincerely hope that their absence wasn't an aus-terity decision. Perhaps it had to do with the interesting way the three on-stage characters came to seem in their isolation like dif-fering aspects of the same personality. But the airlessness is a bit stifling and Bolt's characters attack each other with even more vigour than did French's. The dialogue is very very tightly structured with, for instance, an opening scene in which two characters talk simultaneously about two different topics, making no connections. But the sequence is written so skilfully that each train of thought is clear. Good rhythmically sensitive writing like this gives aesthetic pleasure all by itself.

Throughout, the basis of the humour is in the fact that each character is sealed off from the others so that no matter how vicious the attack it slides off without much pain. If *One Night Stand* was a comedy posing as a suspense shocker, *Escape Entertainment* is a shocker posing as a comedy. Aside from the rapacious dialogue there are recurring moments of physical violence that are deflected into humour (although it's clear that the violence could have followed through). Psychic violence is likewise deflected into laughter. In the last scene there is a violent deflection that I'm not very comfortable with. The characters and the whole play are deflected into a plot wrap-up that is much too cosy with parody to be satisfying: a lark is a lark, a play is a play, and rarely the twain shall meet.

5 January 1981

Nathan Cohen: A Review

Written by Rick Salutin, directed by Paul Thompson.
Toronto Free Theatre

I have an idea that many people will have come away from last night's performance under the impression that they have just seen a bad play enlivened somewhat by the acting of Douglas Campbell. Most people—most spectators and most reviewers—couldn't separate a good play from a bad production if they tried—and they usually don't. The fact is that last night Douglas Campbell appeared in a very bad production of what seems to me a very good play.

It's wonderful that Campbell should be appearing in a new play produced by one of our most established and important small theatres. The indigenous theatre needs actors like Campbell and like Donald Davis (who has appeared at Toronto Free Theatre recently) to benefit from their wisdom and experience. One of the things that is wrong with the structure of our theatre is that William Hutt and

Martha Henry and Douglas Rain rarely collaborate with our younger playwrights and actors in creating new work. Campbell is to be highly commended for helping to break the pattern. He's superb in the part and that's a nice addition.

But the fact is that Campbell is surrounded by a numbing display of self-congratulatory incompetence and bad ginch that—in its own way—is as entrenched and stupefying as the kind of obsessively polished art nouveau posturing that Stratford has been passing off as Shakespeare for years. And as condescending. And as quick with the tongue to the audience's boots.

It is no more than cute and self congratulatory to present a knowingly tacky set (whether or not it's meant to represent an earlier period in this country's theatre) when that set is inefficient and beastly ugly both to the audience's eye and to the actor who has to manage its gawky raked surfaces. I shudder to think of Campbell steeling himself to play scenes behind poorly designed TV frame masks that shadow the face. I shudder for all the actors who have to play a dreadful piece of story mime behind the vilest scrim this side of the Fort Mudge Merrymakers Annual Fish Fry and Stomp Skit Night, who do a halfhearted spoof of Broadway, miming to records piped through some dinky sound system in the rafters and sometimes whispering along. I haven't seen that trick since the Port Nelson United Church Annual Glee Club and Fun Fest of 1965. Nor is it a question of production values here. It's a question of what is theatrically effective and the quality of imagination.

But I think this play should be seen—even in its present manifestation. There is lots to enjoy and lots to consider and Cohen's pronouncements are beautifully integrated. Rick Salutin is an interesting writer, not least because he writes in a style that grew out of the collective approach that Passe Muraille has been instrumental in developing. Salutin worked with Passe Muraille during its halcyon years. The style of *Les Canadiens* obviously benefited from his experience there. And in some way *Nathan Cohen: A Review* tells the same story as the earlier play. There was a collective hero in *Les Canadiens* to be sure, but Nathan Cohen follows the same trajectory of a career. The protagonist fumbles into purpose and power, finally becoming a symbol that focuses an aspect of a nation or a culture. The hero is faced with the fact that the symbolic nature of his role is also his irrelevance. This cruel epiphany visited *Les Canadiens* in the conversation with the woman after the election of the PQ. It visits

Nathan Cohen in a conversation with his culture hero Clifford Odets who is sitting by his swimming-pool, writing a film for another burnt out pawn in the system called Presley. (Incidentally, Campbell plays this scene as an object lesson in how to transfer energy to another actor who doesn't have the same strength or technique so that the scene can play effectively. Good for him.) In both plays there is a final scene that returns dignity and meaning to the protagonist and leaves you happy. George Luscombe was right to cut that scene in his reworking of *Les Canadiens*. In my quiet opinion it was sentimental guff. But the equivalent scene in Nathan Cohen works rather nicely. In it Cohen is permitted to see the beginning of new growth in his theatre.

I feel that this play is an advance for Salutin, whether or not he tells the same story. There are scenes in *Nathan Cohen* that are beautifully conceived. The mature critic commenting on his own life in process, watching impatiently from an audience position as his young self tries to write his first review. In a good production— preferably with Douglas Campbell in the title role once again (he makes of Cohen a fully comprehensible human being and of his aspirations something noble)—several of these scenes would be devastating. But in so many sections, some of them straightforward arguments and encounters, others tricky bits in which more than one action is occurring, Paul Thompson's technical deficiencies as a director trip things up fierce and plenty. And the cast members, with the exception of David Bolt who has a few moments, aren't up to the high style and the technical flexibility necessary for the thing. To the younger actors in the cast and to the director and the designer I say with all good intentions: "Swallow thy pride. Get thee to Luscombe and take you the lessons that you should have taken years ago."

29 January 1981

Rexy!

Written by Alan Stratton, directed by Brian Rintoul. Phoenix Theatre

Jean-Claude Germaine of Montreal's Théâtre d'Aujourd'hui said last fall that he couldn't understand why English Canadians hadn't built a play around Mackenzie King. "He is," quoth M. Germaine, "the biggest nut case you can find." (In fact I know of at least one previous play in which King figured and that was James Reaney's *The Dismissal*. Reaney's play had King as a young U of T student, hopelessly compromised even then by the conflicting forces in his personality.) But I don't know of a full length play about the man. Now—as if to answer Germaine's implied challenge—comes Alan Stratton's *Rexy!* For some reason I had the horrible impression that *Rexy!* was going to be a musical about Mackenzie King. Maybe that had something to do with that title which rubs me the wrong way. It smacks of Broadway vehicles for musical stars geriatric enough to play presidents. I'm sure that in ten years or so the Broadway stage will see a new musical called *Dicky* about Nixon's Watergate travails. In a way *Rexy!* is a Canadian variant on the kind of American play that reduces all history, all intelligence, all play of ideological forces, to the personality of one great figure. It's a Canadian variant because the great figures have become great buffoons. *Rexy!*, although not—thank the Lord—a musical, is a comedy. And at times it almost seems to be pursuing nothing more profound than Germaine's description of King as a nut case. Almost but not quite. Stratton knows enough to keep to a clear line of dramatic action and he does so by telling one story—King's behaviour during the war—and following one series of confrontations—his fight with Colonel Ralston against the use of conscription. The line of things gets a bit muddled in the second act but for the most part Stratton keeps to it, weaving around it King's adventures with the spirit world (his mother and grandfather appear as onstage presences); King's shrewd and petty ability to manipulate anyone with ideals or a sense of fair play; and his total inability to manipulate anyone, like Roosevelt, who understood King's weaselly mind because he had one of his own, only bigger.

There is no mincing of words. King is a contemptible little nub in this play. And were that all Stratton had to say, this would be a contemptible little play. As it is, I find myself uneasy with the author's conscienceless picking through the pockets of history to come up with a play that never quite cuts itself loose from what it purloins. As a rule it exploits fact and historical incident with, mind you, a good theatrical eye. It's grounded in no ideology, offers no real sense of history, nor any interpretation of King's character that hasn't been standard stuff for newspaper columnists for ages. At least it's been standard since the publication of his de-Pickersgilled diaries. Although it is clearly a comedy I am uneasy with derisive laughter inspired by such familiar things as Lester Pearson's lisp and his quaint use of phrases such as "goodness gracious." I'm uneasy because the laughter is elicited very much for its own sake and seems cheap in context.

Despite all this, watching *Rexy!* at the Phoenix, I had as fully enjoyable an evening as I have had in the theatre this entire season. Stratton knows how to put a play together dammit, no mean feat. He is helped enormously by a really fine, sympathetic and self-effacing performance by Larry Reynolds in the title role. The actor—for me at least—removed most of the dyspepsia from the project.

I really think that *Rexy!* will be a very big popular success—and I even feel pretty good about that. In one way *Rexy!* is no better than *Maggie and Pierre*. I found that play excruciating in its earnest, goggle-eyed attempts to transcend its own roots in sensational exploitation. *Rexy!* steps off from the same starting point with no apology and manages to find something fairly interesting. There are a handful of effective monologues by King in which the prime minister tries foggily to come to grips with his own soul. There is at least one speech—on his deathbed—that is fine writing by any standard. Spare, poetic, it jumps out of the play into very interesting territory. The line in which King speaks of having built a ruin with fresh mortar is rooted in a well known incident, and yet it reverberates in its context, and becomes an unforced and suggestive metaphor.

But more than these isolated moments, Stratton has put together his play very very shrewdly. Would it be possible to have made of this material anything but a comedy or, perhaps, a Gothic melodrama played on the edge of comedy? There is pathos in King's life but played straightforwardly for that end, the sight of a grown man singing hymns over the coffin of his dog would not be edifying. Situated as it is in a comedy, the laughter keeps catching in our throats. This is the great shrewdness of Stratton's play. And, finally, its claim to seriousness. This canny employment of scenes based on incidents too funny to be tragic, too pathetic (if not tragic) to be funny, is something to admire. It reaches a marvellous climax with King's death scene. On his deathbed, King grapples once again with his place in history. Always struggling to come through is the terrible light of self-recognition. But soothingly the shadows appear.

The shades of his mother and his grandfather (William Lyon Mackenzie, to whose memory he has struggled to be worthy) lure him to his death by chanting a stupefying little poem from King's diary about his beloved dog, now a lonely dog-angel waiting forlornly for his master to join him. This is stunning theatre. Even in its monstrous pathos, its use of hideous sentiment, it is as gripping as a death scene should be. And in those final moments we get a terrifying sense of a half-aware, brutally deluded sensibility teetering on the edge of truth.

Winter 1981

Plenty

Written by David Hare, directed by Peter Dew. St. Lawrence Centre

I have the feeling I've seen a great play in David Hare's *Plenty*. I won't know until I've seen it again—and I will see it again; the production at the St. Lawrence Centre is a good one. If it isn't a great play it has the feel of one. At curtain you have the sense that wonderful things have been revealed—things that may be simple, may be complex, but resist words. In the best of all radio worlds I would wait and see it again and mull at it a while. As it is I'll muster what I can of my understanding. Unless you are comfortable reducing art to allegory or to the motivations of a single character or to something safe and contained and suitable for party chat, you won't come out of *Plenty* clear about it at all. Which is not to say that the theatrical experience is difficult. There's a tough, clear, hard arc of dramatic action running through a series of self-contained scenes, all of which depict crucial periods in the life of a single magnificent character.

Because the character is a woman who comes out of the second world war marked for life, and because the play follows her career from that point, *Plenty* will be compared to Fassbinder's *Marriage of Maria Braun*. I think there is no real comparison. To these eyes at least, Fassbinder's film remained within its allegorical framework, content to play coolly with irony and melodrama there. *Plenty* dares so much more and achieves very close to what it dares. I think, surprisingly, of Chaplin's *Monsieur Verdoux*, another deeply serious comedy disguised as—and often mistaken for—a social satire. Both works deal with a character whose solipsism is both monstrous and beautiful in its purity. And both central characters shore up a secret and dangerously unreal sentimental idealism and they protect it with violence.

Susan has been a spy in World War II and her idealism is locked into a moment on a hill in occupied France. There she shared her fear with a young paratrooper she had only just met: a perfect moment of union because it is final, free, complete and unpossessive. Her sense of what her life and the world can be is forever tied up in that memory. And she spends her life protecting that unreal image. Her best friend after the war (beautifully played by Nicky Guadagni) is an androgynous would-be artist who lives outside society by embracing a Bohemian existence. But Susan takes a half-route of semi-respectability, working hard all the time to disassociate herself from her surroundings. She tries to have a child free of an emotional entanglement, but the poor stiff with whom she makes attempt after failed attempt gets involved with her and gets shot for trying to press it. Susan has carried a gun since the war, but after the shooting the gun is never seen—as she trades her independence for marriage. Her husband is an old lover who swoops her up out of a mental breakdown. He works for the foreign office and is regularly posted in one or another of Britain's dwindling colonies. Their marriage contains a phenomenon I've never seen given a treatment worthy of it. For this well-meaning guy is truly out to colonize Susan through kindness, through patience (Scot Denton's placid voice and manner are perfect for the part). To her credit Susan never stops seeing through this very nice, self-deceiving guy. But she spends the marriage on the edge of madness. Finally she leaves him after destroying the physical evidence of their life together—their belongings, her clothes.

The play ends with two heart-piercing scenes. Susan, a harridan by now, is visited by the paratrooper who—it is suggested—like her, has never been able to forget that moment of union on the hilltop. Susan falls into a dope-induced dream and we see her once again on a fairytale hilltop in France just after the liberation speaking to a French farmer and filled with a fierce joy. Her last words are "there will be days and days of this, my friend." Whether or not this incident is a dream, there is a painful unreality to this meeting, and John Ferguson's flat cartoon-like setting for this scene suggests this very well.

I think I've said that the Peter Dew's production is a very good one. But, even so, much depends on the actress in the leading part. Dixie Seatle is a very good actress in a part that asks for a great one. Within that limitation she works well and intelligently to fill that part. She does so in quite a remarkable fashion, even when she has to rely on a certain extravagance of technique. But back to the play.

There are elements of allegory at work in *Plenty*—the characters' situations standing for declining post-war society in Britain. And there is, if you insist, a simple implied moral: that to take part in a decaying society and to hold onto one's integrity are contradictory efforts that can only end in madness. But the play goes beyond these things. *Plenty* seems to me to tread the dangerous outer edges of the human spirit where only great art dares to venture.

Winter 1981

Toronto Arts Production: A Capsule History and Unpleasant Diatribe

Way way back not so long ago in the spring years of Toronto theatre, when Toronto Workshop Productions was established enough to send shows like *Chicago 70* to New York; when Theatre Passe Muraille was tilling the soil for its first big homegrown bloom with *The Farm Show*, and Factory Theatre Lab was emptying the drawers of every indigent writer in the vicinity for scripts; when Martin Kinch and Tom Hendry were getting Toronto Free Theatre underway, and Bill Glassco was about to do the same with Tarragon. Way back in the midst of this furious all-of-a-sudden activity there appeared in Toronto a theatrical giant that trod with heavy foot and spoke with a great voice. Its name was the St. Lawrence Centre. It flew the grand old banner of Theatrical Standards, the same banner that most official regional centres have held high since "Our Stratford" showed the way in 1953. And it proclaimed with flourish and fanfare that, despite the coldness of its cement façade and its cement interior set off by royal blue carpeting, despite the 830 seats of its formidable main hall, and the tuxedoed front of house staff, it proclaimed that the St. Lawrence Centre was "The People's Theatre." Now if that puzzles you, consider that the St. Lawrence

Centre was a kind of instant, ready-quik institution, and that the year was 1969 when institutions still quaked at the word "relevance." And the "People," of course, were really relevant.

To prove that it was as good as its name, The People's Theatre opened with a translation of Quebec playwright Jacques Languirand's *Man Inc*. Well right there you've got to ask yourself what "People" the St. Lawrence Centre had in mind. Certainly not the people of the Toronto *Star* with protest letters, every time a tad more than token French appears on their TV screens.

But it was brave of artistic director Mavor Moore in any case. And it was brave to do a season of Canadian plays. But they weren't well received; it wasn't tried again. Mavor Moore left for York University, Leon Major arrived fresh from Neptune, and everyone threw nasty tomatoes at him as he wrestled with that great beast of a theatre for ten years.

From the beginning, Toronto Arts Production had trouble figuring just what it was supposed to do. When it began its slow lumber to existence weighed down by its ungainly stage space, its board of directors, and the other baggage that accrues to any official arts organization, it was clear what Toronto needed by way of theatre: it needed more theatre. There was little enough around. There was George Luscombe, but he didn't say nice things all the time, and he was a socialist to boot. And there were those colonial appendages, the touring houses—the Royal Alex and the O'Keefe. But Toronto didn't have what Halifax, Fredericton, Winnipeg, Edmonton and Vancouver had: an official theatre offering its library services to the region.

However, by the time the St. Lawrence Centre opened its doors, Toronto was popping with theatrical activity of one sort or another, and Leon Major had to find a role for his theatre to play. Inevitably this boiled down to doing plays that the smaller theatres couldn't afford to do—modern classics, new plays from Britain and the States, or neglected larger scale plays. But just as inevitably there was really only one thing that the St. Lawrence Centre was or could be, despite Major's efforts: it was rich. Where else in town could you find anything like the matchstick Taj Mahals designed by Murray "The Set" Laufer? But Major kept plugging, even when later in the decade small theatres such as Tarragon and Toronto Free were cutting the ground under his feet by doing very similar repertoire. When Major left last year, the role of Toronto Arts Productions—as the artistic arm of the enterprise is now called—was no clearer than it had ever been.

I'm happy to report that with the arrival of artistic director Eddie Gilbert, it's clear at last what TAP is. It's the Toronto theatre that can afford to hire Len Cariou to make a ham casserole out of *Macbeth*. (At one point he used, for an entire monologue, a corny stage whisper straight out of radio's old Inner Sanctum series.) It's the Toronto theatre that can afford a large cast of talented actors for the same play, and find incredibly inventive ways of making them look silly. It can even manage a large cast for a *new* play—René Aloma's *A Little Something to Ease the Pain*—so that instead of finding ways to strengthen that script it could turn the stage into a small scale Cuban Carnival for the delectation of the suburban subscribers. It's the Toronto theatre that can afford to hire John Hirsch and allow him to put together a mild prance and giggle show out of that decayed old chestnut *A Funny Thing Happened on the Way to the Forum*. Speaking of decay, TAP can afford to replace a David French play with a shambling old wreck of a Terence Rattigan script, *The Winslow Boy,* coughing and sputtering and spitting into the mothballs.

There is one exception to all of this waste and tedium. David Hare's *Plenty* was a brilliant fragmented melodrama even when guest artist Peter Dews directed it a bit cozily for its own good.

As for Eddie Gilbert, there were no artistic trends visible in his season. I see no sign of personal conviction in his choice of plays. Except for a certain cacophony of acting approaches, and a preoccupation with the naked male posterior, TAP's productions this year bore no stamp at all. And aside from a few pretty effects in the René Aloma play I saw no evidence of a directory in Eddie Gilbert. In fact he's absolutely perfect for an official theatre centre.

No more Leon Major soul searching, no attempts to address society. We can expect a packaging of saleable shows, sold by the presence of stars like Len Cariou or Dixie Seatle or Gerard Parkes. TAP seems to have thought out its position and is on the right track at last. It's a regional Theatre Centre like all the rest, cozy in the death clasp of officially sanctioned culture.

April 1981

For the Dying, for the Dead, for the Living
From Laughing at the World to Living in the World

Two plays by Bertolt Brecht, directed and performed by Ekkehard Schall.
Toronto Theatre Festival—On Stage 81

Brecht wrote about one thousand poems. Only a small proportion of them were published during his lifetime. Until last year, when a good edition of his poems appeared in English, they were not easy to come by. Which is all by way of saying that I know very little of Brecht's poetry. And I would be very skeptical of those critical reports from the English-speaking press that make pretty claims for the power of great acting to transcend the language barrier. Mr. Schall is not here to provide us with a textbook summary of the acting style of the Berliner Ensemble. He is offering a theatrical presentation of a particular literature. Speaking for myself, I estimate that I absorbed only a small percentage of the impact of the show. My eye was forced to hop from performer to translation constantly, and even when I managed that with some facility I still had to be content with an uneasy compromise between words and the quick and precise verbal and physical inflections of the performer.

However I must say that the experience was never frustrating. There was too much of extraordinary interest to take in. First of all the poems struck me as wonderful, even when snatched from page and performer like bits of a fine meal hastily picked at a bus stopover. I was going to refer to the translation of the poem Schall read, but I liked the one that followed it. This is the opening of a poem called *To Those Born Later*.

> Truly I live in dark times!
> The guileless word is folly. A smooth forehead
> Suggests insensitivity. The man who laughs
> Has simply not yet had
> The terrible news.
> What kind of times are they, when
> A talk about trees is almost a crime
> Because it implies silence about so many horrors?

Of course he sang many of Brecht's songs, and it was in the songs that I felt that the real punch of Schall's performance could be imagined through the language problem. The attenuated line of a musical phrase allows you to catch up with the lyric, and the musical structure supplies the necessary bridgework for the ear that's unfamiliar with German.

But, of course, great material or no, for a North American theatre enthusiast there is a lot of curiosity in simply having the opportunity to see Schall. Earlier I made the point that Schall wasn't here to demonstrate the approach of the Berliner Ensemble. But that was surely a major focus of interest for most of the audience, myself included. The thing that immediately strikes you is how spare his performing is. He does several elaborately acted show stoppers, one a song sung by a frightened little creep of a bootlicker, speaking out in the loud voice of the coward who has to justify his actions, the impulses of bravado and of fear springing against each other in jerky escalations of unpleasant compulsiveness. In this and in other songs, Schall paints his pictures vividly enough to print hard the meaning of the character over the natural charm of watching an actor's ability to change. But most of the time Schall's body and his eyes and his voice are used like the most precious of natural resources to point, to underscore, to twist a line in mid-syllable from one sense to another. The convincing fact about his very supple technique in presenting a song, for instance, is how strong, intelligent and invigorating it looks when placed beside the truly ugly, impossibly stupid and embarrassingly vulgar American style of modern musical performing, a style that has all but swamped English speaking musical theatre, eviscerated American popular song-writing and ruined dozens of otherwise talented singers and dancers. That style cajoles, flatters, wheedles and lubricates its audience, does all the work for it, and demonstrates that feelings can be had over nothing. But Schall points with every gesture to something outside the performer, and acknowledges with every throb of his tight, sharply-focused voice that there is a world outside the performance. The strong emotions he elicits are not voyeuristic, but shared responses to that world, its madness and its fleeting pleasures.

May 1981

The Blyth Festival

In 1975 when James Roy, founder of the Blyth Festival, was piecing together his first season, he lodged in place what he thought was a safe piece of insurance. Along with the new or recent Canadian scripts that formed the heart of the season, Roy scheduled Agatha Christie's *The Mousetrap*, which had been running in London since it's-hard-to-care-how-long and had just started a similar run in Toronto. Roy expected it to pull in crowds. But in that same season there was a play by local writer Harry Boyle and, to everyone's delighted surprise, Boyle outstripped Christie by a country mile. If the Blyth Festival people had been looking for a sign that building a Festival on new work aimed at a local audience was a sound one, they had it.

Blyth represents certain things to people who care about theatre. Behind the Festival is the idea that Theatrical Standards—meaning a certain professional smoothness in the technical presentation of theatre—might be secondary to trying to speak directly to a particular audience on particular subjects even if the form the plays take turns out to be a bit rough or unfinished.

This approach to theatre should be put into an historical context. In 1953 the new Stratford Festival became a great benchmark in Canadian theatre. Its major effect was on the technical quality of what little theatre there was here. For well over a decade every Canadian theatre strove to be worthy of Stratford's example. When there was a break from that tradition in Toronto in the late sixties, the many artists—Stratford "rejects," as Tom Hendry calls himself and his compatriots who formed the Small Theatre movement—challenged, partly through expedience, the whole Stratford International Tradition of Quality Theatre. They had to, as its expense and its weight of cultural baggage was crippling to an emerging theatre.

There grew out of this an unarticulated aesthetic of Anti-Quality Theatre that's best seen in Toronto in the kind of work that Paul Thompson still does with the collective at Theatre Passe Muraille.

It's arguable that the Blyth Festival, where many alumni of Passe Muraille work, is now in many ways the Ontario centre of Thompson's rough theatre tradition. I say this even though this last season at Blyth contained only one semi-collective. And that play was not one of the hits of the summer. The play was *Fire on Ice*, which the

Blyth company took from Keith Roulston's musical about Howie Morenz, legendary Montreal Canadien, and also—significantly—a native of Mitchell, Ontario, not far from Blyth.

In the present season of five plays, artistic director Janet Amos included three traditional scripts. One of them was a new thriller by Carol Bolt based—fancifully—on the mysterious disappearance of Toronto Theatre Impresario Ambrose Small in 1919. Perhaps an attempt to hit another *I'll Be Back Before Midnight*, *Love or Money* had a lot of Miss Bolt's strengths—some good nasty dialogue and a whole festering sinkful of repressions and evil motives. It also had a cheerfully gimmick-ridden second act that was a satisfying as popcorn after a good roast of beef.

Two plays by Anne Chislett broke box office records this summer. One was *The Tomorrow Box* which had been such a big hit for Montreal's Centaur Theatre after Dennis Sweeting premiered it in Lindsay last summer. It's a comedy about big city liberal attitudes hitting rural Ontario. The second was *Quiet in the Land*, an absorbing drama about conflict between the generations in a Western Ontario Amish colony during the years of the first World War. Miss Chislett is a good honest writer of dramatic narrative. If we had a decent outlet for TV drama in this country she would easily find a niche writing the kind of nicely crafted TV series the BBC has been sending us for years.

Finally came the biggest box office hit of all; Ted Johns' *He Won't Come in from the Barn*, a reworking of a 1977 Passe Muraille collective about an old farmer who barricades himself against the world of modern farming. The play was directed by Paul Thompson himself, and held over well past Blyth's usual closing date. It featured several live chickens and two well-behaved cows and received roars of approval from its audiences. Great art it wasn't nor was it meant to be. It was—if truth be told—a bit clubby, leaning on audience friendliness to quite some degree.

This summer at Blyth saw the most successful season in a series of successful seasons. It was also a success in making something theatrical out of life in a certain community, as all of the scripts but the Bolt piece derive more or less directly from life in small town and rural Western Ontario.

Whether or not Blyth will ever give us great art is an interesting question. If Blyth does create significant works without losing the intimacy it's enjoyed with its audience, then I think it will have to be recognized as one of the most significant developments in Canadian theatre. But if Blyth fails to do so then it will be because it was satisfied to rest on what it has already developed; on a pleasing chumminess with its audience; on a kind of democratic populism that—whatever its strengths—can be as cloying and smug as the worst kind of theatre elitism; and on an inverted snobbery about its casual, sometimes sloppy stagecraft. I still find Blyth one of the most exciting experiments we have in creating theatre. But if it gets stuck in any one of those grooves it will suffer a theatrical death-in-life that is the perfect mirror image of Stratford's long-time malaise. That would be an irony more sad than funny.

September 1981

Stratford 1981

By any standards the present season at Stratford is miles ahead of last year's marathon of sequined mediocrity. It was produced on short notice by John Hirsch's associate Muriel Sherrin, with Hirsch acting as a figurehead to give newspapers and magazines something to talk about rather than art. Starting in January of this year, three months late, Sherrin—and presumably Hirsch—arranged for five experienced directors to handle the eight plays of the season, and put together a company of actors that was in every way superior to the poor spiritless bunch that crowded the edges of last year's stages looking on with dead or anxious eyes as various star actors took turns milking the audience. There were only a few instances this year in which the larger company was used as poorly as it tended to be during the reign of Robin the Boy Wonder. The 1981 company, relatively lean and enthusiastic, had the initiative to bring life even to those scenes that a director hadn't shaped terribly well. And there was none of that casting of inexperienced, untalented or simply inappropriate actors in key roles that marred even the better Phillips productions.

What Stratford offered us for the most part this year was solid, intelligent work. This is not to be taken lightly. What we have been getting in recent years is bad flashy work. Peter Dews directed *Comedy of Errors* and *Taming of the Shrew* as if he knew that the primary source of inspiration for the actor must be the text. His productions were a reminder that ingenious readings—Phillips' *Twelfth Night* was an egregious example—often betray a want of just those qualities they seek to advertise: a want of imagination, a want of conviction. Instead of straining to be noticed by working against the text, the actors in Peter Dews' productions found their meanings and their working rhythms inside the plays, and that's not as simple as it sounds. As a result there was the gratifying sense of something running free, easy and to a satisfying end.

Jean Gascon gave us two mildly stylized productions. *The Misanthrope*, an attempt at classicism, was not a success, but was fascinating as long as Brian Bedford held the stage. Bedford did what he always does: he used a technique of great precision and economy to seduce the audience into such intimacy with his character that the rest of the production had to be filtered through his emotional centre. He unbalanced *The Misanthrope* with a vulnerable cuddly Alceste who seemed more reasonable than Molière's voices of reason.

Gascon's production of Friedrich Dürrenmatt's *The Visit*, which made use of stylized, representational sets and incorporated some inventive scene changes, was wholly absorbing. Yet the dramatic impact of the piece was oddly muted in a way that is to me the true Stratford trademark. The play requires a certain flexibility of style that the Stratford company has never had. The actors failed for instance to adapt themselves to the subjective nightmare quality of the second act. Even William Hutt, very fine indeed as Anton Schill, could well have used a turn of the expressionist screw. But the muted aspect of the production was best seen in John Ferguson's sets which were clever and picturesque without being particularly expressive of the play's tormented core.

That the characteristic Stratford muting of dramatic experience can be overcome was clear from Brian Bedford's exciting production of *Coriolanus*. No matter how much it was limited by what looked like rigid direction of the actors, by unrelieved declamatory acting, by a certain simplification of the play's dreadful ironies, and by Len Cariou's doggedness in the title role, *Coriolanus* took risks with stagecraft that are rare at Stratford. It often attempted a theatrical poetry rare on any stage and almost as often succeeded. Many of the images, such as the opening slow lights-up on a huge rumbling mass that is revealed to be a restless mob, had great power.

Bedford also directed a production of Sheridan's very slight comedy *The Rivals*, the distinguishing characteristics of which were pretty sets, pretty costumes and a number of Bedford mannerisms distributed throughout the cast. It was deadly. It wasn't a case of simple failure of intention, common enough in theatre. It was that there was no sense of *why* the artists involved were doing the play, let alone *what* they were doing with it.

There were two other slight plays in the season. But in both cases it was clear that the artists working on them had a passion to do so, had something they wanted to say by doing them. I'm speaking of *H.M.S. Pinafore* in which a spirited young company helped Leon Major unleash his own passion for stagecraft, and of *The Comedy of Errors* in which the sextet of young actors at the core of the play discovered elements of meaning and pleasure that are not obvious in reading it. But the particular nature of the failure of *The Rivals* soured my experience of the Festival. It raised old doubts about the possibility of good art flourishing in such an institution as Stratford.

It may seem ungrateful to carp at a generally pleasurable season, produced under duress. Yet my feeling is that things have not really changed at all in Stratford. My suspicions were first twigged by an alleged interview with Michael Schonberg, literary manager of Stratford, that appears in the souvenir booklet under the ingenuous title "Classical Theatre For Everybody." In this little public relations effort (which yearns after meaning like a successful madam yearns after respectability) Mr. Schonberg tip-toes daintily around the aesthetic meaning of the term Classical Theatre. All I could gather from the piece is Mr. Schonberg's assurance that while watching classical theatre you will not be disturbed by anything contemporary. Therefore, presumably, you will be free to dally harmlessly with the Great Abstractions of Art, itself the greatest abstraction of all.

The truth of the matter is this: the term classical theatre means only two things. It refers first of all to plays that have been preserved from generation to generation so that everybody knows their names. Secondly it implies big plays that only rich theatres can afford to do in the still accepted mainstream international style. It has no aesthetic meaning whatsoever. And this is why a piece like "Classical Theatre For Everyone" is defeated before it begins. Where the term Classical Theatre really belongs—and where it is extremely effective—is in the field of marketing. Mr Schonberg's piece is really a clumsy version of the glossy full-page apologias the oil companies have been putting out for years.

Stratford is still straddling two shaky horses. One runs pell-mell after the kind of wide popularity that will fuel a major North American tourist attraction. The other trots proudly around a false altar of Pure Art. Art and popularity are not exclusive. But I see little evidence that Stratford has even considered any route but marketing to attract its audience. As for art, Stratford makes misguided obeisance before a certain conception of tastefulness, the best correlative of which is the middle-brow style of the MGM studios in the thirties and forties.

There were a good many things of interest in the 1981 Festival season. But I suspect their source was largely in the new blood injected into the beast. I suspect also that a similar excitement was there in the first seasons of Langham, Gascon and Phillips. I sincerely hope that John Hirsch will prove me wrong by finding a way to sustain that energy.

September 1981

Jennie's Story

Written by Betty Lambert, directed by Bill Glassco. St Lawrence Centre

What Betty Lambert has tried to do in *Jennie's Story* is a very ambitious thing. She's attempted a genuine contemporary tragedy. She hasn't merely heightened a prairie farm house drama with poetic language, say. In fact she attempts little heightened language at all, and probably should cut the little she has. Nor has she written a psychological dissection of the common man, Arthur Miller style. Lambert has actually ventured into tragedy's world of fate and magic where great forces of good and evil play.

Jennie, the heroine and a natural life force, has roots that go back at least as far as Emily Brontë's Cathy in *Wuthering Heights*. She has lots of antecedents in Canadian literature and drama as well, particularly in prairie literature. I'm thinking of the heroine of Johanna Glass's *Canadian Gothic*, for instance. Lambert's Jennie is a pagan spirit who communes quite naturally with forces too powerful for Christianity to circumscribe. Organized religion in the play is present in the person of Father Fabrizeau, another who is at root a common figure of nineteenth century literature: the failed priest twisted to evil after losing the struggle with his animal nature.

Some years prior to the action of the play, Father Fabrizeau seduced the young Jennie, and although the pregnancy and subsequent abortion were more or less covered up, Jennie was left barren. When she discovers this after her marriage to a laughing Irishman, the pagan spirit at her centre turns against her and eats her up.

Act I only nibbles at the edges of Lambert's serious intentions. It seems a bit lightweight. But Act II opens with a lightning storm, and it ain't kiddin'. Few tragedies are without elements of melodrama, but the second act of *Jennie's Story* is rife with earnest and clumsy melodrama and is difficult to endure.

It was suggested to me after the performance that if Lambert were to cut the play by a third there might be a dramatic experience at the core worth developing. But I suspect that enthusiastic editing would merely reveal the same faults that were apparent in Lambert's political allegory *Clouds of Glory*: a schematic ordering of events and character that chokes any possible artistic life out of the material. *Jennie's Story*, for instance, is structured around the natural progression of the seasons, and each of the seasons is made to carry with it all of its conventional associations. In the autumn, for example, Jennie reaps her harvest of sorrow. In winter she dies with the natural world. In the spring there is a newborn baby and the remaining characters making a new start and so forth. The characters, particularly Jennie and the Priest, retain their emblematic roles to the bitter end.

The real tedium in last night's very tedious play was in the recurrent effort on the part of the characters to clarify their actions, their very nature, long after these things had been made all too clear. A play that doesn't rely primarily on narrative can't afford to give away what's going on in such a profligate manner. Trying to sort out unstated action, and the meaning of it, is the major appeal of most plays, and I'm surprised that an experienced playwright like Lambert should be oblivious to that simple fact.

Despite the failure of *Jennie's Story*, I find myself thinking kindly of it. The author has picked up a genre that Canadian playwrights have made their own and tried to take it beyond the limits of kitchen sink drama. The desire to mythologize (or to seek the mythology behind the things we've recorded) has been present for some time in the work of novelists as diverse as Robertson Davies and Margaret Laurence. If the theatre that we've seen spring up around us these last ten years is to grow in scope and artistic ambition it will likely spring from similar artistic impulses. And these impulses are there in *Jennie's Story*. They just need to be developed properly.

October 1981

The Riddle of the World

Written by David French, directed by Bill Glassco. Tarragon Theatre

David French's new play is a comedy with a number of sharp, funny situations but it's also something of an ideas play. No matter how strenuously the characters hole up in closets, holler through doors, and bang their heads against door frames, the play is still in earnest about its philosophical explorations.

The Riddle of the World is about two new bachelors coming to terms with their natures as men in a world with few signposts of male identity left erect. Ron, who has always seen himself as a bit of a stud, undergoes the humiliation of having his live-in girlfriend refuse to sleep with him when her guru declares her a spiritual being. Steve, on the other hand, is a kind of mirror inversion of Ron. An ex-priest, he's in the process of being divorced by his sexually aggressive wife after it's become apparent that his honeymoon impotence is a permanent condition. The two men move in together and ruthlessly badger and prod at each other's erotic and spiritual natures.

I spoke about the play's philosophical explorations. Perhaps I should have spoken about its use of the explorations of others: notably T.S. Eliot, Alexander Pope and the Prophets of the Old Testament whose writings are quoted at key ironic moments. As read by Hardee Linehan and Joe Ziegler under Bill Glassco's direction, they are also among the most intense moments of the play—true climaxes. This is not a bad achievement when one considers that an important dramatic moment is assigned to Alexander Pope's *Essay on Man*.

The subject of the play is nothing less than the nature of Man. This would seem to make a rather heavy evening of it, but that's not the case. *The Riddle of the World* is, among other things, a farce, and it is such because French finds his subject in that most comic of phenomena: the psychological contortions of the modern male, trying to find a reflection of his nature in something that is not life-denying, simple-minded, or romantically quasi-homosexual.

I'd wondered for some time why nobody had written a play like *The Riddle of the World*. Can it be that the dilemma of the modern male is too painful for a man to contemplate and too negligible for a woman?

I believe *Riddle of the World* is not a negligible play, and I think it is, at least potentially, a very good play, because it roots out the male dilemma not simply to sneer but to empathize honestly, if wryly, and to seek a meaning in it. What French finds in the sad, funny, but ultimately dignified lives of his two unspectacularly endowed men is as old as the Bible. And it doesn't hurt to relate a contemporary sexual anguish to the oldest and deepest philosophical strains in the Western world.

It's interesting to me that by far the best scenes—those scenes that are the most engaging and even the funniest—are those in which French's two central characters really go at each other's opposite perceptions of life. At some moments the play actually reaches the level of Shaw's better work. Where I found the play tiresome was in the frequent exchange of dialogue designed largely to fill out the laugh quota. It was here that I sensed an uncertainty on the playwright's part about stepping out on challenging ground.

I have a grim feeling that *The Riddle of the World* is going to suffer commercially, and I feel sorry about that. It's truly encouraging to watch a good artist like French stretch further. And when a good artist is stretching, his work may for a time lack smoothness and polish. The climate of Toronto theatre right now is very bad for art. Our daily reviewers, whose only real function is to reflect that climate, only look for polished, self-contained entertainments that will not ask of them commitment of any sort. Last spring, during the Theatre Festival, one did not have to be an admirer of James Reaney's *Gyroscope* to be disturbed by a review such as the one in the *Globe and Mail* that betrayed such contempt for art, such ignorance of what art is and can be, that even at this date I recall with horror its clammy, witless tone of entrenched mundanity. David French would have been safer to have tried to repeat *Jitters* than to go out on a large limb where he's a big target for little pea shooters.

But needless to say he's to be valued all the more as a writer because he has done so.

Fall 1981

The Passing Scene

Written by Erika Ritter, directed by William Lane. Tarragon Theatre

Let's start with the obvious and go on from there. In her new play,
Erika Ritter preserves some of the strengths of her recent success of
Automatic Pilot and elaborates on its weaknesses. By that I mean
simply that the ratio between sharp comedy and light drama has
been reversed. In *The Passing Scene* we end up with far too few
scenes of comedy and these tend to act as a hook for far too many
scenes of lightweight drama.

The play tells the story of a small town Canadian writer and a
brash American reporter falling in love after a New York Book
Bash. Writer/film-maker Billy Wilder has a term for the kind of
quick flip shorthand that comedy writers use to get over the sticky
business of lovers meeting for the first time. He calls it "meeting
cute." By that he means there's a snappy twist involving mistaken
identities or wrong assumptions. This sets up some snappy aggressive dialogue between the potential lovers and the audience is left
charmed, breathless and in no mood to question the plausibility of
the situation. The snappy patter is a convention that suggests that
the lovers are souls in harmony despite themselves. In *The Passing
Scene* the lovers "meet cute" at the book party when the reporter
insults the heroine's book, not knowing she's the author, tosses it
into a potted plant and comes up to her hotel room with a bottle of
wine to apologize. It's a neat trick, and it could sustain a brittle
comedy. This comedy could also be serious, the seriousness none the
less real for being deflected by humour. But within half an hour of
the reporter's arrival he has wrung from the heroine an emotional
confession that clearly springs right from the core of her being. Now
the convention of "meeting cute" doesn't prepare the audience or
the characters for this change. It's not the change in tone that's
disturbing. It's that we have been asked to accept the plausibility of
the meeting according to certain comic conventions and we end up

having the relationship developed through no set of conventions at all, save perhaps those of psychological naturalism. As a result of the switch in convention in Act I of *The Passing Scene*, the meeting of the lovers rings false in retrospect. I, for one, wondered what those two saw in each other. I was still wondering in Act II when they meet again on an L.A. talk show, and in Act III when they are married and she confronts him over his infidelity.

Now there is intelligence in all of this. The skeletal structure is carefully worked out. In that final scene, for instance, the roles are reversed and she wrings a confession from him using his Carl Bernstein techniques. During the course of the play, political events contemporary to the action, mostly having to do with Watergate, are meant to reflect their five year relationship. And there is a juggling of private and public roles as the two central characters become celebrities of sorts. I don't think the play is a finished work, but there's a mature, open-ended feel to it that I like very much. This is consistent with all of Ritter's work to date. All of her plays deal with couples trying to stay intact in the face of external forces—religious, political or simply those of fashion.

What's wrong with the play as it stands, and what makes it seem hardly a play at all, but a series of illustrated ideas, is a misapprehension about the nature of content and the nature of seriousness. *Automatic Pilot* is a serious play, never more so than when it's funny. Think of its final scene when the stand-up comic turns her failed love affair into fodder for her act. That monologue should be hard, sharp and funny even though it's a self-condemnation, even though it makes you feel as if someone is screeching nails against a blackboard.

I feel that Ritter is doing herself a disservice in her approach to playwriting. I don't simply mean that she should be writing more funny lines or whatever. I believe she is working with a confusion about what can be important to an audience. She has parcelled her writing into two sections: the serious and the funny. She has labelled the funny section glib, which, as a result, it sometimes is. In compensation, she has overvalued the serious aspect and labelled it sincere and honest. Yet her serious scenes are the least artistically honest aspect of her work. Ritter could accomplish—has accomplished, will accomplish—so much more by using her enviable wit and comic deftness, and this without sacrificing in any way the generosity of spirit that is one of her finest qualities as a playwright.

166

I want to say a word about the production. As countless people
have pointed out to me, Erika has been ill-served by the production
at the Tarragon. In particular William Lane, the director, has
steered with more enthusiasm than he should into the softest spots
of the writing, trying to get at the truth of the material where the
truth is least present. Like many Tarragon shows, the play presents
itself on opening night with a half-rehearsed feeling. If you haven't
seen it, wait a couple of weeks.

11 January 1982

The Saga of the Wet Hens

Written by Jovette Marchessault, translated by Linda Gaboriau,
directed by Michele Rossignol. Tarragon Theatre

It's been a long time since I've seen a Toronto audience explode into
excitement as they did at the end of *The Saga of the Wet Hens* last
Thursday night. This is particularly striking as the audience was
even fuller than usual of the bloodless first night note-takers, the
one-handed clappers of the press, who set the jaded tone for dozens
of dismal no-runs. It's even more striking because the general attitude before hand was "wait-and-see-with-teeth-clenched." After
all, haven't we all long passed the stage where a feminist play about
four women coming together to discover their sense of shared
womanhood can have the slightest impact?

Apparently not. But then *The Saga of the Wet Hens* is directed and
performed with real gusto and a lovely sense of the absurd. Monique
Mercure enters whipping over the audience's head on a trapeze.
Diane D'Aquila is lowered in a birdcage or a chandelier, or both;
I'm not sure. And, like all good plays, *The Saga of the Wet Hens* is
about more than it appears to be on the surface. The play takes a
quartet of novelists—all real novelists from Quebec's history—and
has them meet out of time. Each woman carries with her the cultural role demanded by her time. They use their different experiences to find their common identity as artists and as women who
had each responded in different ways to her time.

In the first meeting, Monique Mercure as Laure Conan, Quebec's
very first novelist, takes the role imposed on her as spinster and

outsider and turns it into comic release. Prancing about as a horse she caricatures the gossip that she is a madwoman, a witch. The scene is crucial to understanding the play. It is the first of a series of confrontations with the inhibiting roles imposed on women by priests, doctors and a patriarchal society in general. Some of these scenes are comic, some are dead serious. But in all of them the women take the negative images implicit in these roles and make them positive. They transcend their personal histories of role playing. The climactic transformation from negative to positive takes place when the four writers drop their individual cultural guises to become the wet hens of the title. Donning hen costumes and clucking about, they defy the casual dismissive insult of the term "wet hens." And in coming together in such a surprising guise they transcend their personal histories of role playing. I'm grieved that a reviewer in the *Globe and Mail* missed the wonderful theatrical irony of this climax. I'm sorry that she felt insulted as a woman, but I'm glad that she was very much in the minority. Judging from the reaction on opening night, most women in the audience took the ending as it was intended—as funny and liberating.

The value of *The Saga of the Wet Hens* is that it produces its effects theatrically. One does not get a feminist lecture from the stage. Even if the feminist arguments are familiar, they are given a theatrical embodiment, valid in itself. Jovette Marchessault's lyrical prose has been translated by Linda Gaboriau. There are some clinkers by way of dead phrase that I'm sure would not have jarred in the original French. When Monique Mercure uses the phrase "verbal diarrhea" in the middle of an angry speech it hits the ear with a thunk. It is simply inexpressive common parlance. But for the most part the translation serves a difficult image-laden script well.

Mercure, as the most vulnerable of the four writers, is wonderful. Even more so in retrospect when details of her performance linger and tug at memory's sleeve. Equally fine is Chappell Jaffe's sharp, edgy, low key performance as Anne Hébert: too sophisticated to be comfortable with the earthiness of the other women. When she at last doffs her evening gown for the hen costume, it is a key moment and she makes it sweet and comic and moving. In the past I have found both Jennifer Phipps and Diane D'Aquila very inconsistent actresses. I had occasional trouble with their performances in *The Wet Hens* as well. But Phipps had some quiet intense moments when she focuses the play's image of mother beautifully. And

D'Aquila as Gabrielle Roy worked with a good clean vigour that often made me forget Monique Mercure's brilliance in the same role in the original French production.

Tarragon Theatre brought designer Meredith Caron from Montreal and apparently gave her carte blanche to redesign Tarragon's small space for the production. She has built a semicircle thrust where the audience would normally be. She's used whatever fly space she could gouge from the ceiling of Tarragon's rambling warehouse. I'm sure that director Michele Rossignol had something to do with the design. I am always amused by the nebulous term "good direction." But sometimes you know it when you see it. Director Rossignol has approached Marchessault's script as if it were a musical score with certain themes and movements to shape, and she's done a brilliant job at it. So brilliant that when I was there she clearly conquered the mistrust a North American audience typically holds for rhetoric, stage or otherwise. I trust the wet hens will survive the soggy blankets of Toronto's press.

23 February 1982

Science and Madness

Written by George F. Walker, directed by William Lane.
Tarragon Theatre

I always look forward to a new George F. Walker play. *Science and Madness* turns out to be not only Walker's most ambitious play to date but also a shameless pseudo-melodrama that trundles through its 90-odd minutes with an assortment of hackneyed theatrical effects, brilliantly handled. Fogs, great flashes of light, ominous organ music; a woman shining in white passes quickly along a dark upper balcony. Hulking figures intrude suddenly upon quiet scenes.

But look past the flashy theatrical qualities of *Science and Madness* and it's as schematic as a morality play. Look past the sardonic humour and it's as serious. It sets out to depict the struggle for Man's soul in the twentieth century. The struggle takes place in the mind of one Benjamin Heywood, a doctor living in a lonely Scottish village at the turn of the century. The other characters exist largely as personifications of his struggle. The tempter and controller of the action is Medeiros, a powerful Mephistopheles-like figure and a cold clinician who represents the inevitable end of twentieth-century man. Under his encouragement, Dr. Heywood tries to free himself from an empathy with human suffering by operating on a poor mental patient named Freddy. Freddy represents humanity helpless in the fact of science and madness and unable to strike back except in stupid acts of violence. Set in opposition to Medeiros are two figures that stand for forces from the past. The weaker is Lilliana, Heywood's sister, a poet and an embodiment of nineteenth-century romanticism. Lilliana is vulnerable to sentiment and attacks of religious fervour. She is forever making some bold statement only to find it turn in her mouth to fanatical pronouncements about God and the devil. She is easily seduced by Medeiros, the new order, and becomes his strumpet, a grim comment on the role of romanticism in this century. Medeiros' true antagonist is young Mary who carries within her the force of the accumulated superstition of the centuries before. In the final battle only Mary and Medeiros, the reasonable man, are left alive.

It's impossible to talk about *Science and Madness* without bringing out this very tight schema. But the way George F. Walker sets it before us is another thing altogether. Walker has always loved to toy with genres. In his other plays, *Filthy Rich, Gossip,* and *Theatre of the Film Noir,* he presented us with delirious variations on the American postwar detective films that French critics dubbed "film noir." This time he has moved laterally from "film noir" to its poor relative, the horror film. On one level *Science and Madness* is a parody of the horror genre, not just films such as *Frankenstein* and *The Mummy,* which dealt in comic book fashion with the struggle between science and superstition, but also—stylistically at least—films like Roger Corman's *The Fall of the House of Usher.*

George F. Walker has one of the most fertile comic imaginations at work in our theatre. One sequence of *Science and Madness* has the eldest character trying to stab Medeiros, his tormentor, in the back. Without even turning around Medeiros uses the power of suggestion to turn the knife against the idiot's own chest. His one hand struggles to pull the dagger away, his other forces it back; he pulls it away, he pushes it back. While this continues, Medeiros coolly explains that he—Medeiros—has merely set forces in motion and is not responsible for the outcome. The idiot's life force is struggling with the destructive force within him. He can stop any time he wants to. "Oh," says the idiot, and does. But only for an instant. The grim joke is that his will is not strong enough to do so without intercession.

Not all of the scenes were so well-balanced. Often the complexity of response that Walker calls for was ruined by misplaced comic lines which become smart-ass if they're not perfectly judged. And there's a problem with the structure. Young Mary who represents the force of superstitious terror is introduced far too late; she seems like an eleventh-hour addition. By the time she's introduced, parody has begun to run wild. "This is Scotland, Ben," says Medeiros, recalling dozens of explanations of supernatural phenomena in dozens of B movies. And the excellent Barbara Gordon is permitted to indulge in a parody of a Tennessee Williams' southern belle, at a point when the action should be flying home. As a result of loss of dramatic momentum, much of the climax simply falls flat.

As for the production, it's very ambitious. It is presented in black and white and garish reds on a revolving stage, the effect of which is as furiously unsettling and as wickedly beautiful as the rest of the movies the play parodies. Movies have arrived onstage in more ways than one. The sequence in which Lilliana seduces (or is seduced by) Medeiros has as its climax a languorous 360 degree revolution of the stage that calls to mind several grand and delirious film moments. It's not just showy, it's stunning, as daring an exercise in style as I've seen onstage for some time. The best of *Science and Madness* has just that kind of impact. Having seen it I know that George F. Walker is still one of our most fascinating playwrights.

1982

What is to be Done?

Written by Mavis Gallant, directed by Paul Bettis. Tarragon Theatre

Mavis Gallant's first play has all of the qualities of her short stories—wit, finesse, tenderness and a delicate civilized irony. But it still amounts to three hours of largely boring theatre. *What is to be Done?* (the title is taken from a socialist tract by Lenin) tells the experiences of two young women in wartime Montreal, enthusiastically caught up in naïve socialist ideology, and finally facing the great disappointment that their brave new world is only business as usual; only worse for them, because as women who've had relative freedom during the war, they will be shunted aside to make room for returning veterans. One of the young women is a rookie journalist; the second is a young mother whose husband has gone to war.

Every scene of *What is to be Done?* is beautifully crafted. Yet they don't give us the sense that we're going anywhere. There is little cumulative dramatic effect. The opening scene tells us everything we'll ever know about the characters.

The obvious thought occurred to me that each scene of the play is like one of a cycle of short stories—like Gallant's own Linette Muir stories, for instance—likewise about a young girl in nineteenforties Montreal trying to break into journalism. In story number one of this cycle of short stories by Mavis Gallant, called *What is to be Done?*, two young women are initiated into a Communist cell and meet two colourful eccentrics. A second has the young women blunder into an Austro-Hungarian hall on New Year's Eve. Cozy in their naïveté (they believe that all Europeans are socialists), one of them calls out a socialist slogan at the stroke of midnight. The hall turns out to house a fascist cell, so the women are forced to beat a hasty retreat, dragging their champagne bottle with them.

Gallant says that her stylistic referent in writing *What is to be Done?* was the mode of *Cabaret*. Director Paul Bettis has taken his cue from this. He's separated the scenes with actors who bust in, in music hall fashion, and pitch the property-ridden set about, to get it ready for the next situation.

One scene ends with a fuse box blowing, sending sparks flying. Immediately two actors in firemen's outfits spring on stage, setting things up at emergency pace. The effect is remarkable only for its air of desperate contrivance.

The *Cabaret* style is hardly pervasive. Much of *What is to be Done?* wanders in and out of naturalism, some of it bordering on rather earnest naturalism. But there are scenes that could have been *Cabaret* monologues if they had been performed better. Gallant is not well served by her cast in this respect. Neither Donna Goodhand nor Margot Dionne, who play the two central roles, can time a sharp laugh line to save their souls. Nor can they give the subtle twist of the wrist that turns the tragic into comedy and back again. Both of them come at an effect dead on, like freight trains. Neither of them is a bad actress; they just aren't suited to the kind of high comedy that Mavis Gallant has written, and the casting is the director's fault.

Watching Mavis Gallant's *What is to be Done?* is a disorienting experience. The dialogue is so finely turned you have the unmistakable sense of a fully developed sensibility confidently unravelling the contents of its imagination. There are scenes that reflect precisely Gallant's sensibility. One superb semi-comic monologue has the Margot Dionne character alternately reading letters to and from her husband, while subtle cinematic lighting alters the emotional content of the scene. And there's a very funny party sequence that's handled wonderfully by Dionne, Goodhand, Rod Beattie and Jack Messenger. The two girls try to fend off the very direct advances of a European wolf. But the effect of these scenes is muffled by the very length of the play. In the end the failure to cut *What is to be Done?* is a large disservice to Mavis Gallant.

1982

Julius Caesar

Written by William Shakespeare, directed by Derek Goldby.
Stratford Festival

Derek Goldby is among the most physical of directors. In the farces that he's best known for, his actors whirl about the stage like cartoon figures looking for a point of rest. His *Julius Caesar* is typically physical. The mobs of plebeians are no compliant observers to the action. Moved by the rhetoric of the play's various leaders, they surge about the stage in great thrusts of movement. Easily swayed, they are not so easily controlled. The pivotal scene in which Marc Antony plays on the crowd, a dangerous instrument, and sets it howling against Caesar's assassins, is crucial to any production of *Julius Caesar*. In Goldby's production, once again, the scene is conceived in physical terms. Goldby choreographs the mob to make the movement of the scene clear, but finally it's up to the actor playing Marc Antony to bring it off.

The fine young actor R. H. Thomson makes his Stratford debut in the role of Marc Antony. In his early scenes, Goldby has Antony bounding about Caesar like a frisky pup. This is intended to set off his eventual emergence as a political force, but it's a dangerous trick. It's more dangerous in the "Friends, Romans, Countrymen" scene to have Thomson's Antony working the crowd on a spontaneous uncalculated level. Thomson leaps up and down the stairs glorying more and more in this successful manipulation and surprised by his own power as a leader—all of this right in the thick of the action, the surging of the crowd, his own rhetoric. When he bounds off the stage proclaiming in surprise and new-found arrogance: "Belike they had some notice of the people, how I had moved them," the play's theme of power as the great corrupter has been vividly realized. This puppy has unleashed the dogs of war, both within the state and within himself.

R.H. Thomson comes through, even if it's a tight squeak. He lacks a strong voice, but he's such an exciting presence, so immersed in the theatrical moment, that the scene belongs to him, as it must. Thomson's Antony is a nice contrast to Len Cariou's dogged, stoic Brutus, whose nobility carries with it a wish for defeat in the face of corrupting power, and to Nicholas Pennell's Cassius, lean, hungry and opportunistic as the Bard intended.

Goldby's production works best when the director's physicality of approach really complements the action: Antony's speech, or the assassins nervously manœuvring Caesar for the kill, Pennell's Cassius edgily checking his false starts. And the protracted painful scene following the assassination, the conspirators awkwardly proclaiming "freedom and liberty" in voices that are hoarse and horrified by the deed. This assassination sequence flirts daringly with nervous comedy.

On the debit side, Goldby has a habit of setting up obstacles for his actors to overcome, with the idea that their effort will give the performances immediacy. In the scene in which Cassius and Casca meet during a storm, the sound and lightning effects were too extravagant for the actors to compete with; the dramatic momentum was lost. Similarly Thomson's Antony is made to shriek above unnecessarily loud mob noises. I fear for these actors' voices, and for Susan Wright's who has been pushed to unnecessary shrillness as Portia.

There have been complaints by reviewers about an overabundance of swordplay and gore in this production of *Julius Caesar*. In fact there is very little swordplay and no more gore than the play calls for. I suspect that it's Goldby's attempt to make violence vivid and realistically banal that raised the complaints. This is not a grand and classical *Julius Caesar*. It's as grim and gory and unheroic as the play itself. Taken on its own level, it's a strong, flawed production.

The Mikado

Libretto by W.S. Gilbert, music by Arthur Sullivan, directed by Brian Macdonald. Stratford Festival

Now we turn to Stratford's Gilbert and Sullivan offering. Last season Leon Major gave Stratford a very spirited *Pinafore* that was hampered by some weak acting from performers who were primarily singers. Major clearly cast *Pinafore* for the music first. This season Brian Macdonald, director of *The Mikado*, has taken the opposite route. In several instances he has cast actors who are only passable singers but who bring an actor's presence to the roles. Thus we have Richard McMillan only more or less singing the notes, but mugging delightfully as Pooh Bah. I'm used to rotund pompous Pooh Bahs, but McMillan is an elongated preening fun-house version of Trudeau. He runs away with everything that's not tied down, and might have stolen the show were it not for Marie Baron's witty Yum Yum. Ingenues are not supposed to steal shows, but this one does.

The production is fast, funny within its limits, elegantly and wittily staged, very, very handsome to look at, and almost too clever for its own good. I must say a very little of this sort of thing goes a long way with me.

But *The Mikado* was a rousing success with the first night audience. One moment should be recorded for posterity. In the famous patter song "I've got a little list," Ko Ko catalogues people whose heads could be removed with impunity. Eric Donkin's Ko Ko included in the list a Toronto journalist, and in the next line referred to her as "she." The audience roared its approval. They recognized the reference to a reviewer deeply resented by the Stratford and Toronto theatre community for her biased reporting. Who would have thought she could have provided such an exciting moment in the theatre—even if only indirectly.

Summer 1982

Cinema

Le Vieux Pays ou Rimbaud est Mort

Directed by Jean-Pierre Lefebvre.

Jean-Pierre Lefebvre has been making films in Quebec for sixteen years. The mere fact that any filmmaker working in this country can have succeeded in creating a substantial body of work—seventeen feature films before his fortieth birthday—is striking enough. But according to critic and teacher Peter Harcourt, who is preparing a book on Lefebvre, it is a very distinguished body of work.

Until last week, when I was prompted to see *Le Vieux Pays ou Rimbaud est Mort* at Toronto's Festival of Festivals, Lefebvre was no more than a name to me. Nor can there be many Canadians better informed about this remarkable artist. His work has been rarely seen in this country outside of Quebec, and even in Quebec Lefebvre is hardly better known than he is in Vancouver. I have no experience of his other work to draw on. I can only testify that after seeing *Le Vieux Pays ou Rimbaud est Mort* (henceforth to be referred to as *Le Vieux Pays*) M. Lefebvre has instantly become one of the handful of artists in this country whose work carries indispensable weight in my attempts to understand what it is to exist in the civilization that has spread itself so thinly across the northern half of the North American continent. If that particular aspect doesn't interest you, let me add that *Le Vieux Pays* is clearly the work of a mature artist, with an impressively clean and economic mastery of his medium.

Le Vieux Pays tells us of a wandering Quebecker in France named Abel, who is seeking his connection with the civilization that spawned his own and then abandoned it. On another level the film is about the search for the father (or the father country) as well as the need to reject or leave the father in order to make one's own connection with life. The literal fathers one meets in the film have all abdicated responsibility to life through alcohol or art or false patriarchal ideals. And in Abel's ironic eyes the father country France is no more than a dying civilization—an imperialist power that no longer has any connection with its enforced offspring, including Quebec. Abel himself hasn't seen his own father in twenty years, and in the course of the film he avoids a potential father/son relationship with a confused adolescent. Through loving relationships with two very different French women, Abel comes to see that his nearly uninhabited homeland of snow and trees is his real father. But in a sense we the audience may ask ourselves whether the idea of fatherland is not a harmful one, and whether Abel isn't carrying around his problem with him wherever he wanders. In the scene which introduces the central character, his little garret room is explored in a deliberate 360-degree pan which has Abel at its centre. As the shot suggests, the likeable Abel, played with a fine sympathetic edge by Marcel Sabourin, is in certain respects a closed personality, wearing his Quebecois identity as armour against the world. Although he is a warm, accessible personality to women, his relationships with them stop short of responsibility. In fact Abel himself might be a prototypical abdicated father, recreating his inner experience in the outer world. On the other hand, in light of the film's attitude toward fathers, Abel's circumspection regarding the role may be justifiable. This ambiguity extends to Abel's relationship to his own culture. In one of a series of very funny encounters, Abel interrupts a folksinger singing of Les Gloires de France by hollering an off-key extemporaneous folksong about how all Canadiens love Madeleine de Verchères, scourge of the Indians. The term "Canadiens" is ironically used, for de Verchères is a discarded heroine of the old colonial days in Quebec. Further, the French people that Abel meets ignore his wishes to be referred to as Quebecois, calling him Canadien instead. Abel carries about with him a hand-drawn poster titled Kebek (with a K), consisting of a blank surface in a crude frame. This itself is an ambiguous image. Is it snow? Or is it just nothing? Nothing may be preferable to the crowded surface of a civilization choked on its own glorious past. But if the film suggests that Abel's wandering has been an extended adolescence, prolonged by an obsession with fathers and by his defensive sense of being Quebecois, the final image is hopeful. Behind the credits there is the striking spectacle of ice breaking on a river.

In a way, I'm doing this film a disservice by imposing a reading on it. Le Vieux Pays is generous in its response to people, subtle and searching in its ambitions. And it has an openness rare in a film so hard and intelligent in its perceptions. The film will mean many things to many people. But I can't help thinking that it will mean something very particular to those who struggle to define the nature of our life and history on this blank poster of a land, the parts of which are known by many names to many different peoples, but which share a common isolation one from another and by extension from the world. *Le Vieux Pays ou Rimbaud est Mort* speaks calmly and wisely to the centre of our contradictory natures as a people. Like a few other great works of art of the last decade, like Margaret Laurence's *The Diviners*, like George Luscombe's production of *Les Canadiens*, Jean-Pierre Lefebvre's film deserves a special response from the Canadian artist, a response that says: "Yes, that's been said at last. Thank you. We can go on from here now."

1980

Henry Fonda: 1905-1982

For me, Henry Fonda will always remain the centre of several memorable images and scenes in the films of John Ford: Wyatt Earp clumsily asking his lady fair to dance at a church consecration in Monument Valley in *My Darling Clementine*; Abe Lincoln kneeling at the grave of his lost love in *Young Mr. Lincoln*; Tom Joad's lean frame disappearing over a morning skyline after the famous goodbye scene in *The Grapes of Wrath*.

As a movie star Henry Fonda was a kind of complement to John Wayne, who shares the distinction of being John Ford's other favourite actor. Violence, the inevitable outlet for male Hollywood action heroes, was a release for Wayne, often a joyous one. For Fonda it was more complex. The tension between repressed violence and basic decency charged the Fonda persona. There was a reticence in Fonda's screen acting that spoke of a willingness to use violence only as a last resort. The reticence in Fonda's action-hero could, and was, easily transferred to his middle-aged personifications of men of state. Henry Fonda was Hollywood's favourite presidential candidate in the early sixties, or so it seemed with films like *Fail Safe*, *Advise and Consent* and *The Best Man*. Finally, Fonda's reticence contributed to an image of extraordinary rectitude.

Henry Fonda was around for so long doing the kind of work that is usually called "dependable" that we think of him as one of the biggest Hollywood stars of his era. In fact, all through his career he often played second leads to his peers like John Wayne, James Stewart or Richard Widmark, or to actors far less talented such as Tyrone Power and Tony Curtis, or he played leading man opposite the grand dames of the screen such as Bette Davis, Joan Crawford, and even (later) Audrey Hepburn. In retrospect this seems another aspect of his integrity. He was one of the rare Hollywood stars who was more interested in his role than his billing. Perhaps this marks him as a man whose first love was theatre.

There's a wonderful story about Fonda appearing for the first day of shooting on King Vidor's *War and Peace*. He was wearing glasses and a little pot belly to suit the role of the ineffectual Pierre. The producers had none of that. Fonda was Fonda and he'd better look like Fonda.

For a younger generation Henry Fonda is the father of Jane and (for the children of the sixties) Peter. Like the Kennedys, the Fondas became a focus of liberal feeling in their time. The agonies and successes of the Fonda's public and private lives followed, to a re-markable degree, the progress of liberal thought in America. Jane and Peter went through their public rites of passage and Henry, like liberal America, somehow succeeded in accommodating himself to their changes.

It's fair to say that Fonda only became a superstar after Peter and Jane grew up and the mythology of the Fonda family took hold. There was always something stubbornly ego-less about the man. Peter and Jane completed him as a star.

His films are there, more good ones than a Hollywood actor has a right to expect: Ford's *Drums along the Mohawk* and *Fort Apache*; Fritz Lang's *You Only Live Once*; Preston Sturges' *The Lady Eve*; William Wellman's *Ox-Bow Incident*; *Twelve Angry Men*; *Firecreek*; Leone's *Once upon a Time in the West*; Don Siegel's nasty little cop melodrama, *Madigan*.

Perhaps the film that epitomizes Fonda the actor is Hitchcock's *The Wrong Man*, a quasi-documentary in which Fonda completely submerged his star charisma to play a mundane little man. But the film that epitomizes Fonda the star is Ford's moving *The Grapes of Wrath*. It's this film that shows us, if we need to be shown, that Fonda, like James Stewart, like Spencer Tracy, was one of the very finest of the American Actor/Personalities.

Summer 1982

Friday the 13th Part III

Directed by Steve Miner.

I have to confess that before I saw *Friday the 13th Part III* I had never seen a modern horror movie. I'm referring to films like *Halloween,* in which rampaging psychopaths cut gory swaths through the principals, letting the corpses fall where they may. There are no rules about who gets it in films like *Friday the 13th Part III*. They are the illegitimate children of Alfred Hitchcock's *Psycho*. In *Psycho*, Hitchcock broke the rules of narrative and audience identification by killing his leading lady in a shower a third of the way through the film. After *Psycho*, no one in a horror film was safe. Mind you, things have changed in the 23 years since *Psycho*. That film depicted two (count them) two murders. *Friday the 13th Part III* gave us twelve, if I counted right, and a lot of peripheral violence.

Friday the 13th Part III is in 3-D, so you can't turn your head away from the ugly parts without losing your glasses, hurting your eyes and risking a splitting headache. It's peculiar, but a movie filmed in 3-D is much less involving than an ordinary film. You'd think it would be the opposite, but no, the little dolls on the screen pose and chatter—it's more like a puppet show than a movie. Or like looking through one of those viewmasters that used to fascinate me as a child.

The peculiar unreality of 3-D is perfect for a film like *Friday the 13th Part III*. Unlike *Psycho*, in which Janet Leigh's graphic murder, even in stark black and white, contained all the horror of senseless death, and evoked the sweetness of life as a bitter aftertaste, *Friday the 13th Part III* dispatches its characters with brutal snaps of the finger. Death is clean, sudden, almost abstract, almost bloodless in fact. The victims don't writhe in their death agonies. The axe sinks into the man's forehead with a thunk and he topples slowly like a felled tree. The pitchfork is thrust into the girl's stomach and out the other side as if through warm plasticine, and she sinks to the ground, her face fixed in painless surprise. How easy death seems. How easy too it would be to join in the audience applause that greets the filmmaker's ingenuity at finding new ways of dispatching people.

I spent much of the first hour of *Friday the 13th Part III* watching nothing but medium shots of people's faces exploring cellars and dark corners. Round 3-D heads turn slowly, shyly, defenceless against the weapons that seem to lurk in every shadow. When will they fall? This whole section relied on simple shock devices. Its suspense was mechanical and repetitive. Who will get it next? How will he get it? The last murder actually fought past my adult defences and "grossed me right out" (to use a favourite expression of a ten-year-old friend of mine). The killer grabbed this guy, see, and skroonched up his 3-D head, so that his 3-D eyeball squirted right into my lap. But the final section of the film in which the girl destined to survive scrambled away from the psychopath was so gripping that one can't entirely write off the movie as a crude shocker.

Like a nightmare, *Friday the 13th Part III* has a meaning if not a message, and it's time to talk about that. So I'll tell the story. Six teenagers go to stay at an isolated farm. Without parental supervision they have fun. They take skinny dips, smoke dope, and make love or talk about it. It gets dark and one by one the children are killed by a monstrous hulk in a hockey mask. He has a name but it escapes me. Seeing as how the monster acts as an avenger of permissiveness, a convenient projection of repressed feelings of sexual guilt, let's call him Herpes. Herpes is a mad father figure asserting that you can't get away with that and if you try here's what will happen to you! There's a sequence which I'm told is common to this genre, in which a couple make love and are promptly punished by being butchered. It's significant, I think, that the one survivor turns out to be the girl who has misgivings about sleeping around and abstains from lovemaking despite the prompting of the randy clod she's with.

Friday the 13th Part III is a poisonous fairytale for teenagers — and for youngish teenagers at that. It's disturbing that a film that toys with such volatile fears in its intended audience should come out on the side of repression, encouraging an almost paranoid fear about the danger of exploring one's own sexuality. The oppressive nature of this violent little tale frightened me much more than the lethal pitchforks and the squirting eyeballs.

1982

183

Careful He Might Hear You

Directed by Carl Schultz.

The central figure of *Careful He Might Hear You* is a five-year-old boy being raised by one of his dead mother's sisters, the wife of an Australian labourer. The boy's life is disrupted when his rich aunt, young, beautiful, cultured and anglified, returns from England to take control of his upbringing. The ugly battle for the boy's affection that ensues has several levels: it's a class struggle, a war between simple Aussies and snooty Anglos, and it's a demonstration of certain rather baldly stated Freudian tenets.

The flaws in the script and acting are all but subsumed in the great melodramatic rush of the presentation. The emotions are big, the actors play them big; the images are lush, the camera movements are sweeping, rhetorical. Even the music is big, it sounds a bit like Mahler and it's locked into the narrative as surely as the old Max Steiner scores for Warner Brother's film melodramas such as *Casablanca*. The difference is that the music of the old Hollywood illustrated and underlined the action, whereas in *Careful He Might Hear You* the lush music makes an ironic commentary both on the tawdriness of the story and on the genre of family melodrama to which the film belongs.

Careful He Might Hear You is an almost delirious exercise in style. This will surprise those who have seen previous Australian films such as *Breaker Morant* or *Gallipoli*. By and large the Australian cinema is in the mainstream of commercial narrative film. *Careful He Might Hear You* could have been told in a more direct and accessible style, but as it is it has more in common with opera than with other Australian films or with the current Hollywood cycle of homely family melodramas such as *Ordinary People*. *Careful He Might Hear You* has a European flavour; its expansive style is actually the work of a Hungarian director, Carl Schultz.

Schultz belongs to that tradition of film-maker, like Orson Welles or Fellini, who uses the camera as an active voice. In *Careful He Might Hear You* there's a horrifying scene in which the rich sister, in an erotic trance, molests the child. We experience it from the boy's viewpoint; the aunt becomes a beautiful monster, a succubus. There's a misogynistic edge to the film here and elsewhere but Schultz redeems it somewhat in the last section of the film. When the child begins to fight his aunt back with some mental cruelty of his own Schultz suddenly switches viewpoints so that we experience the film from her eyes. At this point, *Careful He Might Hear You* shows itself to be more than just another interesting Australian film; it becomes the work of a very promising film-maker.

Careful He Might Hear You comes highly recommended from this quarter. Just don't go expecting *Ordinary People*.

August 1984

The Cotton Club

Directed by Francis Ford Coppola.

The Cotton Club, Francis Coppola's 60-million-dollar gangster musical, opened to reactions that swung from pan to rave. This might have been expected because *The Cotton Club* is really two movies in one: a movie and a simultaneous commentary on the movie.

The movie runs straight down Hollywood's throbbing heart line. It shows us gang wars among the most colourful sets of mobsters since the Warner Brothers/First National days. It gives us musical numbers, lovingly performed and brilliantly integrated; racial tensions (black vs. white, Irish vs. Jew); family tensions (two pairs of brothers at odds); three (count them) three major bad guys plugged or punished; two love stories; three happy endings. And all of this presented in an atmosphere so rich you can taste it: a shabby Harlem flat; a vulgar, opulent gangster bash in a penthouse; outside, inside and backstage at the Cotton Club; a smoky after-hours speakeasy where the real jazz is played; a renegade gangster's hideout close with fear and sweat; the fabled Hoofer's Club, Harlem tap in all its glory. This furious mix of colourful ingredients is on the screen like a dream of Harlem in the twenties made real, and peopled with characters that are equally vivid.

But there's another side to Coppola's film, one that only asserts itself at the end. Two events, simultaneous but happening in different places, are crosscut repeatedly; one, the murder of Dutch Schultz, head honcho in the heavy department; the other, a solo tap dance by Greg Hines performed at the Cotton Club. Coppola's handling of these involves the most obsessive display of crosscutting since D.W. Griffith put Lillian Gish on an ice flow and sent Richard Barthelmess hollering silently into the storm. But Coppola's crosscutting is not done for suspense purposes: the effect is aesthetic. Because Coppola holds the sound of the tap dancing over the murder scenes, the murder is forced into the structure of the dance. At the end we see Hines finish his dance, whereupon Coppola cuts back to Schultz slumping on a table, dead, and holds this image while we hear the enthusiastic roar of the Cotton Club patrons. A stunning distancing effect to find at the climax of a commercial film, and a brilliant cinematic conceit.

Coppola extends the conceit in the next and final scene. While Cotton Club performers dance in front of a mock train station, the lovers, Richard Gere and Diane Lane, are reunited in a real train station where people are also dancing. Coppola makes it difficult for us to tell when we are in the Cotton Club and when we are in the real station. The same music blares in both scenes; he even goes so far as to superimpose Cotton Club dancers onto the real train station. The final shot: Gere and Lane on the platform of a real caboose but shot in romantic tableau to look as artificial as a valentine.

At this point the movie has left behind the documentary impulse of the earlier sections and leapt into fantasy. The Cotton Club (the place, not the film) was where fantasies were acted out, white fantasies of black sexuality, black fantasies of making it in the white man's world. When the Cotton Club fantasy is imposed on the film's real world and its characters, that world is revealed for what it is: a Hollywood fantasy, bigger than anything the Cotton Club could manage. Gere's last line:

"Here's to happy endings, kid."

The Cotton Club is a brilliant film. Its images match the tricky, vibrant and mysterious early music of Duke Ellington which sets the tone for this movie. There is a certain element of parody in the early Ellington compositions. In his early career and particularly at the Cotton Club he was forced to cater to white folks' perceptions. He didn't do it without a wink and a nudge. Coppola likewise has to please us popcorn eaters. He does so, never quite falling into outright parody of his genres. But he has also made *The Cotton Club*, as he did *Godfather II*, as a multi-million dollar art film. I hope that Coppola is not destroyed by that contradiction.

1984

Wings

Directed by William Wellman.

In 1927 Charles Lindbergh captured the world's imagination with his solo flight to Europe, the first of its kind. 1927 was the year in which airplanes were imbued with a romantic fascination they have never had before or since. Paramount could not have chosen a better time to release *Wings*, a hymn of praise to the men who flew flimsy biplanes, airborne death traps, during World War I.

It's a marvellous thing, going on 60 years later, to be able to view a silent movie like *Wings* on home video. Paramount has even provided a musical score performed on a Wurlitzer organ. Historically, *Wings* is a fascinating film. As you mentioned, Terry, it was the first movie to win an Academy Award, but it was also the last silent movie to do so. In that same year, 1927, Warner Brothers blew the silent film away using the considerable lung power of Al Jolson in *The Jazz Singer*. So *Wings* was the last of its breed, the last of the great silent war epics. Perhaps that's why its title has always had a certain romantic cachet. *Wings* has remained better remembered as a title, if not as a film, than the infinitely better movie that preceded and inspired it, King Vidor's *The Big Parade*.

Wings was directed by William Wellman, Wild Bill Wellman, a director who, in his day, had a reputation for making no nonsense, tough, men's pictures. Today Wellman's work tends to look a bit unfocused or flat when put beside his contemporaries King Vidor, John Ford or Howard Hawks. His best film is probably *Public Enemy* with James Cagney, still one of the best gangster films ever made (although critically unfashionable at the moment).

Wings tells the story of two young men who go to war and become fliers, beetle-browed Richard Arlen and cherubic Buddy Rogers. Both men love the same girl, a little doll in Mary Pickford curls. Rogers, however, the boy next door, is loved from afar by the girl next door, spunky Clara Bow, the famous, flirtatious "it" girl. Bow, who gets top billing, is clearly in *Wings* for the marquee value. Her major scenes seem to belong to another film, another very bad film. Director Wellman clearly found nothing interesting in her character.

What Wellman did find interesting and therefore makes interesting for us, are the details of camp life, the training, the fighting and the bonding between the two leading men. The male love story is brought to a gruesome climax that may be intended to demonstrate the horrors of war or may simply derive from some scriptwriter's feverish grasp of the principle of irony.

But the real love affair of the film is not between Bow and Rogers, nor Rogers and Arlen, but between director Wellman and the airplane. The flying scenes have never been surpassed. Wellman served in the Lafayette Flying Corps in World War I, and he put his experience to good use in *Wings*. He imaginatively recreated the dogfights so that we experience them both from a distance as a pattern—almost an aesthetic pattern, of swooping, dodging airborne craft, now and again one spiralling off in a sheet of flame, and from right inside the cockpit with the flyer, dreadfully exposed and waiting for the next volley. While much of *Wings* is now an expansive curio, the dog-fighting scenes leap over the years. They are suspenseful and uncomfortably brutal and realistic. Anyone who has a fascination with the early days of flying will want to see *Wings* or own a video copy. Seeing *Wings* today offers the film buff reverberations unintended by its makers.

Knowing that *Wings* was one of the last big silent epics, it's a shock to see Henry B. Walthall in a small role. Walthall was the lead in D.W. Griffiths *Birth of a Nation*, the film that marked the coming of age of the silent film. And as a portent of the future we are soon introduced to a familiar lean figure who slouches from a bunk to fill the screen with his shy presence. Anyone familiar with the first 30 years of American sound films might well think that here at last is the hero of the film. But no, Gary Cooper ambles off to die in a plane crash after his one short scene, leaving us with the suddenly inadequate figures of Arlen and Rogers, both of whom were to be relegated to B pictures with the coming of the talkies. Gary Cooper still makes the mark he must have made in theatres in 1927. But today seeing him in *Wings* he seems both as familiar as an old shoe and as fresh as something come upon for the first time.

March 1985

The Last Dragon

Directed by Michael Schultz.

The late director Nicholas Ray, when asked to describe his wild proto-feminist Western *Johnny Guitar*, chuckled and said; "Baroque, very baroque." The term could well be applied to *The Last Dragon*, another wild genre film that manages to remain straightfaced in front of its own outrageousness.

It has a perfectly conventional Kung Fu plot about a youth who leaves the tutelage of his wise, oriental master to come of age in the streets of Harlem. And it ends with a fine Kung Fu bash-out.

But *The Last Dragon* is shot through with wonderfully tasteless play on racial and ethnic stereotypes. The hero, for instance, is not Oriental but Black: his name is Leroy yet. Leroy's idol, and, if we are to believe *The Last Dragon*, the idol of most of Harlem, is that James Dean of Kung Fu, Bruce Lee. Our hero is sometimes called Bruce Leroy by his adversaries. Leroy's teacher has filled him so full of inscrutable orientalism that he has shucked off the Harlem jive talk of his soul brothers and leans instead to the speech patterns of Charlie Chan. "You do not understand, honourable brother," he tells his sibling, a street-wise kid on the cutting edge of puberty who thinks Leroy is a cracked fortune cookie.

Oriental characters in *The Last Dragon* tend to talk Harlem jive like they were to the watermelon born. There's a young trio of Chinese thugs who spout pure soul talk and breakdance furiously, if not well. Their ghetto blaster plays something like "Sukiyaki sock it to me/ I'll sock it to you." There's further ethnic confusion in Leroy's family. His father, Leroy Sr., owns the first black pizza shop in Harlem ("Take yo' feetsa to Leroy's Pizza") and wears a red and white Italian Chef's outfit. What's black and white and red all over? Leroy Senior on the job.

The best scene in *The Last Dragon* takes place early on, in a Harlem movie theatre, where a rowdy audience of whites, blacks and orientals is loudly appreciating an old Bruce Lee flick. In the midst of this colourful throng sits our hero Leroy in the Chinese peasant clothes that he wears throughout. A huge coolie hat balances serenely atop his black head. He is eating popcorn with chopsticks and absorbing the onscreen action with the dedication of an acolyte. Wham! Into the theatre, accompanied by a vivid assortment of cronies, comes the villain of the piece, a bad black dude and a mean Kung Fu master, the Mighty Shogun of Harlem. The Shogun's name? What else? Sho'Nuff. "Am I the baddest?" "Sho'Nuff!" "Am I the meanest?" "Sho'Nuff!"

Now I don't want to send everyone who takes pleasure in this kind of flip humour rushing out to see *The Last Dragon*. The movie is more fun to tell about than it is to see. It is, in the final accounting, an elaborately produced children's film. It has a chaste hero, a sexy but unthreatening leading lady and an army of kiddie Kung Fu fighters who burst in to save Leroy when there are too many bad guys on his plate. At its best it's a hip fairytale. At its worst it's arch and tedious. Its white villains, for instance, are simple-minded scenery chewers right out of an old Walt Disney Herbie movie.

The director of this heaping bowl of chop suey and black-eyed peas is Michael Schultz. But it's billed as Barry Gordy's *The Last Dragon*, and it's clearly the Motown King's movie all the way. Gordy's recording artists, like Stevie Wonder, flood the soundtrack and sometimes appear in the film, as does Lebarge, a scruffier Michael Jackson who seems to have borrowed Michael's emasculated voice. Further the heroine is a Barry Gordy discovery called Vanity. Vanity plays a video/disco queen who sets the tedious subplot in motion. (Let's not talk about the subplot.)

There's a small cultural footnote here, for Vanity turns out to be none other than D.D. Winters, a gorgeous southern Ontario kid who had a brief moment in the spotlight a few years back when someone with less clout than Barry Gordy tried to market her. Now here she is once again looking like double dynamite, singing passably, dancing a bit jerkily and photographed to suggest that she might be black. As for her acting, one gets the uneasy feeling that they did a lot of looping to get a passable performance from her small Ontario voice. As they used to say, you can take the girl out of the country but you can't take the country out of the girl.

The better parts of *The Last Dragon* find that certain giddiness of invention that some trash grooves into when it knows that no one is likely to pay serious attention to it. It doesn't seem to be breaking Box Office records, but I have a strong hunch that in ten years *The Last Dragon* will come into its own as a minor cult film. Remember, you heard it here first.

April 1985

Last Reviews

Fred Astaire: The Man, the Dancer by Bob Thomas

I was not expecting much from this book. There's that portentous title, for one thing: *Fred Astaire: The Man, the Dancer*. For another, author Bob Thomas has shown himself many times with many books to be the kind of journalist who pounces on the famous dead before the body is cold to dash off quickie biographies. Besides I've read a lot on Astaire, who is very much alive at 85, and most of it has been dull. The only portrait that really gave a sense of the man was that in Ken Barnes' *The Crosby Years*. Barnes produced a Crosby/Astaire album in the middle seventies and he provided an extended, almost comic, account of two friends who happened to be the two classiest popular artists of their generation, at odds in their approach to work: Crosby's loose, improvisatory, throw-me-the-ball-and-I'll-hit-it approach against Astaire's tightly controlled Nervous Nellie. Actually Astaire's sister Adele, with whom he spent years on the stage, called him Moaning Minnie. This aspect of the man, this fierce passion for perfection, comes through well in Thomas' book.

Moaning Minnie happens to be one of the three or four greatest popular artists of the century and, except for Chaplin, the only one who managed to keep control of his career from beginning to end. The boring plots and creaky comedy that surround even the best of Astaire's movies are not his province or responsibility. But when the films flower into dance the ineffable Astaire comes into his own. For the 25 years or so that Astaire danced on film (until he was almost sixty), there was no poor, fair or even pretty good Astaire dance, there was only great Astaire and greater Astaire. And who would dare say which of his many dances was the greatest? Even when he was saddled with an inadequate partner, if you kept your eye on the man he had his own integrity. Always at the still centre of whatever joy, passion or anger his dance expressed—and his range was both deeper and more varied than is acknowledged in words such as elegant or dapper—there was Astaire controlling fury with what looked like the least possible effort, a Prospero of dance. His nearest rival, Gene Kelly, like the car rental people, was number two, tried harder, and it showed.

But where did this passion for perfection, this imagination that, at its best, whipped poetry out of thin air so that his whole body was one plastic metaphor, where did all of this come from? Not, if Bob Thomas' biography is to be believed, from his life. By all accounts, including his own, Astaire has been a quiet, domestic, even dull man. He admits to no tensions save from his work, or grief at the loss of loved ones. Those things we all suffer. Like Crosby he had few close friends and took his pleasure and camaraderie from golf and horses. He never drank excessively, married happily twice: the second time at the age of 80 as a long-time widower to a 35-year-old jockey and divorcée. He seems to be a man who has sublimated everything into his work. He has few words of wisdom about it to share, certainly no theorizing, which he would call pretentious, no apparent interest in his own or anyone else's psychology.

Bob Thomas is quite content to take Astaire at his word, so the book shares the unexciting qualities of the man and none of the brilliant qualities of the dancer. It entirely ignores his recording career, an important aspect of Astaire's work. Yet it is relatively free of error and burnished to a kind of dull professional gloss. It quotes from a number of co-workers and uses Astaire himself as a kind of "aw shucks" chorus, pooh-poohing anything excessive.

Fred Astaire: The Man, the Dancer is probably the best Astaire biography around. It's also one tenth of the biography that the man and the dancer deserve. However, as it says in the song, "It'll have to do/Until the real thing comes along."

January 1985

Eubie

Music by Eubie Blake. Warner Home Video.

Eubie Blake was one of the great exponents and composers of popular rags. In the early years of the Jazz Age he joined forces with his vaudeville partner, Noble Sissle, to write and produce a series of Broadway revues, plotless shows stringing together songs and sketches into an evening's entertainment. Their first show, *Shuffle Along*, was a sensation in 1921. It brought the black revue into vogue on Broadway. It was in *Shuffle Along* that blacks were first allowed to sing a serious love song onstage and to wear formal clothes instead of clowning about in Jim Crow rags.

Eubie, the Broadway show, is part of a recent revival of the black revue. Once again, with shows such as New Orleans' *One Mo' Time* and *Ain't Misbehavin'*, based on the recorded works of Fats Waller, black revues are being performed for predominately white audiences. *Eubie* was a big enough success that Warner Home Video has picked the filmed show for its catalogue.

Eubie is not really about Eubie Blake. It merely riffles his pockets for old songs. Nor is it really about the old Negro revue. For unlike *One Mo' Time*, which was a stunning re-creation of black vaudeville, it makes no pretence to historical accuracy. It is simply a grouping of Eubie Blake's songs performed energetically by a talented cast. In fact, like many revues, *Eubie* is really about itself and how much energy it can generate for and with an audience.

This sort of thing probably works better live than on television, particularly when, as with *Eubie*, there's been little attempt to re-think the show for video. What you get is simply a filmed live performance, with the performers presumably aiming as much at the live audience as at the camera. There are times when the strain shows: the camera peers in on the acrobatic fat man, traditional to black revues, dancing to a song called "I'm a Great Big Baby." And it's ruined. Up close you can see the effort he has to make to appear graceful. Even the exceptionally gifted Gregory Hines is handicapped to a certain extent by having to perform at one and the same time for a live audience and a TV camera. He sings and acts "I've Got The Low Down Blues" with marvellous conviction, but sometimes in closeup looks as if he's about to have a coronary.

But for the most part the great energy of the performers works for them. And so do Eubie Blake's songs, which run the gamut of popular styles of the day: "Roll Jordan," a really convincing pseudo-spiritual, the raunchy "My Handy Man's Not Handy Anymore," the delicately raggy "Goodnight Angeline." Finally, there's "If You've Never Been Vamped By A Brown Skin, You've Never Been Vamped Before." That should go into anyone's list of great song titles (I will make mine available on request). The performers are also helped by a few pretty ideas—very few—from the otherwise unexceptional choreography. They are definitely not helped by the tacky orchestrations that sound as if they were written for the June Taylor Dancers. Nor by the director when he insists on cutting in closeups during dance numbers where we should be seeing the whole body of the dancers.

Thanks to the performers, *Eubie* is fun, on first viewing at least. But were it not for one element it would not be worth owning. That element is Gregory Hines. He and his brother Maurice have a couple of wonderful displays of tap, and Gregory himself does a great goofy solo to the song "Hot Feet." In fact everything that Gregory Hines does on screen—acting, singing, dancing—is so effortlessly right that you know that he could perform for six mediums at once and still come out glowing. I don't wish to take anything away from his talented co-stars, but Greg Hines makes this video worth the price. He is one of the few musical performers around with a style that seems new, freshly minted and totally his own.

January 1985

Albertine in Five Times

Written by Michel Tremblay, directed by Bill Glassco. Tarragon Theatre

In 1979 Michel Tremblay announced his intention to retire from play writing until he had something to say again. He had just completed a cycle of fourteen plays in as many years. In them a style was perfected—let's call it Quebec Gothic, a powerful brew of sensation melodrama shot through with an original theatrical imagination. Tremblay took from the Greeks, from Tennessee Williams, from Beckett, from popular television, but it all came out Tremblay.

In 1981 he presented a minor work, *Remember Me*, a conventional two-hander about a pair of estranged lovers exploring their pasts. *Albertine in Five Times* is, even more so than *Remember Me*, a memory play. And I would guess that it's the beginning of a whole new cycle for Tremblay. The melodrama is back, if only around the fringes, and Tremblay, the master of multi-levelled theatrical form, is back. But in *Albertine,* Tremblay is no longer tearing at his society with satirical rage, making it laugh while slipping the knife to it with images that describe the warping effects of Mother, Church and Repressed Sexuality.

Because *Albertine* is a memory play, Tremblay can distance himself from his passions, and he uses that distance to make peace with one of the major demons that shrieked through his earlier plays, Mother. Albertine, 70 years old, a monumentally failed mother, spends her first night in an old-folks home. She finds herself with unbidden company in the form of her earlier selves:

Albertine at 30, a widower and already hating men, exhausted by rage and frustrated by ignorance. She has been sent to her mother's farm for a short rest after nearly beating her eleven-year-old daughter to death.

Albertine at 40, a snappish shrew, ignored by her mad son and her sluttish daughter, unable to deal with the relentless guilt she feels over her failure as a mother.

Albertine at 50, determinedly happy. She's washed her hands of her children, has a job as a waitress and is enjoying a taste of independence.

Albertine at 60, miserable and resigned, daughter dead, son locked away. She's retreated to her bed and pops pills to push away guilt.

The voices of these women bicker in counterpoint and in chorus, in duet and in trio. Well, that could well describe Tremblay's first major play, *Les Belles Soeurs*, with its choruses of bickering women. Has he come full circle? Well, yes and no. The difference is in his approach to them. Tremblay mocked and rejected his *Belles Soeurs*. But in *Albertine* all of the women collapse into one and Tremblay tries to embrace them, tries to make his peace with them.

He even invents a saintly intermediary for them. She is Madeleine, Albertine's impossibly good sister, a perfect wife and mother. Apparently happy in her submissive role, she is selfless, generous, bovine and complacent. Susan Wright, who plays Madeleine, is good at conveying the hidden corners of this shaky paragon's life. Tremblay will tell Madeleine's story in a subsequent play.

All the actors do well in their roles: Susan Coyne, Albertine at 30, fear knotting up her thin body; Claire Coulter, Albertine at 40, resigned in her fury, a dried, malignant dumpling in a rocking-chair; Pat Hamilton, Albertine at 50, perched on her stool in an attitude of brightly painted cheeriness; Joy Coghill, Albertine at 60, a sedated spider full of poison and guilt. Presiding over them all is Doris Petrie's Albertine at 70, the only character who must be a real woman. (The others are bigger than life, essences of Albertine.) Petrie is superb, her performance is unfussy and unmannered. In it she suggests that hard-won intelligence may be the only consolation at the end of a tragic journey.

A very bleak play, but not of course without magic or humour. When Petrie is first surprised by her younger self clumsily waxing poetic on a farm porch, her reaction is unsentimental. "You talk funny," she says, not to deflate but to acknowledge the faultiness of memory. This moment, and others like it, defy the preciousness of the play's whole conceit (a woman at the point of death, talking to her past selves) without destroying its theatrical power.

It remains to be said that director Bill Glassco has guided his actors with assurance and sensitivity through the world of Michel Tremblay (familiar to him through six previous English language premieres). It's a world that's slightly altered now; it's more reflective, more compassionate, perhaps more open. Let's sum it up with this: In the play *Albertine in Five Times*, Michel Tremblay permits his mother figure to grope toward a state of grace. That in itself is a remarkable way to begin what I hope will be a second cycle of Tremblay plays. May it be as rich as the first.

April 1985

The Madwoman of Chaillot

Written by Jean Giraudoux, directed by Wendy Toye. Shaw Festival

First the bad news: *The Madwoman of Chaillot* amounted to a very uncomfortable night in the theatre. Jean Giraudoux's whimsical postwar fairytale tells how a quartet of paradoxically sane madwomen save the world from a conspiracy of evil, money-worshipping men, thereby making the world safe for dogs and cats, flowers and birds, and for people who like them. Like one of the madwomen in the play, this little fable is far too sweet to be sincere. It's open to any number of interpretations, ecological, political, anarchist, populist, left, right, centre, or all of the above. But when, at the climax of the play, *The Madwoman of Chaillot* happily sends all the evil men of the world to their deaths in the Paris sewers, I found it hard to forget that Giraudoux was a willing collaborator with the Vichy government, that he believed in the Final Solution, and hewed firmly to a long tradition of anti-semitism that has recently resurfaced in our own backyard in a high school near Red Deer, Alberta.

The actors in Wendy Toye's production of *The Madwoman of Chaillot* seem largely embarrassed, with the glorious exception of the ineffable Frances Hyland. Had Hyland played the Madwoman instead of Irene Hogan, who Hermione Gingolds the part to an extravagant death, she might have brought out some of the play's elusive Gallic charm. To my taste, it's a charm that might just as well be eluded, but onward and upward, out of the Paris sewers and onto more pleasant ground.

Heartbreak House

Written by G. B. Shaw, directed by Christopher Newton. Shaw Festival

The good news is that *Heartbreak House* on opening night was very close to wonderful. Shaw's great play, with its brilliant exploration of sexual intrigues among a group of idiosyncratic characters in an eccentric household, is as difficult a play to bring off as *The Madwoman*. At the beginning of the evening I was very much afraid that the company was not going to manage it. Director Christopher Newton's jumping-off point for the production worried me.

When, in his production, Ellie Dunn, Shaw's hard-headed heroine, falls asleep in a chair waiting for the Shotover household to take notice of her, the walls of Michael Levine's peculiar set rise a good ten feet. This is meant to signal an altered perspective and that the body of the play is to be Ellie's dream. For a few relatively ineffective moments, Marti Maraden's Ellie becomes Alice in Wonderland confronted with strange creatures: Jennifer Phipp's potty nurse, Goldie Semple's Hesione Hushabye, a gorgeous witch-like creature in flowing black lace, and Douglas Rain's distracted Ancient Mariner, Captain Shotover.

The play's dream motif is an important undercurrent, but it's distracting when such a thing is imposed so directly on the action. I was relieved when this somewhat twee interpretation was absorbed into the flow of things, and I was astonished and delighted when the Festival's production proved to be a definitive reading of *Heartbreak House*.

Heartbreak House requires great ensemble playing, and that is the real strength of Newton's production. There are fine individual performances: Rain, Semple, Robert Benson as Boss Mangan, Fiona Reid, superb as Lady Utterwood, and Norman Browning, who gave a wonderful reading of Hector Hushabye, comic and tragic in equal proportion. But good as these people are, no one of them dominates, and this is exactly the way it should be. The characters emerge from the fabric of the play and disappear back into it when someone else comes to the fore. The ensemble playing is so strong that the few weak members of the cast are hardly noticeable.

Finally the cast has not succumbed to the inevitable temptation to play Shaw on his wit alone, as if he were some cranky cousin of Noel Coward. *Heartbreak House* is a distillation of Shaw's bitter experience on the home front of World War I, and Newton's cast has dug into the play to find the despair that is at the core of *Heartbreak House*, with its powerful, cynical women, and its enervated, emasculated men. The mark of their success is in the final scene, a scene that has never in my experience worked onstage, not in last year's New York production with Rex Harrison, not in John Schlesinger's Old Vic production of 1975.

It's a scene of poisonous enchantment; the characters sit in a garden and watch a zeppelin burn in the night sky as if it were fireworks, and listen to the explosion of bombs as if it were Beethoven. In any production I've seen, this moment has jolted, as if Shaw himself had suddenly intruded from inside the scene to underline the callousness of his otherwise charming characters. But in Newton's production, it is made terrifyingly clear that these self-indulgent people, who have left the ship of state to others less intelligent and humane, are waiting in terrible self-hatred for their ship to run aground, are longing for their own private apocalypse. The final lines of the play are spoken by Ellie and Hesione as they hope breathlessly that the enemy will return the next night. This is not just, as it's often played, the cry of two suddenly silly women, hungry for excitement. It is an unconscious shriek of despair, and a longing for hopelessness and self-hatred to be brought to an end with violence.

As the curtain descended, I found myself murmuring aloud, "They've done it." And so they have. The Shaw Festival's 1985 production of *Heartbreak House* is not to be missed.

Spring 1985

Chaplin: His Life and Art by David Robinson

The fruitful career and eventful life of Charles Spenser Chaplin have been the subject of at least fifteen biographies, half a dozen memoirs, and more critical books and articles than I care to count. Chaplin himself published four autobiographical works. Yet, with all the biographical water under the bridge, David Robinson's *Chaplin: His Life and Art* is a major publishing event. It's a hefty volume, pushing 800 pages, and in its scope and ambition it stands alone among biographies of entertainment figures. The usual treatment of movie folk, in particular, is to give them the once-over-lightly, plundering a few interviews or press clippings. Worse than that is the sordid truth approach, the kind of thing that makes you want to take a shower after each chapter. Chaplin certainly had his share of scandals, or near scandals; two shotgun weddings to very young brides, a vicious divorce action launched by his second wife in which a truly excessive amount of dirty linen was scattered about, and a trumped up paternity suit (blood tests had demonstrated that Chaplin could not have been the father of the child). About all of this Robinson is direct, tactful and largely non-judgmental. Likewise, he shows admirable restraint with regard to his subject's psychological make-up. In his preface he states:

Readers who like biographers to supply post-Freudian inter-pretations for every action and incident may be frustrated. I have no personal liking for that genre of biography; I do not feel qualified for psychoanalysis; and finally I think that Chaplin's singular life story would defy the process.

Indeed it would. Robinson recounts how (not why) a genius flourished in a London childhood so deprived and unstable as to make virtually every biographer or commentator reach in desperation for some variation of the term "Dickensian." Chaplin had a mother who was periodically mad, and a father, a music-hall performer of some note, whom he rarely saw, and who died from drink at age 37. He had little schooling and was in and out of the orphanage until he was old enough to establish a career in the theatre, first at age ten, as a clog dancer, then as a child actor (his major part was Billy in Sherlock Holmes, a role which he repeated several times). By the age of sixteen, he was well enough respected to be present among the elite of the theatre at the funeral of the distinguished actor Henry Irving, and to appear as an entry in the first edition of *The Green Room Book or Who's Who on the Stage* where he was listed as "impersonator, mimic and sand dancer." At the age of twenty he was a leading comedian in Fred Karno's famous comedy troupe. By 1914 he had jumped the Karno ship, while the company was on tour in America, to make films for Mack Sennett's Keystone Company. By the end of that year Chaplin had made 35 films and was one of the most famous figures in the world. He was 25.

The remarkable story of Chaplin's early years has been told many times before, nowhere better than in Chaplin's *My Autobiography*. Robinson correctly asserts that the "first eleven of its thirty-one chapters can stand comparison with any autobiography for their colour and vitality." This acknowledged, Robinson does not try to compete with *My Autobiography*. He sets out to complement it, filling in details and confirming dates and names against the London public archives and theatrical sources. To Chaplin buffs, one of the more interesting side effects of his research is to exonerate Chaplin from the often-repeated charge of exaggerating his early life for dramatic effect. *My Autobiography* is revealed to be astonishingly accurate.

Aside from corroborating or correcting Chaplin, Robinson set out to be as comprehensive as he could about the early years. Reading the early portion of the book, it sometimes seems that every major document pertaining to the Chaplin family that has been uncovered by researchers is reproduced in the pages of the narrative. For instance, Robinson provides us with a quarter-page reproduction of the handwritten minutes of the Southwark Board of Guardians (1896) instructing "the collector...[to] collect the sum of 15 p per week from Charles Chaplin [Sr.] of 15 Gunders Grove, Fulham, in respect of the maintenance of his two children Sydney, aged twelve and Charles, aged seven, about to be sent to Hanwell School." This sort of thing, and there's a lot of it, may not satisfy the immediate thirst for narrative, but the antiquarian in us is gratified a thousandfold.

Whatever the strengths of *My Autobiography*, even Chaplin's greatest admirers will agree that it deteriorates after the account of his early years. Robinson can and does improve on Chaplin by filling in the sparse details he left us regarding the making of his films. Robinson has the advantage on previous biographers. Not only did Lady Chaplin throw open the vaults so that Robinson had complete access to working papers, letters, and studio records, but he benefitted from the co-operation of Kevin Brownlow and Brendan Gill, whose superb television series, *Unknown Chaplin*, retrieved outtakes, unissued films and discarded sequences.

Robinson's account of the making of the film is the single most valuable and fascinating aspect of his book. Chaplin is revealed as an extraordinarily intuitive artist who worked through trial and error, was willing to shoot miles of film to get what he wanted, and just as willing to drop whole sequences, even when his fierce perfectionist nature had pronounced itself satisfied. For *City Lights*, he spent seven days shooting a routine with a piece of wood wedged between the bars of a grating. By the time he had worked out theme and variation to his satisfaction he had a beautifully developed seven minutes of film comedy. Yet he cut it from the final print of the film, claiming that it detracted from the main story: "It was a whole story in itself," he explained.

Chaplin once told an interviewer, "An idea will generate enthusiasm and then you're off! The enthusiasm only lasts for a little while, and then you wait another day. It replenishes itself and you start again." Sometimes Chaplin's fluctuating enthusiasms led him into major structural changes, or even changes in subject matter. Surviving outtakes reveal that an early masterpiece, *The Immigrant*, which tells a simple story of two penniless Europeans who land in New York, began as a "serio-comedy—set in the Parisian Latin Quarter" (Chaplin's words).

To follow Charlie Chaplin's three feverish years from the crude Keystones to the brilliant Mutuals of 1916/17 (*The Pawnshop*, *Easy Street*) is to follow a one-man evolution of the two-reel comedy from a rough and raucous entertainment to a minor art form. Chaplin paved the way for the brilliant Buster Keaton, the immensely clever Harold Lloyd, and the others, outlasted them all, and finally steered his art into ambitious areas seemingly alien to his rough beginnings in Fred Karno's *Fun Factory*.

During the period of his early maturity, from *A Dog's Life* in 1918 to *City Lights* in 1931, he made fewer and increasingly longer films. This was the time of the great comic melodrama, *The Kid*, and the great comic epic, *The Gold Rush*, as well as *A Woman of Paris*, an anomaly in Chaplin's career, a drama with comic/ironic overtones, and still one of the most impressive and sophisticated of Hollywood silent features.

Chaplin, whose lowly origins in baggy pants knockabout were always proudly displayed, was nevertheless one of the American cinema's great poets of feeling. His protean sensibility worked its way toward the creation of vivid images, luminous with expressed emotion, comic but all the more intense for that. The final close-up of *City Lights* in which the tramp recognizes himself for the first time in the look of a flower girl, is a mixture of revelation and simple curiosity. Chaplin's words, quoted by Robinson, on one of the greatest moments ever captured on film, characteristically relate to the actor, not the camera:

I was looking more at her—interested in her, and I detached myself—standing outside myself and looking, studying her reactions and being slightly embarrassed about it.

After that moment of self-revelation the tramp's seeking is through. He makes a reprise appearance, sharing the spotlight with Paulette Goddard's waif in *Modern Times*, but then Chaplin retired him and entered the world of the talking picture, ten years after the rest of the film industry had done so. From this point on he was to make a handful of flawed and fearless works. *The Great Dictator* (1940) splits the tramp into two characters, a gentle Jewish barber and Adenoid Hynkel, Chaplin's parody of Hitler. In the final scene of the film the two are brought together in the face and voice of Charles Spenser Chaplin, hiding imperfectly behind the toothbrush moustache that the tramp and the dictator share. For six minutes he harangues the crowd in Hynkel fashion, but pleading in tramp fashion for peace.

The Great Dictator was an uneasy mixture of buffoonery and political satire, but the dark side of Chaplin was out. Chaplin explored it as bravely as he had everything else in his artistic life. His next film, *M. Verdoux* (1947), was told from the point of view of a mass murderer. Verdoux's cold irony alienated Chaplin from what was the single largest international audience before which any artist had the mixed blessing to perform.

There was to be one last major film, *Limelight* (1952), Chaplin's talky, pretentious, more often profoundly moving elegy for the Victorian/Edwardian popular theatre that was always his source of inspiration. Just before its release Attorney-General James Mc-Granerey, in an extraordinary and cowardly move, rescinded Chaplin's re-entry permit while he and his family were away on vacation. The action was taken under a law which permitted the barring of aliens (Chaplin had never taken out American citizenship) "on grounds of morals, health or insanity, or for advocating communism or associating with communist or pro-communist organizations." Chaplin had been the victim of a war of lies and innuendo, fostered, in part, by the FBI. The FBI files on Chaplin, which Robinson summarizes in an appendix, are a compendium of idiocy from which Chaplin himself would have had trouble making comic sense.

Chaplin spent his long twilight years in Vevey, Switzerland, pottering about with his screenplays, autobiographies, composing musical scores for reissues of old films and raising the eight children whom he had by Oona O'Neill. Early on Christmas morning in 1977, Charles Spenser Chaplin died in his sleep.

David Robinson quotes J.B. Priestley as saying in 1957, the year of the release of *A King in New York*, Chaplin's bitter commentary from exile:

> [Chaplin] has turned film clowning into social satire and criticism, without losing his astonishing ability to make us laugh.... And Charles Chaplin has stature. He is, in fact, one of the most remarkable men of our time. To begin with, he is one of the very few men who have compelled the film industry to serve them, who have been its masters and not its slaves. Sooner or later most film men, no matter how brilliant they may be, are beaten by the front offices, the distributors, the exhibitors, the trade.... Chaplin, like most genuine artists, is at heart a genial and gentle anarchist and the laughter he provokes only clears and sweetens the air.

The quotation captures the duality of Chaplin's heroism. Robinson's book is a testament to it.

Globe and Mail, 20 July 1985

Afterword

Bruce Vogt

Christ! What am I doing scribbling down my experiences in the nether world of free association to someone who won't even appreciate it in all its subtlety and nuance. Besides it will probably reappear in some embarrassing form in a volume called *My Brother Gordon* by Bruce Vogt when I am rich, famous and irrevocably middle-aged and stodgy. *{March 1970}*

It's been over twelve years since Gord's death from a brain tumour at the age of 37 and I haven't yet entirely lost the habit of silently discussing things with him, whether it's a personal difficulty, a political issue; or sometimes I find myself arguing with him about a film, a novel, a play, whatever. For a few moments his voice seems as alive and characteristic as ever. We argued and discussed for much of our shared childhood and on from there and it doesn't seem to have entirely ended with his death in 1985.

*   *   *

Gord's last years—the years in which he produced the reviews in this volume—were blighted by his struggle against illness and despair. But to begin by dwelling on the melancholy facts of his premature death would be to give a very false impression of his character or his life. In fact Gord was—even in those last years—unaffectedly engaging and engaged. He delighted in his family, friends and acquaintances, in their lovable qualities as well as in their quirks and foibles. His conversation had a striking intensity that was leavened by an easy and wide-ranging sense of humour. The way in which he effortlessly combined high and low forms of humour was unforgettable—and unforgettably Gord. And when you were with him there was never any doubt that your time together, your conversation, was important. It was animated, sometimes heated, and he would be surprised when someone took personally the intensity with which he insisted on a point of view. Conversations about life, art, about anything, mattered.

For the last twenty years of his life we were rarely in the same city; in rereading the many long letters this distance evidently made necessary, I am still surprised to find so much about books, movies, musicians—enthusiastic rants or detailed criticism. Sometimes a Hitchcock, Ford or Bergman film would inspire many pages of argument back and forth.

It was the popular arts that first mattered in this way to him. From early childhood he was an obsessive movie-watcher; from this came a love for the great American cinema pioneers. John Ford, for instance, "…was simply the greatest filmmaker there was, and, like Chaplin's, his work gets richer and deeper the more you see of it." {19 April 1976}

But after a time he seemed to have seen most any movie that mattered—Hawks, Hitchcock, Sturges, Capra, Renoir—and many more that didn't. And we would have found it impossible to imagine surviving childhood without the Marx Brothers. Later there was Chaplin, Keaton, Lloyd, and the dozens of other lesser figures from the hypnotic anarchy of the silent comedy world. He loved Walt Kelly's Pogo and with Kelly as his model, Gord became, by his early teens, an excellent caricaturist.

Later, he made his obsessive way through a great number of jazz and popular recording artists. He surely had one of the two or three most complete collections of Bing Crosby recordings in the world. But there was also Astaire, Dylan, Armstrong, Beiderbecke, Venuti. Typically he'd feel compelled to collect, evaluate and catalogue everything they'd done and then extract their greatest achievements. This usually took the form of a very lengthy reel-to-reel tape—a few choice friends would then be privileged to get a copy. One example: I still have a copy of his Astaire tape along with an enormous booklet, perhaps 150 pages, of Gord's wide-ranging hyper-kinetic commentary.

This immersion in popular culture made him very suspicious of intellectual snobbery of any kind. But he was just as suspicious of the kind of reverse snobbery that would deny a Shakespeare or Shaw his due. Later on, this allowed him as a critic to avoid posturing either as an over-bred intellectual or a cant-destroying populist. His response was highly informed but it was not pre-ordained by ideology.

*   *   *

I realize now how much of my sense of myself relied on this sense of a myriad of talents that I could develop when the time was right. I now know that the time will never be right and there has to be a leap into the dark if I am to accomplish any-thing in this very possibly truncated life of mine. *{October 1983}*

Even in high school, Gord showed talent as an artist and musician, and he always wrote with precocious ease. By the time he reached his mid-twenties he knew he wanted to be a writer. His struggle to become one was painful. It usually is, of course, but for him it was made a great deal more so by the disease which was affecting him long before it was diagnosed. He noticed at times a weakness in his right arm or a sagging of the right side of his face—symptoms which, as it later became clear, were directly related to the brain tumour.

But was the disease also the source of his agonizing morbidity, his obsession with the past? For Gord did have a depressive side to his nature which could easily lapse into a kind of self-laceration. In his late teens, he had learned to curb his emotional nature and perhaps it was this effort of self-suppressing that left him prone to melancholy. Or perhaps it was already the brain tumour—who knows when it first began to do its work? Could it have been the central cause of the periods of morbid paralysis which punctuated his life from late adolescence onwards? Or did these tendencies lead to the disease which killed him? It's hard not to be impatient with those who would find a psychological source for every disease—a simplistic philosophy which serves primarily to reassure the healthy. But toward the end of his life, Gord was willing to entertain quite a number of possibilities. In February 1984, he wondered if his illness could be "...a reflection of nascent emotional blockages that would eventually erupt in this physical symptom? Of course [this] is to assume that a tumour is a symptom as well as a physical thing...."

* * *

Briefly again, Agee's book is a changing point in my whole life and thought—and one of the problems which keeps me from my work is the terrifying responsibility to keep my integrity and the integrity of his book intact and still write something which will fulfill the requirements of a thesis for this ticky-tacky cream-of-wheat institution. The other problem is an almost annihilating sense of my own inadequacies as a writer. *{July 1972}*

In 1973 he finished his Master's in English from Queen's University. He did not feel particularly suited to student life but he read passionately and avidly, developed some important friendships and learned from a couple of worthy mentors, so perhaps university life suited him a great deal more than he could ever allow. Besides, his thesis was on James Agee's monumental *Let Us Now Praise Famous Men*. Anyone who has read Agee will recognize the strong influence on Gord's writing: the intensity of the prose, the moral wrestlings, the poetic rhythms.

For part of his undergraduate years, he was a theatre major and he continued to work in theatre after leaving university. Immediately after graduation he became resident playwright and actor for a Kingston troupe, Theatre 5. It was after leaving Theatre 5 in 1975 that he moved to Toronto and began the struggle to be a writer. Out of this came a number of short stories, some plays, plus various sketches for shorter and longer works. The only employment he could find at first was menial clerical work. And then for a while he taught English as a second language. In the meantime he continued to write:

> As for the writing, I know now that I have ability. Of its nature I know a little but not much—it tends to lean on larger structure and overall form rather than density of language—it is strong on rhythm and weak on rhetoric (by which I mean there's lots of it and it's not very good). But whatever's there, it's worth seeing what will come of it. *{February 1975}*
> I've been sitting and staring at an empty sheet of paper for most of the morning. That story which I mentioned a while back is now about two-thirds finished. The third section has hung me up a bit.... I know I have a strong sense of shape which has always imposed itself on everything I do, and, by attempting to write what, for want of a better term, I must call original material, I'm discovering what lies behind that sense of shape. But as to whether I have a sense of form (which is an entirely different problem and not necessarily related in some important ways) I really don't know. On one very practical level, this doesn't matter at all for I still must explore whatever I've got to the fullest degree. And whether this means that what I write will ultimately only interest me, disturbs only that small and rather laughable part of me which

would like to be the James Joyce of Canadian letters. So on-ward and perhaps upward, but, at least onward. *{January 1976}*

If I can start looking on these things as exercises to improve my writing rather than potential masterworks to justify my existence, I'll be a lot better off. It may very well turn out that I haven't the long-range talent to be the kind of writer I want to be, and I'll just have to adjust to that when and if it turns up. *{June 1976}*

*   *   *

The opportunity to do some radio came along in 1978 and he soon became a regular reviewer for *Stereo Morning*, the CBC-FM's 6 am to 9 am program. At first it was strictly theatre, but later he did some film and book reviews. CBC did have a larger role in mind for him which would have involved travelling across Canada to review Canadian theatre regionally. However, his illness made such travel impossible and, except for a two-hour *Ideas* program about Quebec theatre, his reviews were limited to productions from southern Ontario, particularly the Toronto scene along with the Stratford and Shaw Festivals. Occasionally he would have a day or two to prepare the reviews but the usual pattern was this: after seeing a play, he would write the review that same night, get up at 5:30 the next morning to make revisions and then record it in dialogue form by telephone with *Stereo Morning*'s host, Terry Campbell.

He remained rather ambivalent about writing criticism: journalism had never figured in his ambition. In 1983, in the middle of his fight against his illness, he wrote to me:

I have little sense of vocation anymore—if I ever have had. The urge to write, for instance, is a taunting ghost which re-appears sporadically. This is partly due to the fact that I haven't been settled enough to put concerted daily effort into it. But my lack of energy won't allow me any hope in that direction. I have always had—except for one period in the middle 70s—excuses not to write—sometimes, often, I have had reasons. Looking back on the dozens of reviews I wrote I think they were the last things I should have done for I do not respect them. I do respect even the least of my efforts in fiction.

There's a tendency to see the critic's common ambivalence about being a critic as a kind of conceit: a fine artistic sensibility is kept from original work by some romantic Hamlet-like flaw, or simply the prosaic need to make a living. But perhaps this ambivalence shows a realistic awareness of how dangerous it is for anyone's integrity, this taking on the mantle of the critic. Perhaps the only way to avoid becoming an inflated faun's ass is to venture into criticism with fear and trembling. Certainly Gord never entirely lost his reluctance—a prudent and fearful self-consciousness—about his critic's mantle.

And yet he finally did come to feel some sense of belonging to the artistic community—the possibility that he was making a certain kind of a contribution.

> The odd thing is that the room was full of people that I knew, not as intimate friends to be sure. But I must have had pleasing conversations with a dozen people and said hello to several more. I even had a fan. This stunned me. I had to ask him to repeat what he said. This tall eager-looking fellow came up to me and said something about how much he admired me for being literate on the air. I told him my producer thought I used too many big words. He said he appreciated my words and used to stop what he was doing to listen to me and further that it was refreshing to hear something that had actually been written and sounded like it. It turns out that this guy had been among one of the many people Stereo Morning has tried in my place [during his illness]. It was strange to realize how many lives in the theatre community here that I've touched one way or another. As I write this I think of James Stewart in the nightmare segment of *It's a Wonderful Life*. It's an absurd self-dramatization, but it comforts me. I think I'll let it do so. {*October 1983, after a post-production party attended by many theatre people*}

* * *

It's not possible for me to say how grievous the loss to our culture was Gord's early death or to try to evaluate his achievement or his potential. Yet how prescient his criticism seems in so many areas. Stratford—which Gord sardonically suggested should be funded by the Ministry of Tourism rather than Culture—has become even more of a tourist industry. He was spared the overblown kitsch of mega-musicals, but he certainly anticipated them, as well as the harm they would do to—to *real* theatre, one is tempted to say.

*   *   *

I have started to see that there are two planes of endeavour as far as I and, I think, you as well, are concerned. Put in a kind of Baby's-First-Reader fashion, there's a linear plane of achievement which we value perhaps too much and there's another plane of achievement which we have trouble seeing, let alone valuing, and which is hard to describe (particularly now as I'm literally nodding off as I write this). But it has to do with sensitivity toward others, consideration of ethical concerns, a philosophical attitude to life, and (slowly emerging perhaps) a sensual grasp of the moment. *{March 1983}*

There was in Gord an instinctive suspicion about people—or art— that placed too much value upon the achieving of worldly prestige, particularly when it is at the expense of other qualities, qualities that may be more valuable. Like most aspects of his life, these feel- ings intensified and came under much greater self-scrutiny as a by- product of his battle for life.

The word dignity shows up a great deal in his criticism. He had a strong sense that both the actors and the audience must be chal- lenged, must not be allowed to feel condescension toward each other or toward the material. But the audience must not be abused either. This is a fine line and Gord was as sensitive to it in art as he was sensitive to others in life.

*   *   *

When Gord's brain tumour was finally diagnosed in June, 1981, he was told he likely had about five years to live. In fact, he had only four—and his ordeal was to be at times absurdly Kafkaesque. In the winter of 1982, suffering from periodic seizures and neglected by his doctors, he went to yet another well-known neurosurgeon, who gave him a very different diagnosis—that he had merely scar tissue in his brain, not a tumour at all, and he could expect a long and healthy life. Gord was of course euphoric:

As for whatever happens in the future, you know that I am always here (and for longer than we thought a while back) with my imperfect understanding and my own confusions but also with the love you have every right to expect from your friend and your brother. *{April 1982}*

But he soon began to doubt this new miracle:

I entered this hospital without conscious fear, with even a certain amount of relief. But now I'm a bit like the criminal who is to be hanged and approaches the rope with dignity, and who, when the rope breaks and he finds himself alive at the foot of the scaffold, is lost to the fear of death and must be carried screaming to his second hanging. *{April 1982}*

When he began to lose more and more strength in his right arm and his speech became more and more untrustworthy, he knew before it was medically confirmed that the first diagnosis had been the correct one. He was blackly resigned and despairing when he went into the hospital in January 1983 for surgery to relieve pressure on the brain. But even before the surgery took place, the enormous number of visitors, the great outpouring of love from so many, completely transformed his outlook, and his hospital room became a rather unlikely place of celebration. After the surgery he felt renewed and hopeful once again as he began a series of radiation treatments.

But during and after the radiation treatments there was still the struggle to regain his strength: "I feel like I'm being slowly poisoned like Ingrid Bergman in *Notorious*...." *{March 1983}* For quite a number of months afterwards he was left weakened, lethargic and fighting depression.

Gord had told me when he first learned of his condition that he feared, even more than death, a sense that he might leave this life with a grim conviction that it had been wasted, that he had squandered the many gifts he'd been given. Now, with physical weakness making the fight against despair all the more difficult, this concern became greatly intensified:

I don't know whether I'll send this because, unlike many of the others whom I call my intimate friends, you are far away, and it may be difficult for you to hear from me when I'm in a sad state for it would hit you undiluted with seeing me at other times and in other moods.

I find myself overwhelmed at times by feelings of loss and sadness. And these feelings seem to hit me more and more often as my weakness drags on. I am still unwilling to step outside my close circle of family and friends. I feel, most strikingly, a loss of possibility. I'm sure I would be wrestling with this in any case, as my mid-30s melt into my late-30s, but my weakness makes it harder to deal with—harder to find the energy or optimism to fight my characteristically fatalistic way of thinking and harder to see my future as anything but illness upon illness.

...I am left wondering why have I, with my natural gifts, not been able to focus on them as have [so many other] people. It's not a new question, of course. I've been asking it for 15 years at least. Perhaps the very asking of it denies the possibility of solving it—or perhaps simply sees to it that the pattern will be re-enacted over and over again as if I were one of the characters in *No Exit* (Hell is myself).

There is one new wrinkle. I do not use the question as a scourge. And I no longer sneer at the things that others do (which is a symptom of sneering at what you yourself do). I am less threatened by the successful actor, the successful performer, writer etc. The danger now is to be overwhelmed by the feelings of loss or sadness that I described at the beginning of this letter....

And in the meantime, the clichés are often true, I do have a hell of a lot to be thankful for; you for instance, and that host of troublesome friends of mine and the very fact that I'm around at all, able to enjoy this life.

Even as I write this the sun has gone behind a cloud and the wind has sprung chill. Now it's out again. I guess a warning was sufficient. (Just after the sun disappeared I experienced the mildest of mild seizures as if the warning from the natural world was not enough.) {*October 1983*}

Within a few months his energy level and spirits had improved considerably.

...As a matter of fact old friend and brother, I am quite happy for the most part, resting, reading, getting lost in various and largely inconsequential tasks. I have come to a realization: Doctors aren't worth a fuck (come to think on't, a fuck is not to be sneezed at) until such time as some mechanical endeavour is required. I have come to be quite an expert on my own body. I don't need a doctor to tell me whether or not my recovery pace is normal or abnormal as I can tell that I'm getting better—no matter how slowly. If I sense deterioration that's another matter altogether. But otherwise I'm going to make my own rules and not worry about that crude and imperfect body of knowledge called medicine. I will however take my appointments seriously. I'm not setting my back against doctors. But I'm going to keep them in their place. {December 1983}

* * *

I have already touched on Gord's special gift for community, his talent for friendship, his unforgettable sense of humour—the last a quality perhaps common to many melancholics. And if humour most fundamentally springs from an awareness of the incompatibility between life's preciousness and its relatively trivial nature, then it's not surprising that his illness only served to dramatize this and to deepen his sense of humour.

* * *

Around the time Gord began working for CBC in 1978, he joined an early-jazz band which became known as The Rainbow Gardens Jazz Orchestra—or simply RGO. They specialized in arrangements from the twenties: their musical model was the early bands that formed around Bix Beiderbecke. As Gord struggled to regain health and vitality, singing and drumming with RGO became all the more important. In the early nineteen-eighties they played in a number of venues, more or less regularly, before settling in at Gracie's Restaurant. Gracie's is gone now, but it was located on the north side of Queen Street just east of Bathurst. It was there that they developed a regular following. They also appeared on various radio shows, did a Caribbean cruise, were invited three times to the Bix Beiderbecke Memorial Jazz Festival in Davenport, Iowa and played a few times at Harbourfront in Toronto: they kept a pretty busy schedule for the last few years of Gord's life. In 1984 they made their first and (sadly) only recording. He was at times very irritated with some of his fellow band-members but he was also extremely fond of them.

Gord was the second of four siblings. The other three: David—his senior by two years, myself—his junior by 2½ years and Lynn, 3 years younger still. As much as any family we were a group of very different individuals. That we remained—and remain—close was certainly largely the result of Gord's energy and insistence. It was he who would mediate, touching on the essential nature of our shared affection when any particular disagreement or aggravation would threaten to create some angry incident between family members (anyone from a large family knows the kind of thing I refer to). And even from an early age it was he who insisted on the importance of celebrating our shared lives. The imagination and care he brought to our Christmases, birthdays, indeed any gatherings, kept us in touch with our identity as a family. To the end of his life, each of us felt a special closeness to him. This shared experience of Gord was a large part of how we defined ourselves as a family. It seemed to me that Gord held a strikingly similar position within the RGO, able to enjoy an affectionate and particular relationship with each of the members—even as they exasperated him—and thereby holding it together emotionally.

In any event, Gord's work with the band became a major part of his life as he struggled to get his writing activities going again. And RGO was certainly more than an occasional recreation for him. It allowed him to explore and indulge his love of early jazz, of singing, of making music with others. However unpretentious the band members might have seemed, in fact they were very serious in their determination to do justice to the music, to bring it to life in a genuine way. Gord instinctively acted upon the belief that unpretentiousness should not be an excuse for shoddiness or carelessness or parody—the last in particular a sin of many early-jazz groups.

Some of the time, Gord was the front man for the band and he had an easy unaffected way with an audience. He was also the lead singer and for this he was blessed with a fine natural singing voice. But he took great care to develop it and extend its range and expressive possibilities. His performances were understated, simple—music and lyrics seemed to have their effect without him getting in the way. When Gord wrote the following in his review of Ekkehard Schall, he could very well have been describing unconsciously his own aspirations as a singer:

> The convincing fact about [Schall's] very supple technique in presenting a song...is how strong, intelligent and invigorating it looks when placed beside the truly ugly, impossibly stupid and embarrassingly vulgar American style of modern musical performing, a style that has all but swamped English speaking musical theatre, eviscerated American popular song-writing and ruined dozens of otherwise talented singers and dancers. That style cajoles, flatters, wheedles and lubricates its audience, does all the work for it, and demonstrates that feelings can be had over nothing. But Schall points with every gesture to something outside the performer, and acknowledges with every throb of his tight, sharply-focused voice that there is a world outside the performance. The strong emotions he elicits are not voyeuristic, but shared responses to that world, its madness and its fleeting pleasures.

*   *   *

In January, 1985 he was told by the doctors they considered him cured.

> Good news on health front. Latest CT scan shows yet more shrinkage. Feeling happy, thankful and lucky beyond belief. Things are almost back to normal after over four years. *{January 1985}*

By then he was able to plan some radio work and the prospects for more interesting and challenging possibilities seemed excellent. And he had begun a new and very loving relationship. Life indeed seemed blessed.

> The most important thing for me is that I've come to see my course is the right one. There are lots of possibilities there. It's up to me to take advantage of them. And to recognize them. I don't pretend to be doing either terribly well. I do insist, however, that I've been doing both with less angst (very little in fact) and more determination than I ever have in my life. That's the good news. And I'm at least very close to having my Ideas series accepted (I've got an inside channel) and

should know within the week or so, perhaps before I finish this letter. Plus I sat down one day last month and wrote a complete draft of a story within three hours. It's finished (please find last draft enclosed). If nothing else it should amuse you.... The big news is that Luscombe has officially named me as the co-writer of his major production for next year [a play about Jelly Roll Morton], to be premiered at the end of the season almost precisely a year from now. We talked about it over a few beers last week. I am excited, wary and feel sure that I am in for a real roller-coaster ride. Luscombe is a wonderful man when he's relaxed, but when it came down to brass tacks about whose show it was, he didn't mince words. I hope he's taken on more than he bargained for in me. I have an advantage. As Luscombe himself said: I'm sure you've heard that I've got a reputation for being a bastard to work with. I assured him I had. I know what I'm getting into. Aside from all that, it's the chance of a lifetime. Ten years ago when I came to Toronto, the only theatre that I submitted my resume to was TWP. It's only taken a decade. I think, however, that I needed that long to get ready for him.

...Judi's upstairs reading books on computers and falling asleep. The children have been fun lately. The house is peaceful except for the racket this typewriter is making. I'm going to finish off this letter and slip into bed. I'm very, very happy.... *(28 April 1985)*

On 18 June the RGO was playing at Gracie's as part of the du Maurier International Jazz Festival. At the end of the second set, Gord began to stumble over his words. He knew immediately the troubles had returned and he told one of the band members with bleak emphasis that he would never sing again. Six days later a CT scan revealed that the tumour had metastasized. Surgery was performed on 28 June to relieve pressure on the brain. This provided some relief for a few days but his condition quickly deteriorated and on 10 July he died.

* * *

When I arrived in Toronto from the west coast on 25 June to see him before what was to be his final surgery, on his desk I found an unfinished letter addressed to me:

...At what I hope is the tail end of a monumental depression, perhaps brought on by tiredness (who knows with these things?). A fierce crisis of confidence about most everything. You know the kind?

...Last night (a Sunday) Mom and Dad brought Rebecca [my 3-year old daughter] to see the second set at Harbourfront [of the RGO]. I saw her during two breaks, sat and let her steal my nose and the like. At the end of the second break I made a faux pas. I asked her to kiss me goodbye. Her little heart bust right in front of me and she spent the next five minutes bawling into grandma's dress. She too, Dad said, was tired. I was so gone myself that her tears would have had me bawling on somebody's shoulder if there had been one handy. As it was I got up and acted as energetic as could be for an audience mostly of geriatrics and weird people. One of the latter was sitting next to Rebecca and Mom. She was a sad crippled woman, lost and probably lorn, with a happy grin. Every time I waved at Becky she waved back with a big grin. After the last set she came up to me and asked for an autograph and kept asking me where I was going now. In my state of mind the question had monumental significance.... {3 June 1985}

*　*　*

I retain a number of vivid images of those last days: a lengthy conversation three days before he died about certain tendencies in Canadian journalism, a conversation that was sustained through our habits of many years even though he could no longer speak more than a couple of words at a time. I remember also his last day at home, two days before his death, being repeatedly and violently ill, yet looking up from his misery to flash a smile of encouragement to yet another friend who had arrived to join the vigil. He had feared a lack of grace in his final struggles. Such concerns were characteristic of him. Of course the fears were groundless.

A few days after Gord's funeral, we had a kind of wake at TWP. The RGO played and everyone partied and danced with a desperate euphoria. Some of us were strangers to each other yet there was a kind of shared intimacy: each of us felt we had a special relationship with Gord. And each of us was right.

20 January 1998

GORDON VOGT was born on 17 September 1947 in Cornwall, Ontario. As a child he showed unusual promise in art, music and literature, and graduated with an MA in English from Queen's University in 1973 after completing a thesis on the American writer and critic James Agee. During his university years he was much involved with theatre, and after graduation remained in Kingston to work with Theatre 5, a local troupe for which he was resident playwright and actor and for whom he wrote a number of plays and stage adaptations.

In 1977 he began to do freelance work for the CBC, including a number of *Ideas* programs on both Canadian theatre and American cinema. In 1978 he became the theatre critic for the CBC arts program *Stereo Morning*. In June of 1980 Vogt was struck by the first of many epileptic seizures and a year later was diagnosed with an inoperable brain tumour. During the four years remaining to him his health was often seriously compromised, but he continued to write and broadcast until his death on 10 July 1985.